# PAMELA ALLARDICE

*feel*
# GOOD

## LITTLE CHANGES TO SIMPLIFY YOUR COMPLICATED LIFE

A SUE HINES BOOK

**ALLEN & UNWIN**

FOR MY MOTHER, WHO TAUGHT ME THERE'S NO SUCH WORD AS 'CAN'T'.

First published in 2001

Allen & Unwin
83 Alexander Street
Crows Nest NSW 2065
Australia
Phone: (61 2) 8425 0100
Fax: (61 2) 9906 2218
Email: info@allenandunwin.com
Web:  www.allenandunwin.com

National Library of Australia
Cataloguing-in-Publication entry:

Allardice, Pamela
    Feel good.
    ISBN 1 86508 511 1.
    1. Self-care, Health – Popular works. 2. Naturopathy –
    Popular works. I. Title.
    613

Cover design by MAU Design
Cover photography by Monty Coles
Text design by Gayna Murphy, Greendot Design
Edited by Sonya Plowman
Typeset by Pauline Haas
Printed in South Australia by Griffin Press

10 9 8 7 6 5 4 3

The publisher thanks Marbletrend (www.marbletrend.com.au) for the generous
loan of the clawfoot bath used in the cover photograph.

# I.   START AS YOU MEAN TO GO ON

'Yesterday is ashes; tomorrow wood.
Only today does the fire burn brightly.'
**Eskimo proverb**

Every day presents a new opportunity to feel good about yourself — and how you actually get up can profoundly affect the rest of that day.

When you wake up, don't leap out of bed. Lie still, and spend a little time gradually becoming aware of how you feel. Stretch, and slowly flex your arms and push your feet down to the bottom of the bed. Remind yourself of what it means to become and stay truly 'awake' to your life and experiences. Visualise yourself as bright-eyed, bushy-tailed, ready to go — and lucky to be alive.

Take three breaths, clear yourself of stale air and shake off the residue of yesterday. Say out loud: 'I'm putting aside any negativity I feel', swing your legs over the side of the bed, and then stand up. Feel your feet connecting with the strong, quiet power of the earth beneath you. Lift your arms, take a deep breath, and imagine sunlight streaming in through the top of your head, filling you with hope and joy. Drop your arms and clasp your hands and say a simple affirmation out loud, such as: 'Today I will try to bring truth and kindness to others, and to do the best I can.'

## 2. JUMPSTART YOUR DAY

What's the quickest and easiest way to greet the morning with feelings that at least approximate vim and vitality? Bouncing on a rebounder! As well as boosting your energy levels, toning your muscles and giving your cardiovascular system a terrific tune-up — it's fun! (Remember bouncing on the bed when you were a kid? It's not a lot different from that!)

1. Firstly, warm up by bouncing gently in the middle of the rebounder, without lifting your feet. Keep your knees, shoulders and arms relaxed and loose.

2. Next, move into a gentle walk on the spot. Let your arms swing gently, left arm coming forward as you raise your right heel, then right arm moving when your left heel rises.

3. Now you're ready to move into a pacy little jog — put your arms down by your sides and kick your heels up at the back, attempting to hit your hands.

4. Move into a series of jumping jacks. Try to kick your legs out so they are further than shoulder-width apart, at the same time that you swing your arms up, straight, to shoulder level. Jump back, with ankles together and hands by your sides. Repeat.

5. Start your slow-down with a series of side-to-side jumps. To get the rhythm right, imagine you're skiing, with your ankles together and elbows tucked in at your sides.

6. Finish up with the Twist! Just like the dance, keeping your feet together and only jumping up an inch or two, but vigorously twisting your hips and torso in opposite directions as you do.

## 3.    SQUEEZE A LEMON

Stodgy meals and foods can clog the lymphatic system. When this system becomes blocked, toxins cannot be released effectively from the body. The build-up puts strain on the liver, kidneys, and digestive and immune systems.

Starting the day with a glass of warm water with the juice of one lemon and half a teaspoon of freshly grated ginger in it is one of the healthiest ways to take the load off your lymph, cleanse your system and detoxify your cells. The lemon juice helps flush the liver and colon, while providing vital phytonutrients and beneficial natural enzymes. Plus, if you're concerned about your cholesterol levels, lemon juice could be the answer. One study has shown that lemon juice reduces the level of low-density lipoprotein (LDL or 'bad' cholesterol) by over 40 per cent, compared with drinking only water. Lemon juice also contains vitamin C and antibacterial and antiviral agents that help ward off colds. The zingy scent of fresh lemon boosts your energy, too.

# 4.  OPEN YOUR HEART

If you're under too much stress, you'll inevitably feel the result in a tight, constricted chest and too-shallow, rapid breathing. This simple yoga exercise will relax your chest and rib muscles, help you open your lungs and take pressure off your heart.

Roll a towel into a long, narrow tube shape, and fold in half; it should be approximately the same length as your torso, from the base of your tailbone to the base of your neck. Fold another towel to act as a small pillow for your head, and roll a third to form a thick bolster to raise your knees slightly off the floor. Lie back, lengthwise, over the long, narrow roll, placing the second under your head, the third under your knees.

Flop your arms out to the sides, palms up, slightly bent at the elbow. Relax, and breathe steadily. Imagine that your chest and lungs have actually opened up and outwards, as wide as your hands are apart. Sense how your heart seems to open and beat more strongly, now that it is not hemmed in, and how your breathing becomes so much deeper and fuller as the towel roll gently forces your torso out of that crushing, inward-pointing posture and holds it open to receive fresh oxygen.

# 5. LOOK OUTWARDS, NOT IN

'Happiness is contagious.'
**Ralph Waldo Emerson**

Concentrate on external factors rather than dwelling too long on your emotions. Research from Washington University shows that looking inwards too much makes you insular and broody, and means that you are more likely to feel depressed. Boost your happiness rating by taking time out to appreciate the world around you — concentrate on colours, shapes and fragrances.

# 6.   LAUGH MORE

'A good laugh is sunshine in a house.'
**William Makepeace Thackeray**

Here's a riddle: what is something that boosts your immune system, relaxes your nerves, and makes you feel great? (Extra hint: kids do it about 300 times a day; adults a stingy 17.) Give up? Laughter!

Laughter really is the best medicine: it can lower your blood pressure, relieve stress, revive a sluggish circulation — it even increases your body's production of natural 'killer' cells, which attack incoming viruses and bad bacteria. And as if that isn't enough, studies have shown that laughter supports the body's production of the chemicals in the brain that are needed for alertness and memory. So, if you're thinking of embarking on a computer course, or taking driving lessons, read or watch something funny first. And resolve to:

Send funny cartoons to friends at work.

Re-write captions on cartoons, making it refer to you and your friends.

Sticky-tape cartoons, funny cards and jokes to the inside of the pantry door, or some other spot where you can stand and see them often.

Write down jokes or buy a joke book so you can learn a few favourites off by heart.

Go to funny films.

Watch your favourite comedy programs on TV more often.

# 7.   SAVE MONEY ON FOOD

So — one of your New Year's resolutions is getting your finances in order? Here are some of my favourite budget-stretching ideas. Some are tried-and-true old favourites — but others will surprise you. And they really do work!

**Bring back the Sunday roast**. Not only is it tasty and nourishing, but you'll get at least two meals out of the leftovers.

**Have at least one 'vegetarian' day a week**. Vegetarian meals can be just as interesting and healthy as meals based on meat, at a fraction the cost.

**Declare war on waste**. Even the most humble ingredients can be transformed into delicious dishes: onion skins, for instance, which are usually chucked away, add colour and flavour to soups.

**Use less milk**. The difference between a recipe made with all milk and the same thing made with a 50:50 mix of water and milk is not a lot.

**Do you have a cat or dog?** Then find a wholesale pet goods barn. Buying pet litter and food in bulk every three months will save you a small fortune.

**Buy a secondhand freezer**. Stocking up on specials and bulk-buys when they come up makes for excellent long-term savings.

**Buy generic or 'house' brands**. Buy as many of these products as you can, especially the basics: toilet paper, tissues, flour, sugar. They can be up to half the price of products with premium brand labels but are the same inside the packet — in fact, most are contract-manufactured by the same companies!

**Invest in a breadmaker**. You'll really notice the difference in your shopping budget if you have children. It's easy — and it makes the house smell wonderful!

**Buy a food drier**. (You will find them in health food stores.) By drying fruit and vegetables when they're in season, you'll save heaps on things like muesli bars and kids' snacks.

**Get together with friends or family to bulk-buy meat, or fruit and vegetables**. There are many entrepreneurial greengrocer cooperatives that even do home deliveries at no extra cost. Look them up in your local telephone directory.

**Shop with a list**. You will do less impulse buying.

**Ask yourself every single time:** Do I absolutely need this purchase?

**Save time, energy and petrol by consolidating shopping trips**. Go to the supermarket no more than once a week, preferably once a fortnight.

# 8. ↘ FIGHT CANCER IN THE KITCHEN

Here's a statistic to make you think twice about what you eat: an unhealthy diet may be behind up to one-third of all cancers. It's vital therefore to increase your intake of fruit and vegetables. They contain phytochemicals and antioxidants, which countless studies have shown help to protect, block or suppress cancer-causing cells and tumours. Many help to protect against specific cancers, too:

**Broccoli** and **cabbage** contain glucosinolates, which break down to fight lung and colon cancers. (Tip: if you can't stand broccoli, but want its cancer-fighting properties, look for broccoli sprouts, available in health food stores and some supermarkets. They've got a tangy yet delicate taste, and they contain up to 50 times the concentration of the protective chemical sulphoraphane found in mature broccoli.)

**Citrus fruit** is high in antioxidant flavonoids that protect against stomach and oral cancer.

**Garlic** has been shown to reduce the size of colon tumours.

**Grapes**, or rather, their skins, contain resveratrol, which inhibits cancer development.

**Soya** contains a naturally occurring plant oestrogen that mimics the action of the anti-breast cancer drug tamoxifen.

**Tomatoes** contain lycopene, which protects against cancer-causing pollutants and helps guard against stomach and prostate cancer.

**Watercress** contains a substance called phenethyl isothiocyanate, which preliminary research findings indicate may help prevent lung cancer.

# 9. ENJOY NATURE

'Earth's crammed with Heaven.'
**Elizabeth Barrett Browning**

No matter what — if any — religion you follow, you can always find spirit in nature. The 'ribbit' of a frog, the fragrance of jasmine clambering over a fence, and the diamond glint of sunlight on water all infuse our lives with tenderness, joy and appreciation for life. Spirituality surrounds us in the air we breathe and the ground upon which we walk, in mountains and rivers, in animals and plants, within the seasons, and within ourselves. It is no accident that many of the world's great spiritual teachings, including Buddhism and Christianity, urge us to explore and honour nature. Sadly, if you're surrounded by concrete and smog every day, it's easy to lose touch with the natural world. Try these stress-busting tips to restore a sense of connection with nature:

**Focus your attention on a particular plant**. Observe in minute detail its shape, colour and texture. Look again, and see it in harmony with other plants, the landscape and sky.

**Get a room with a view**. Looking out on to a natural landscape can make you calmer and healthier. One study has even shown that patients recovering from surgery took fewer doses of pain medication and were less depressed when their room looked out on trees — but those with a view of a brick wall were more doubtful and negative. If you can't manage a view, put up posters or photographs of waterfalls and forests.

**Space out**. Make time for a brief walk some time during your day. Look around and find something natural that captures your imagination. If you're in a park, look at the trees and grass. If you're in the city, notice the clouds rolling by.

# 10. DITCH THOSE CRUTCHES

Recognise smoking and drinking for what they are: coping strategies. The more stressed you are, the more you'll rely on them to supposedly help you cope. The irony is, smoking and drinking only add to the toxic load your body's got to cope with, putting you under even more stress, meaning you've got even less energy for everything you're trying to do. So, contrary to popular belief, smoking and drinking do not relax you. In fact, smokers and drinkers actually have higher stress levels than anyone else. Not only that, but:

Smoking can shorten your life span by as much as 15 years.

Heavy drinking is the most common cause of liver damage and is a critical factor in other conditions, such as heart disease. The 'safe' limit for women is two standard drinks a day, no more.

Both habits absolutely ruin your skin. Cigarette smoke contains over 4,000 toxins which restrict the oxygen supply to the skin and cause a breakdown of collagen and elastin — the proteins that keep skin firm and supple — leading to thinner skin (sometimes up to 40 per cent thinner) which is more prone to wrinkling as well as discolouration. Alcohol also ages the skin before its time, first stripping the cells of vital moisture, and second, inhibiting the absorption of nutrients, especially vitamins A, C and the B-group vitamins, zinc and fatty acids.

# 11.  BALANCE YOUR ENERGY FLOW

Jin shin do is an ancient Oriental therapy, based on the principle of massaging pressure points that relieve pain, revitalise organs, and balance your energy. Try jin shin do hand massage to release tension and stress.

Hold the middle joint of the left middle finger lightly between the right thumb and fingers. Hold for a few minutes. Reverse, and do for the other hand. Hold the fourth and fifth fingers of your left hand between the thumb and fingers of your right hand, the thumb on the palm side of your left hand. Reverse, and do for the other hand.

Hold the thumb of your left hand with the fingers of your right. When you feel a steady pulse in your thumb, release and hold the index finger of your left hand in the same way — again until you feel a pulse in the finger. Work your way through all the fingers. Then repeat with the other hand.

# 12. ⚜ Detox regularly

'The first wealth is health,' wrote Ralph Waldo Emerson. The key to maintaining health is regularly giving your system a rest. It helps rid the body of toxins, a major drain on energy, and perks up the system generally.

Once a month, spend a day eating just fresh fruit and drinking mineral water. You can eat as much fruit as you want and you should aim to drink at least two litres of water. Try not to do too much. Make it a day for pampering yourself. Have a long bath and give yourself a facial . . . you'll feel cleansed and energetic afterwards.

Twice a year, preferably in spring and autumn, try this weekend detox regime. At the end of this three-day eating plan you should feel full of vitality. During the three days:

Cut out junk food, ready-made meals and processed foods in favour of raw, organic and natural ingredients. That means no tea, coffee, cow's milk, sugar, cakes or chocolate.

Eat as much organic brown rice as you want — it's full of vitamins and helps to cleanse the colon.

Drink eight glasses of filtered water each day.

For snacks try rice cakes; nuts and seeds; fruit; raw vegetables; unsalted popcorn.

Start each day with skin brushing and a three-minute burst of cold water before your usual shower. Drink a glass of filtered water with a slice of lemon.

**DAY ONE:**
*Breakfast:* Eat as much fruit as you like with either sheep or goat's yoghurt.
*Lunch:* Organic brown rice; steamed vegetables; salad with nuts and seeds; multivitamin supplement.
*Dinner:* Salad; organic brown rice.

**DAY TWO:**
*Breakfast:* Eat as much fruit as you like with either sheep or goat's yoghurt.
*Lunch:* Salad with tuna, nuts, seeds, beans and raw vegetables.
*Dinner:* Organic brown rice; nut roast; vegetables.

**DAY THREE:**
*Breakfast:* Eat as much fruit as you like with either sheep or goat's yoghurt.
*Lunch:* Salad with salmon, nuts, seeds, beans and raw vegetables.
*Dinner:* Organic brown rice and roast vegetables in olive oil.

# 13.   SCRUB UP

'Your body is the harp of your soul.'
**Kahlil Gibran**

Dry skin brushing is one of the simplest yet most effective techniques for recharging your body and improving your health. It stimulates the lymphatic flow (an essential part of the body's immune system) and circulation, and removes dead skin cells and toxins.

You'll need a soft natural bristle brush with a long detachable handle, so you can reach your back. Begin with the soles of your feet and toes, then brush up the front and back of your calves, knees, and thighs, with smooth, long strokes. Pay particular attention to the groin area, a major site of lymph nodes. Next, brush up your buttocks and over your hips to your lower back. Then brush your hands, up your arms, across your shoulders, gently over your breasts, and down the back of your neck and upper back. Use a circular movement to brush your tummy, avoiding the genitals or any irritated skin. Brushing clockwise will stimulate the colon.

Follow your dry skin brushing with a brisk shower.

# 14. LISTEN TO YOUR INNER VOICE

Psychic ability is one of our best-kept secrets. Children learn all too soon that to follow their intuition or make predictions is eccentric, weird, or, worse, crazy. As adults, many people won't share their psychic experiences for fear of being thought odd. Yet our intuition is a vital part of our nature, enhancing all our other faculties — physical, emotional and spiritual.

Many psychologists are now referring to intuition as the sixth sense — until recently it was dismissed in favour of logic and rational thought. Intuition is the ability to connect and act positively upon feelings of *déjà vu* and flashes of inspiration that have seemingly come out of the blue. A good intuitive sense can make you a better decision-maker and judge of character.

Test your intuition: when you first meet someone, make a mental note of what your intuition tells you about them. Match this to what you learn as you get to know them properly. And take it slowly. By expanding your comfort zone and building your confidence gradually, you'll ultimately be ready for any big risks you have to take. Take little risks from time to time and listen to your intuition as well as your logical mind: for example, when choosing a friend or a new job. As Walt Disney said: 'It's kind of fun to do the impossible.' Follow your hunches and call up a friend you fell out with ages ago; move up from the beginners to the intermediate step class, or try out a new recipe if a friend is coming around.

Speaking of friends, keep an eye out for a 'psychic buddy', someone who believes in this aspect of life and supports its importance. It is safe for you to grow and expand in their presence. All of us need to find people who support our being as sensitive, psychic, and guided as we really are. We need a buddy we can confide in and compare notes with. This kind of support is very powerful. Very often people don't so much doubt their instincts and intuition as their ability to follow it. This is where friends, the right kind of friends, come in. 'Trust yourself,' these friends should say. 'Try it and see what happens. Maybe your intuition is right.'

# 15. LOOK AT WHO YOU ATTRACT

Do you have a history of attracting partners or friends who make you unhappy? Or of ending up in jobs and relationships that, ultimately, are going nowhere? If so, it's a pretty safe assumption that, on some level, you feel that you're not worthy of a better situation; or that, for some deep dark reason, you don't deserve it. It will probably be painful — at best, confronting — but if you're going to break out of this pattern, you need to have a good long think and try to understand why you choose people or situations that are inappropriate for you in some way. Alarm bells should go off if you recognise yourself in any of the following:

Putting your own wishes last so as not to upset others, or get in their way.

Turning a blind eye to physical or verbal abuse — even somehow thinking that you were to blame for it happening.

Only feeling comfortable when you're not called upon to do or say anything that will take you beyond your comfort zone.

Whether at home or at work, relationships involve baring yourself in varying degrees of physical, emotional and spiritual intimacy. Look at who you are trusting to see your body, hear your thoughts and share your dreams, who you are allowing to affect the way your life falls.

# 16. ASK THE HARD QUESTIONS

> 'Lovers don't finally meet somewhere. They are in each other all along.'
> **Rumi**

In your relationship, aim to get the basics right: the ability not to have any taboo areas stops a relationship from going stale. Make sure you tell each other about the good things that happen to you, as well as the bad. Realise that both of you will change, and accept and respect this. Share key values: set aside time to talk and check that you and your partner continue to want the same things. Be honest about your needs, wants and desires.

Knowledge is the key to revitalising your feelings and cultivating long-term commitment. No one can tell you how to have a good relationship or put the zing back in your sex life. There is no answer but your answer. So — ask yourself these questions. Your responses and those of your partner will unearth deeply held beliefs and hopes — and also identify any rocky areas. Some might only take a few moments to answer. Others will take days, and still others may just not have answers. However, from every question — even the ones you can't answer — you'll learn something important about your relationship.

What do we need to make our place feel like home?

Who looks after it?

How do we celebrate holidays and activities?

Were we raised with any spiritual traditions or practices? What place do they play in our life together?

How much money do we need individually and together to feel secure?

Do we keep our money separate or together?

Who is responsible for the housekeeping? For making investments?

Will we have children together? Who will care for them?

It is the process of responding to these questions together — not the answers themselves — that's important. Your situation and feelings about issues may change, but being able to be open and intimate is a wonderful opportunity to create a deeper connection.

# 17.   DEAL WITH CRITICISM

This means not only dealing with comments directed at you, but also being more clear when you are criticising others. When you're on the receiving end, it's important to separate criticism for what you've done from you, the person. When giving criticism, same thing. And use your best skills in delivering the message. For instance, if you are good at discussing an issue, you can use that style in your criticism: 'On the one hand, this could be seen as a good idea; however, it's important to look at . . .' Don't assume that other people will react badly. People are often far more resilient than you think, if you tell them something straight.

# 18. CULTIVATE A STATE OF GRACE

'See the false as false, the true as true. Look into your heart.
Follow your nature.'
**The Dhammapada**

Your spirit needs to be nourished, just as your mind and body do.

Get started by inspiring yourself with the stories and wisdom from spiritual traditions that are unfamiliar to you. Go to your local library or New Age bookstore and ask to see the Sufi parables, or the sayings of Confucius or Lao-tzu. Study the Bible or the sermons of Buddha, or the simple paperback teachings of the Vietnamese Zen master Thich Nhat Hanh. Such stories and sayings will give you greater insight and perception, and may even inspire you to sign up for a study in a course in philosophy or spiritual development. And, as you feel your levels of spiritual energy growing, you will become more confident in your abilities to handle obstacles thrown in your path.

## 19.   LEARN TO FORGIVE

'Nothing is more costly, nothing is more sterile, than vengeance.'
**Winston Churchill**

Clearly, when he wrote 'Hell is other people', Jean-Paul Sartre knew something about how it feels to hold a grudge. It's only natural to find it difficult to forgive someone when they have done something awful to you, but it's imperative that you try — and succeed — otherwise you are just re-injuring yourself. You cannot move on in life if you continue to pick at old wounds, and go over and over something that happened in the past.

Vengeful thoughts hurt you mentally, making you discontented, cynical and preoccupied. They also hurt you physically, and they sever you from your spiritual side, making you feel disconnected from life, a dried-up old husk with no juice, no essence. It's no accident that every single great religious tradition of the world has taught that forgiveness is the most important first step on the path to spiritual fulfilment and true contentment.

Try to find another way of looking at that which you need to forgive. It's often easier to at least understand someone else after you've 'walked in their shoes'. This is why so many people often develop a better — or at least a different — relationship with their parents after they have had children themselves. Remember that everyone brings different strengths and weaknesses to any situation, that most people do the best job they know how to do, and that it is difficult to move beyond the genetic and life skills they have inherited: they are what they are. Also, remember that forgiveness doesn't mean that you're saying what someone has done to you is acceptable — or that you're going to forget about it. Forgiveness means that you are not going to let your anger dominate you anymore. You're releasing yourself.

# 20  SAIL THROUGH WITH SHIATSU

This simple shiatsu exercise can help you maintain your concentration and keep you alert and focused.

Rub all over your head briskly and then tap all over it with your fingertips. Gently tug your hair then release your hands.

Pinch all around your jawline. Then tap firmly all around your jaw with your fingertips. Clench your jaw, open your mouth wide and say 'Ahhh!'

Close your eyes and breathe deeply for a few minutes.

## 21.   EAT MORE WHOLEGRAINS

According to recent studies, regularly eating wholegrains can significantly reduce your risk of developing Australia's two biggest killers: cancer and heart disease. Wholegrains use all of the grain, which means you're not only eating more fibre, but more vitamins and minerals as well.

It's easier than you think to bump up your daily intake of wholegrains. Having wholegrain cereal for breakfast is a terrific start. It's a great fibre provider, which promotes a healthy digestive system, along with iron, calcium, B vitamins and oestrogen-modifying compounds, called lignans. Fibre helps prevent bowel cancer, while lignans are known to protect against breast cancer. Recent research from America also suggests that cereal fibre is associated with a lower risk of heart disease in women. Plus, you can still enjoy sandwiches, toast, chilli con carne and curries — just substitute wholemeal bread for ordinary, and have brown rice instead of white.

Get some seeds into your life, too. The omega-3 fats in flaxseed and pumpkin seeds help to burn other kinds of fat, and also contribute to keeping your skin healthy, stimulating your metabolism and boosting your brain function. Try to aim for two servings of one tablespoonful a day. They're tasty sprinkled on breakfast cereal, or a salad.

# 22. Become a better citizen

> 'It is a painful thing to look at your own trouble, and know that you yourself and no one else has made it.'
> **Sophocles**

Too many people fall into a category that could best be described as 'politically resigned'. Record numbers of people aren't even registered to vote anymore because they claim to be so disgusted by politics and politicians. That's quite reasonable, given the state of play amongst most of our leaders — but is it responsible behaviour? Is it mature?

If you don't like the mean-spiritedness of politics as we know it, it is up to you to change it, even on a small scale. Consider becoming involved in a citizenship gathering, say on a weekly or monthly basis. Start one up if there's nothing in your area. It doesn't matter who at the meeting considers themselves to be Liberal, Labor, neither, communist, or apolitical. Nor does everyone have to have exactly the same opinion — this is about citizenship, not politics. The idea is that those present speak from the heart about subjects that matter to them and their community, whether it's fighting the closure of a local school, the installation of a sewerage vent or the development of local wetlands. And the ideal outcome should be your group drawing up an action plan and aiming to lobby successfully for an item or action that will benefit that community, and counter the activity that you don't want to see happen. Aim for specific lobbying actions — organising a petition, sending letters to an elected official, putting up posters, or gaining media exposure.

# 23.   GIVE YOURSELF FLOWERS

> 'If of all your worldly goods, you are bereft, except for one loaf of bread
> — sell half and buy a hyacinth to feed your soul.'
> **Spanish proverb**

For years, I had a very bad habit of thinking of flowers as a luxury — something I would only buy if people were coming over, or that I would wait to be given on a birthday or anniversary. I thought only green-thumbed gardeners and people with plenty of money could afford to be lavish with flowers on a regular basis. But you can buy a bunch of flowers from your supermarket for about the same price as a packet of tea. Stop denying yourself pleasure. Give yourself a bunch of flowers every week — the nourishment they give your spirit pays for the purchase price many times over. They cheer you up, scent your room and add colour. Experiment with containers, too: jam jars or old bottles lined up on the windowsill, teapots, tall spaghetti jars ... Remember to change the water every day; that will mean they'll last at least a week.

## 24. ᴸ EAT CHOCOLATE

Above my desk I have pinned a quote from the chef and philosopher Anton Brillat-Savarin: 'It has been shown as proof positive that carefully prepared chocolate is as healthful a food as it is pleasant, and that it is above all helpful to people who must do a great deal of mental work.'

In case you require further coaxing, a study from the National Institute of Public Health in the Netherlands has found that dark chocolate has high levels of the mineral magnesium, which helps control blood sugar levels, and catechins, antioxidants that are thought to help combat heart disease and cancer. Plus, there are these words of wisdom from ARISE (Association for Research Into the Science of Enjoyment): 'Chocolate has psycho-tonic effects, enhancing concentration and performance. Chocolate increases euphoria by releasing endorphins (the body's feel-good chemicals) in the blood supply, and may even have a positive effect on stress-induced heart disease.'

Make your fix as healthy as possible by choosing a plain bar of organic chocolate; that way, you're avoiding pesticide traces such as lindane, which have been linked with breast cancer.

# 25.  MAKE GRATITUDE AN ATTITUDE

'To me, every hour of light and dark is a miracle. Every cubic inch of space is a miracle.'
**Walt Whitman**

Take a moment every day, and think of everything you have — family and friends, maybe children, good food to eat, special and sentimental possessions, your work, study or interests — and then think how you would feel if any of it were taken away from you.

It's not really good enough to have to experience a guilty twinge when we see footage of a disaster on TV in order to remember what we have to be thankful for. Gratitude is a habit that should be practised on a daily basis, a lesson that needs to be reinforced as often as possible. If you're all caught up with chasing after goals and objectives that you're hoping to obtain in the future, it's all too easy to overlook the wonderful gifts you already have in your possession.

# 26. HEAL YOUR HOME

Over a lifetime, the average person spends over 25 years at home. Here's how to make yours healthier:

**Put plants in every room**. They help clean the air of toxic chemicals. Peace lilies, for example, soak up benzene (from dry-cleaned clothing), and spider plants absorb carbon monoxide.

**Use chemical-free paint**. Look for 'milk paint' for walls and furniture, which contains only natural pigments. Just mix the powder with water and brush it on.

**Use natural light**. It is easier on the eyes than fluorescent light and can improve alertness and boost mood. No daylight? Use full-spectrum light bulbs, which mimic natural light.

**Sleep carefully**. Permanent press bedding is sometimes treated with formaldehyde, a suspected human carcinogen, to prevent wrinkling. Choose chemical-free cotton bedding instead.

## 27.   TRY AN IONISER

Ions are electrically-charged particles found in the atmosphere. In the countryside or near the ocean, a healthy balance of positive and negative ions exists — which explains why breathing fresh air outdoors makes us feel so good. However, the air inside our homes and offices contains a higher amount of positive ions — emitted from electrical equipment such as computers and televisions, air conditioning and heating. Many experts believe that too many positive ions in the atmosphere can lead to tiredness, lack of concentration, headaches and more colds and flu than usual and, in particular, result in the fatigue and energy slumps in air-conditioned offices. An ioniser can help remedy poor air quality, clear the atmosphere and boost vitality. It works by increasing the number of negative particles in the air, which helps to raise energy levels. Some brands of ionisers also have the added benefit of filtering out pollen and dust.

## 28. BAN SMOKING

Hopefully you don't smoke — but even if you don't, you need to remember that passive smoking is a real threat, too. It's estimated that at least 400 people a year die of lung cancer related to passive smoking. Children who live with smokers are more likely to suffer from asthma, bronchitis and even glue ear; while tobacco smoke is thought to be a cause of Sudden Infant Death Syndrome (SIDS). And once you've banned it from your home, try to avoid smoke in other places — go to pubs and restaurants that have non-smoking areas.

# 29.   GO ORGANIC

After years of quietly building momentum, organic foods (and wines and beer) have finally made their mark. Organic foods are healthy and disease-fighting, cannot be irradiated, genetically modified or produced with hormones or antibiotics. They also have the edge when it comes to disease-fighting phytochemicals, such as the lycopene found in tomatoes and sulphoraphane in broccoli.

Not only are organic foods better for your health but, for those of us increasingly concerned about the impact of pesticides, herbicides and the like — none of which are used in organic farming — it's also better for the environment. (Who can forget the story of DDT? Banned in 1972, residues still remained in the soil, on plants and in our bodies for up to 30 years!)

A common reservation people have about organic produce is its appearance — they're not used to seeing normal, natural fruit and vegetables! However, I now lean the other way. I have become wary of perfect produce: it often takes heavy spraying to make fruits and vegetables look plump and big, not to mention the shiny wax coatings that give them their glossy look. Learn to love the little blemishes and imperfections that are natural.

Nor does organic food necessarily have to be more expensive these days: organic farmers are banding together in collectives to minimise costs for themselves and pass the savings on to the consumer. You can also choose from a rapidly growing number of community buying groups and internet suppliers, which also save you money. If you buy local organic produce, you may not pay more or even less than non-organic produce.

Plus — possibly most important of all — organic food tastes better. Ultimately, with each organic product you buy, you're doing something good for yourself and your family, and giving back to the land.

# 30. ~ Cut fat, not flavour

There are two common complaints that I hear all the time when people are trying to ditch unhealthy eating habits: one, that low-fat food tastes bland and two, that you have to buy special, expensive ingredients. Well — it doesn't have to be that way. Here are some easy ideas to put in place:

**Make your own salad dressing**. Commercial dressings can add as much as 10 g of fat to an otherwise healthy salad. If you simply have to have a creamy dressing, try this one: blend one tablespoon of soft tofu with one of balsamic vinegar and a teaspoon of Dijon mustard. It gives that lovely smooth texture without a whisker of fat.

**Thicken soups, stews, sauces and gravies with vegetable purées** rather than butter and flour.

**Use stock instead of oil**. Whenever a recipe says: 'Heat the oil in the pan', change it to: 'Heat the stock in the pan', and use a bit of stock to cook up your onions, garlic, or spice mixture.

**Use an oil and water spray**. Fill a small plant mister with water and a little bit of oil. When you need to fry food, shake, and spritz the pan.

**Whip up your own ice-cream**. Some dairy-based ice-creams contain up to five grams of fat in each scoop. Here's a quick and endlessly creative option which, I think, actually tastes better than many ice-creams on the market, and has a fraction of the fat: using a food processor, whiz together half a cup of low-fat fromage frais, a quarter of a cup of jam or fruit preserve, a dash of vanilla and a handful of frozen berries.

# 31.   SPICE UP YOUR LIFE

Adding spices to your diet boosts the nervous and digestive systems. They're inexpensive and make all the difference to whether a dish is delicious or so-so. And remember, fresh is always better than dried. Eat more of the following:

**Caraway** Frequently used in bread, they can also be added to soups and casseroles. They go well with root vegetables, especially beetroot, and add good flavour to sauerkraut. Add when boiling cabbage or cauliflower to improve flavour and reduce kitchen smells.

**Cardamom** Add to dishes of lentils, pulses, rice, chicken and meat. Add their distinctive flavour to pancakes, waffles and biscuits. Sugar which has been kept in a closed container with crushed cardamom pods is lovely when sprinkled over pastries and other desserts.

**Cayenne** Its sharp flavour is ideal for adding heat but not taste to seafood dishes and salad dressings. It is a great seasoning for creamy soups and delicately flavoured vegetables such as asparagus, and for egg and cheese dishes.

**Chillies** Fresh chillies can be added to Eastern-style curries and Latin-American and Mexican dishes.

**Cinnamon** Although this is a sweet spice, it can also be used in savoury dishes. Cinnamon sticks will readily impart their flavour when infused with milk or poached with fruit. They can be cooked with curries, rice or spiced dishes of the Middle East.

**Cloves** Add three or four whole cloves to the pan when boiling beans, or add a pinch to nut roasts. Add them whole or ground to apple pies, mincemeat, and cakes or add them to herb teas.

**Cumin** It can be added alone to curries, stews and casseroles and is often used to flavour rice and couscous. An excellent flavouring for lamb, bread and cakes.

**Juniper** Toss the crushed berries into cooked cabbage or add it to sauerkraut. A savoury butter containing juniper makes a yummy topping for baked potatoes.

**Nutmeg and mace** Add a blade of mace and a pinch of nutmeg when poaching or baking white fish. Add it also to pies and spinach.

**Paprika** Use it to flavour dried beans and dishes of mixed vegetables, and also in salad dressings.

**Turmeric** This goes well with fish, chicken, curries and rice, and can be added to savoury butters and vegetarian dishes.

## 32. ❧ SING OUT LOUD

Take a deep breath, open your mouth and enjoy yourself — singing really lifts your spirits.

Sing along to the radio. Sing in the shower. Sing lullabies and songs you learned when you were little: 'Frère Jacques', 'Twinkle, Twinkle Little Star', 'Inch Worm', 'All I Want for Christmas (Is My Two Front Teeth)' and 'Six White Boomers'. Sing loudly, especially if you're in the car, and even more especially if you've got your kids with you!

Vary your music collection. Keep a wide repertoire of music to suit all your moods, and note how different sounds make you feel. Opera may be stirring and sophisticated but every so often almost everyone needs a blast of energising rock 'n' roll or a sentimental dose of country music.

Take things to the next level and consider joining a local choir or singing group: there's plenty of research to show that the musical experience has a positive effect on mood and health.

# 33.  THINK BEFORE YOU BUY ANYTHING

'Advertising is the rattling of a stick inside a swill bucket.'
**George Orwell**

Contrary to what the zillions of manufacturers of clothing, CDs, ornaments, food, alcohol, jewellery, cars and much, much more would like you to think, spending money is not the way to peace of mind.

That's not to say that you can't have the things that you really do want and need, provided you can afford them. But it does mean thinking about how often — and in how many, many different and subtle ways — we are told every day that it is normal to just keep buying stuff, all sorts of stuff, whether we have the money or not, whether we need it or not, whether we even want it. There aren't too many advertisements that say: 'First check your bank balance, and see whether you've got enough for this gorgeous watch . . .' And this more-more-more mentality isn't just the domain of advertising. Watch pretty much any TV show about a family, and you'll see a house that's bigger and better appointed than what's really the average.

For years, anthropologists have been fascinated by the custom of 'hexing', found in indigenous cultures around the world. Think of the Australian Aboriginal custom of 'pointing the bone' at someone who, knowing that this has happened, simply curls up and dies as a result of the suggestion. Similarly, we have 'bones' pointed at us every day that tell us it's normal to buy stuff we don't need with money we don't have — and then have nothing in particular to show for it!

# 34. ＼ AIM FOR FINANCIAL FREEDOM

'Neither a borrower, nor a lender be,' said Hamlet. My mother always adds the caveat that there may be situations where you can give or receive money as a gift — but that you should avoid either borrowing or lending it with a view to getting it back. She's referring mainly to the tensions that can result if loans between family and friends aren't repaid, but it doesn't hurt to consider her advice from a broader perspective.

Have you got credit cards? How many? Are you involved in hire-purchase arrangements, or leases? Have you borrowed money from family and friends? If you are serious about reducing your debt then it's a no-brainer to figure out that you shouldn't spend money you don't have. Nor should you borrow against money that you are going to receive, but haven't yet. Until you see it in your hand or your bank account, it doesn't exist. Spending before you receive is, simply, gambling.

Obviously, if you've got a mortgage, the best you can hope for is to pay it off as soon as possible. However, there's no need to make the situation worse by becoming a credit-oholic. Consider the purchases you've made or are planning to make on credit. If you suspect they are indulgences to solve problems — or to escape from the ones you can't solve — you may need help. Do whatever it takes to stop creating more debt. Here are some quick tips to start you off — do at least one today:

> If you've got a mortgage, don't fix it. Or consider an each-way bet with a 50 per cent fixed, 50 per cent variable rate.
>
> If you've got health insurance, check out the savings you can make by setting up your own fund.
>
> If you've got more than one credit card, investigate which is the best one for you. Different cards offer cash rebates, free flights, hotel stays, and meals; some have quite different rates of interest. Choosing the right card requires careful thought — then cut up the others. Did you realise that having too much credit can actually harm your credit rating and keep you from getting a mortgage or other big loan? Not to mention the risk if your wallet gets stolen. The only way to win the credit card game is to use it for everyday purchases and pay your balance in full every month.
>
> Pay quarterly bills monthly.

# 35.   QUESTION WHAT YOU DON'T UNDERSTAND

'I was gratified to be able to answer promptly, and I did. I said I didn't
know the answer.'
**Mark Twain**

Embarrassment is a waste of time. And if you're afraid of appearing stupid, you'll
probably get caught out anyway if you pretend to know or understand something
you don't! Open your mind. Stretch yourself. Don't lose your curiosity and never
be afraid to ask questions. Be willing to trade a few minutes of temporary
discomfort for permanent knowledge.

# 36. ` Ponder your memorial service

As the old saying goes: do you really want to be remembered for putting in extra time at the office?

Think about how you would like to be remembered by family and friends. Consider ways to make your reality reflect your vision. Putting together a list of things you'd like to be remembered for makes for interesting reading. For instance, you might want to be remembered for being able to grow beautiful roses — but not necessarily for having a big house. And you'd probably prefer to be remembered for being generous with your money — not for having a big stock portfolio.

As well as coming up with ideas for inspirational and meaningful things to do with friends and family, consider how to use and leave your money and possessions: in trust for your grandchildren's education, perhaps, or should a part go to a charitable cause that you all hold dear? Other ideas include ongoing donations held in trust so that a tree is planted in your city in your name every year for the next century, or perpetual support pledges for animal shelters and schools. Be remembered as being worthwhile, being happy, and for having lived a good life.

# 37. GIVE GUILT AWAY

'Drag your thoughts away from your guilt. By the ears, by the heels, or any other way you can manage it. It's the healthiest thing a body can do.'
**Mark Twain**

Guilt is very common in women, and it's really just a roundabout way of saying you don't like yourself. When we feel guilty we feel inefficient, bad and wrong. We feel guilty for eating, for spending too much money (or not enough), for not giving enough time to our children (or for smothering them), for working (or for not working hard enough). A no-win situation that is very bad for your health, making you feel sad and depressed.

Guilt is almost always triggered by low self-esteem ('If I were cleverer/ faster/better, I would be able to . . .') It also goes hand in hand with a fear of not being good enough, or of not being worthy, with a willingness to put yourself down — and sometimes even with a superstitious fear that happiness is automatically followed by disaster or problems as part of some sort of natural balance. If any of these ring a bell, give yourself a break.

First, make a guilt checklist: jot down every time you feel guilty about something — then put a line through everything that isn't actually your fault. Second, realise that people won't reject you if you do something wrong. Finally, where appropriate, try getting good and mad instead of feeling guilty — it's much more empowering.

## 38. Learn something new every day

> 'It is not because things are difficult that we do not dare. It is because
> we do not dare that they are difficult.'
> **Seneca**

Learning activates passion, and passion is power — in fact it is one of the
strongest forms of energy that we can generate within our body. Passion is a
connection to life itself, giving us a reason to want to see tomorrow. Start small,
by learning a new skill: take up 'mind sports', such as crosswords or other word
puzzles, which require you to think; board games like chess, which teach you
patience; or, learn to play a musical instrument and practise it on a daily basis.
This will slow down degeneration of brain cells and may even prolong your life.

# 39.   BE SPONTANEOUS

'Why not seize the pleasure at once? How often is happiness destroyed by preparation, foolish preparation?'

It may surprise you to learn that these words come from someone you probably wouldn't regard as having a particularly passionate or free spirit: Jane Austen. Prim author or not, her advice is wise indeed. Any occasion you have the opportunity to up and do something quite different — do it. It doesn't matter if it's something big — an unexpected job, or moving house — or something really small, like trying a new place to buy your fruit and vegetables.

As any well-travelled friend will tell you, there's a world of difference between tourists and real travellers: the real travellers don't just follow the guidebook. They get off the main roads, and explore side streets and alleys. They talk to people in shops or on buses and find out about the little out-of-the-way places that aren't on the maps and certainly aren't advertised. That's how they were able to swim at the beautiful waterfall that only the locals go to, or shop at a dazzling, noisy night market, or photograph rock paintings in an ancient part of the forest that's usually closed to the public.

And another thing: real travellers rarely travel in a straight line, and they don't stick rigidly to a pre-arranged timetable. They stop and start, often going back to look at something again. They change their minds, and go round in circles accidentally-on-purpose. But even if they decide to take the scenic route instead of the expressway, they still manage to get to important pick-up and departure points on time.

It's a good analogy to keep in mind. Move off the beaten track: risk being surprised, delighted, shocked — even being disappointed or getting temporarily lost. But it's only when you take a risk that you can break a habit, and open up a new direction in your life. In your life, be a real traveller, not a tourist, whenever you can.

## 40. Try hand-y yoga

Mudras — yoga movements involving only the arms and hand gestures — are wonderfully effective and easy to do. Here is a mudra which is said to increase happiness. Try doing it twice a day.

Sit comfortably with a straight spine. Curl the ring and small fingers and press them into your palms firmly but gently with the thumbs. Keep the first two fingers pointing straight up. Keep your spine straight and lift the elbows to the side and away from the body. Take long, deep, controlled breaths. Hold this position for three minutes.

# 41.  HELP THE ENVIRONMENT

Ever since, as a little girl, I curled up in a chair and read and re-read *My Family and Other Animals*, *The Bafut Beagles* and *A Zoo in My Luggage*, I was a devoted fan of the British animal conservationist Gerald Durrell. I was so saddened by his death. An ardent 'greenie' long before anyone had ever coined the term, Durrell's thinking was very much at odds with his times, when exploitation of the environment went hand in hand with economic progress. In explaining the motivation behind his work, he once said: 'To me, life is like a superlative meal and the world is like the *maître d'hôtel*. All I am doing is the equivalent of leaving a reasonable tip in gratitude.'

Durrell was also one of the first conservationists to realise that the future health of the environment lay with lots of small lifestyle changes and choices being made by individuals, rather than relying on governments around the world to act in anything other than their own self-interest. Here are three things you can do right away that will make a positive difference:

Put a bottle of water or a brick in your toilet cistern and save up to ten per cent of water every flush.

Take your old plastic carrier bags back to the shops to fill up next time, and try to avoid foods with unnecessary plastic packaging (pre-packed fruit and vegetables, for instance).

Minimise draughts and save energy while cutting your heating bills. Invest in heavy curtains, or shutters.

# 42. LEARN TO LIVE WITH WILDLIFE

With the growth of the human sprawl, we increasingly find ourselves sharing our habitat with other species — from possums nibbling in our backyard to bats swinging in our laundries.

Learning to live alongside wildlife sometimes means knowing when and how to help. If every household familiarised itself with local wildlife rescue organisations, we might be able to think of our backyards as part of a wider circle, a neighbourhood Noah's Ark. So, next to the fridge with all your emergency numbers, put the phone number of the local wildlife rescue service.

# 43.   USE LESS PAPER

Waste paper amounts to tonnes of unnecessary garbage nationwide. Some waste-reducing ideas you may not have thought of are:

Instead of wrapping kids' presents, hide them unwrapped — and plant clues to where they are, like a treasure hunt.

Get off the junk mail circuit. We waste huge amounts of time dealing with unsolicited catalogues and annoying offers that cram our letterboxes. Put a sign on your letterbox and then send a letter to the major senders of junk mail telling them to take you off their lists. Or, use their toll-free number to stop unwanted mail.

Use faster film speeds, such as 400 or 800. This will extend battery life.

Send electronic cards to family and friends who are online. I like the ones at www.egreetings.com and www.BlueMountain.com.

## 44. `PICK UP SOMEONE ELSE'S RUBBISH

Every little bit helps. If you're going for a walk or a run, by yourself or with friends — take a plastic bag. While you're out, aim to pick up at least six pieces of rubbish — drink cartons, pieces of paper, store catalogues that have got stuck under a hedge. The bad news is it's always easy to find at least six pieces. The good news is, you're helping clean up your environment in a practical, no-fuss way.

# 45. DESIGN A SUPPLEMENT PLAN

A basic daily plan, including anti-ageing herbs and nutritional supplements, for someone who is already in reasonably good health might include:

**Vitamin A and the carotenoids:** 5,000 IU of vitamin A plus 10,000 to 15,000 IU total of beta carotene, lycopene and other members of the carotenoid family.

**Acidophilus:** For healthy gut flora.

**Vitamin B complex:** 50 mg each of B1, B2, B3, B6, choline, inositol, and PABA, plus 50 mcg each of B12 and folic acid.

**A bone building supplement** containing calcium and magnesium plus the trace minerals manganese, boron and silica.

**Vitamin C with bioflavonoids:** 500–1,000 mg, more when you are under stress. The best known antioxidant.

**Coenzyme Q10:** 30–100 mg for energy production.

**Vitamin D:** 400 IU. One of the best sources is cod liver oil. And try to get some sunlight every day to help protect your bones.

**Digestive enzymes:** Take with all meals.

**Vitamin E:** 150–400 IU. An antioxidant and a cardiovascular wonderworker.

**Garlic:** Either in capsules, or one to four fresh cloves.

**Ginkgo biloba:** For good circulation and brain power.

**Selenium:** 200 mcg. A cancer-fighting antioxidant.

**Zinc:** 15–30 mg. An immune booster and wound healer.

## 46. HONOUR YOUR SIGNIFICANT OTHER

If you're in a relationship, it can be sobering to take a simple inventory of how you treat them. How much time did you spend together this week? Of that time, how much of it (if any) was 'quality time'? What did you talk about — was it chit-chat, family business, or something more significant? Pay attention to this most important of all your relationships. Give it the significance and respect it deserves. Pay them the same consideration you would a friend, or even a stranger. Don't forget to say please and thank you — every single time — and try to speak calmly and kindly, even when you're absolutely furious. Here are some ideas to improve the quality of your relationship. Try at least one today:

Read to each other from your favourite books.

Sing silly love songs to each other.

Keep your partner's favourite foods on hand.

Find a secluded beach, or a lookout near a lake or river. Not only is it romantic, but looking at the water soothes the soul, improves mood and stimulates your immune system.

Work out together. Exercise is not only an aphrodisiac, but studies show that exercising with a partner increases your odds of sticking with it.

Start a hobby together.

Give your loved one a massage.

Raise a pet with your partner. Couples with pets are happier and healthier than petless ones.

Surround yourself with happy couples: they'll leave you feeling refreshed and hopeful. Avoid unhappy ones: they bring you down.

Send your partner a letter once in a while, even if you live together. Everyone loves to get a little fan mail!

Drink champagne.

Go parking.

Get intimate: buy each other gorgeous — or outrageous — underwear and leave it on the bed, with a rose.

## 47.   PICK POWER FLOWERS

If your life is beginning to feel like an impossible juggling act of work–house–kids, and you feel like dissolving into tears at the slightest provocation, try gentle flower essences — liquid remedies that help restore emotional and spiritual balance. These are the ones most often recommended for stress relief. When you're:

**Fearful**, hypersensitive, frequently troubled; paralysed by doubt, or plagued by nagging worries, try Mimulus.

**Panicky**, appearing cheerful on the outside, but inside you're stressed about money or never finishing projects or some other fear, or lacking confidence and not really believing in yourself, try Agrimony.

**Bitter**, feeling angry, resentful, or being pettish and over-critical, try Beech.

**Tense**, irritable and impatient, doing other people's tasks because you know you can do them better, or always rushing, try Impatiens.

**Exhausted**, feeling completely lacking in strength, or not coping with the tasks ahead of you, try Hornbeam.

**Indecisive**, swinging from one idea to another without really settling to a task — which makes you even more stressed and anxious — try Scleranthus.

**Worried**, mentally agitated, suffering from insomnia and restlessness, or having difficulty feeling objective, try White Chestnut.

# 48. SHOW YOUR LOVE

'Put your arms around me like a circle round the sun.'
**Arlo Guthrie, 'Stealing'**

The success or failure of a relationship doesn't rest on the big things, the grand gestures, the extravagant gifts, but on the little things. Here's how to make daily life together just a little bit more special:

Brush each other's hair.

You don't have to write great poetry or love letters yourself. Quote from William Shakespeare, Billy Joel or Paul McCartney instead.

Hide notes and small gifts under the pillow, in the glove compartment, under the dinner plate, frozen in ice cubes.

Place a flower under the windshield wiper of their car.

Have their portrait painted from a photograph.

Take a shower together.

Get funky with birthday presents. Thirty years old? Send 30 pink roses. Forty? Send 40 balloons. Fifty? Fill a jar with 50 licorice all-sorts. Sixty? Wrap up 60 sunflowers.

Use those Valentine Conversation Heart sweets to spell out a romantic message on the kitchen table.

Listen to a lush, romantic musical album together, like *The Phantom of the Opera*.

Carve both your initials in a tree.

Put a written message inside a balloon, then attach a pin to the string.

Draw hearts on the eggs in the fridge.

Go for a walk in the moonlight.

Read aloud together.

## 49. GET SOME MARINE MUSCLE

Kelp *(Laminaria)* is a thick brown seaweed that grows in cold waters. In traditional Chinese medicine, kelp is used to treat an underactive thyroid, symptoms of which may include fatigue, depression and weight gain. This is thought to be because, compared to other seaweeds, kelp is especially rich in iodine, which helps to regulate the thyroid gland. There has also been one intriguing study indicating that fucoidan (a complex sugar found in kelp) may stimulate cancer-fighting cells in the immune system.

You can buy kelp (sometimes called kombu) in dried strips in health food shops or Japanese grocery stores. Store it in a dry place as it can get mildew if it gets damp. To use, cut the dried kelp into small pieces and simmer in water for 15 minutes. (Japanese cooks use this as stock.) It's enormously versatile — add pieces to all manner of soups, stews and casseroles for extra taste as well as nutrients. Tip: if you cook kelp with beans, it will make them easier to digest. Kelp is also available in tablet form.

## 50.  TRY GINSENG

Doctors of traditional Chinese medicine (TCM) call ginseng 'the root of life'. It has been used for many centuries to nourish *qi* — the body's vital life force — boost energy, and, especially, to help patients recuperating from illness to get their strength back. Many footballers take it at half-time to boost their energy levels. It's also been used as a sexual tonic and is said to enhance fertility in both men and women.

Ginseng is known as an 'adaptogenic' herb, meaning it helps the body adapt to stress and fatigue by stimulating the nervous system and therefore improving reasoning and concentration skills. It also stimulates the circulation and increases the oxygen supply to the brain, making you feel more awake. There are many forms of ginseng available: Korean or Siberian types are the strongest and are best taken for general loss of energy, while the American type is more gentle, making it suitable for tiredness caused by nervous conditions or insomnia. Look for a brand which lists the standardised ginsenosides (active ingredients of ginseng) which are present in the tablet or tea on the label. Otherwise you may be getting an inferior or stale product. Avoid ginseng if you have high blood pressure or are pregnant.

## 51. MAKE VACUUMING A SCENTUAL EXPERIENCE

Like death and taxes, dust is always with us. Vacuuming is a job that just has to be done or your home ends up looking like an old saloon . . . so, if you can't enjoy it, at least you can do it with style! Sprinkle a couple of drops of essential oil onto your vacuum bag before vacuuming. Many have antimicrobial properties, which makes them excellent for killing germs. And there's a wonderful side effect — friends always remark on how great my house smells! I like varying the oils with the seasons. In autumn and winter, I use rich, heady patchouli. Lighter, uplifting lavender and lemon are nice in spring and summer. Eucalyptus and rosemary are good all-purpose disinfectants for any time of year.

# 52.   CHOOSE QUALITY OVER QUANTITY

Instead of having half a dozen knives that never feel right in your hand and just don't cut or slice as well as you'd like, invest in one absolutely superb knife that sharpens like a dream and feels perfect in your hand. This is smart shopping, and will save you money — and aggravation — in the long run. Rather than a dresser full of odd-shaped plates in trendy colours and patterns that don't match and aren't well-finished, have one set of durable, beautiful white plates that never go out of style. Same goes for all manner of household appliances, furniture and commodities, from cars to candlesticks. If you're going to spend life-energy and money on something that you do need, then choose to spend it once on something that does the job perfectly and will last.

It's an easy philosophy, and one which supports your aim to de-junk and de-stress your life. By buying well, you are more likely to have everything you truly need, and the time to satisfy your inner wants. After all, it's excess, waste, clutter and useless stuff that doesn't work that are the real deprivers of time and quality of life.

# 53. FIND QUIET

'Stop the words now. Open the window in the centre of your chest, and let the spirits fly in and out.'
**Rumi**

A spiritual key to de-stressing and de-junking your life is to seek and find silence. Indoor pollution is a major factor in stress. This can take many forms, including the noise from computers, phones, fax machines, photocopiers at work, and computer and phone at home. At work, suggest changes that will keep your immediate environment quieter, such as siting the photocopier away from desks. The results will be better levels of concentration and increased energy. At home, for one day a week, try going through a whole day without anything in the background: no radio, no TV, no phone. If you have an answering machine, monitor your calls. Return only those you must. Don't speak unless you're spoken to. Don't make small talk. Stay inside and shut the door.

You may be uncomfortable with the silence at first, it can be quite confronting if you're not used to it, and it's natural to react to such a significant change in your environment. However, the more you practise being silent, the less it will bother you — and the more you will look forward to it, crave it, even. When you are silent, you can finally hear your own inner voice. You are more likely to get in touch with your inner feelings and sense of purpose when you take time out from the noise of the world. New ideas and thoughts flood to the front of your mind when you actually have the time to hear them. It's amazing how much calmer things become when you literally 'switch off'. Have you ever had the electricity go off and noticed how much softer and more intense the silence is? You hardly notice the hum of the refrigerator during the day and night, but when it's no longer there, the silence becomes so much more profound.

Consciously try to incorporate quiet time into your daily routine. Many spiritual practices recommend allocating time to be silent at the beginning and end of each day: try it, even if you don't wish to pray or meditate. These brief periods of silence will bring you closer to yourself, make you more conscious of your senses and allow your mind to rest. If you can't get the quiet time you need where you are, take a walk alone. Listen to your thoughts as you walk. Breathe deeply and walk some more. Give yourself this gift and defend it every day.

## 54.   HAVE A MASSAGE

The touching therapies are vital to self-nurturing. It's simply not possible to give yourself a really good back massage, and it's one of the few things guaranteed to create a deep, relaxed feeling and a sense of harmony and wellbeing that can last for hours. If you're impossibly busy and can't spare an hour, contact one of the seated massage specialists who offer workplace massages that can take as little as ten minutes. The deep-tissue massage — which increases blood flow and endorphin production — is given in a specially designed chair, and you don't even have to get undressed. It's a fantastic idea if you spend a lot of time clamped to a computer, and have the typical side effects of a stiff neck and tension in the upper back. You might even be able to convince your employer to introduce on-the-job massage as part of a staff incentive program! It's certainly less expensive than having to pay sick leave benefits.

The seated massage practitioner does not use scented oils. However, you can still enjoy their benefits by putting a few drops of your favourite one on a tissue and inhaling it during your massage. Different oils can alter how you feel emotionally, and can make a difference to your productivity.

**To relax**, try chamomile, clary sage, lavender or neroli.

**To sharpen the mind**, try basil, lemon, peppermint, pine or tea tree.

**To lift your spirits**, try bergamot, hyssop or orange.

**To get more energy**, try eucalyptus, grapefruit or pine.

**To boost intellect and morale**, try cedarwood, rosemary or thyme.

## 55.  FIND YOUR INNER ARTIST

'Open a new window, open a new door — there are things out there
you've never seen before.'
**'Auntie Mame'**

A recent survey at Arizona University found that school students who said they
came from happy families — irrespective of the structure or size of that family —
tended to have parents who had creative hobbies, such as art, writing, music and
photography. Also, when asked whether their parents encouraged their ideas and
endeavours, these kids were a whopping five times more likely to say 'yes' than
those whose parents didn't have some sort of some creative outlet.

But you're not artistic, you say? Haven't a creative bone in your body?
Couldn't draw or paint to save yourself? Think outside the square: pick a class in
pottery, woodwork, jewellery, beading, screen-printing, quilting, knitting, drama,
or making potpourri and wreaths of dried herbs instead. The important thing is
to find out about your creative side — everyone's got one, and it's usually stifled.
Don't worry if your pots are lopsided or you can't get past plain-and-purl, either.
That's not the point. 'Creative' or not, you are responsible for creating all aspects
of your life. Exploring and expressing your creativity is about opening up
windows of possibility, not about having to be 'good' at an activity. And it's fun:
you get a real thrill knowing that you've gone out there and tried something
different, that you've put your energy and time into a project and come up with
something quite new.

## 56. BE INSPIRED BY THE CLASSICS

In *A Room of One's Own*, Virginia Woolf wrote: 'Masterpieces are not single solitary births. They are the outcome of many years of thinking in common, of thinking by the body of the people, so that the experience of the mass is behind a single voice.'

This is why the great works of artists of times gone by — the painters, writers, and sculptors — have the power to comfort a bruised heart or ego, and to enlighten and clarify when it seems nothing else can. Their work has stood the test of time because it has identified common threads in the human adventure, and spoken to generations of souls. Great artists are great because they are able to mirror us — to give shape to our self-expression. Think of an artist whose work has touched you to your very core. Go back to your schooldays, if necessary: there will probably be more than one whose work really resonated with you, even if you didn't know why. Now — visit your bookshop or local library and look up everything you can find about that person and their work. Look at it, and let it touch you. Let it add colour and shape to your life and help you give shape to your feelings and emotions by reminding you of all that is tender, noble, striving, productive and timeless.

# 57.  REDISCOVER POETRY

'A book is a garden carried in the pocket.'
**Arab proverb**

Most of us had poetry utterly spoiled for us at school. Gazing out the window
while a teacher recited boring words that didn't seem to mean anything.
Struggling over essays on completely incomprehensible poems, or slavishly
copying someone else's crib notes. Worse still, having to write your own poem, or
having to learn one off by heart. These are all very effective ways of stripping
poetry of its precious intimacy and passion, probably resulting in a lost
opportunity for you to make a lifelong friend. That is what poetry can be: the way
for one soul to communicate with another. Such a terrible waste.

Nor is there such a thing as 'good' poetry. Be it classical, Japanese haiku or
Afro-American street-rap, a good poem is the poem that's right for you, the one
that says exactly what you're feeling over a lost love, an ageing parent, a troubled
child, war, fear, disappointment, or a glorious triumph. For all those times when
you haven't a clue what to say, you will probably find that a poet has already said it
for you. Remember the lines of grief and fury from the W.H. Auden poem 'Funeral
Blues' recited at the funeral service in *Four Weddings and a Funeral*? 'The stars are
not wanted now; put out every one; Pack up the moon and dismantle the sun . . .
For nothing now can ever come to any good.' Those extraordinary words must
have made thousands of non-poetry-readers think twice about the gut-wrenching
impact and healing power of poetry.

To rediscover poetry, you need first to 'deprogram' yourself, to shed all those
high school associations. Pick up your chosen book of poetry and sit somewhere
comfortable and quiet. Read the poem in your head to begin with, slowly. Then
read it again, out loud this time, but still just for yourself. Really listen to the
words. Why did the poet choose those particular words, and not others? Notice
their sounds, their rhythm. What images come to your mind? Do they change
when you read it again? Whatever you do, don't pick and analyse, looking for
meaning as you were told to do at school. Instead, be open to the flow of the
words, how the poem makes you feel, how you react to it. Not every poem will
speak to you, but you'll find many will give you messages of strength and
inspiration just when you need them.

# 58.  BALANCE YOUR BLOOD SUGAR

Foods that rate high on the glycaemic index, such as white potatoes and corn flakes, rapidly elevate your blood sugar and may result in you producing more insulin than you need. This, in turn, can result in lower levels of HDL cholesterol (the 'good' one), ramp up your blood pressure, and put you at a greater risk of heart disease and weight problems. A huge study of over 75,000 women, published in the *American Journal of Clinical Nutrition* in June 2000, showed that there was a dramatic link between a too-high intake of high-glycaemic foods and a greater risk of coronary heart disease. Your best bet is to avoid highly refined foods, such as white flour and sugar, and white flour-based pasta and bread altogether. Get into the habit of choosing whole-grain versions instead.

# 59. LIE DOWN

For many people, the idea of putting a rest stop in their day is a confronting one. Resting is often misconstrued as being lazy. In fact, you need periods of stillness in order to calm and replenish yourself.

Yoga is particularly restorative. In the pose below the body is completely supported, allowing complete relaxation. It also increases blood flow to your head, improves memory and concentration, and stimulates thyroid function, which helps regulate mood and energy levels. Spend about ten minutes in the pose, then lie flat for about two minutes. As you explore the pose, allow your breath to become long and slow. Listen to the sound of your breathing and let it soothe your system. Feel utter relief as you begin to let go. Practise the pose at least three times a week, preferably once a day.

## Legs-up-the-wall

Find a space next to a wall. Lie down with your buttocks as close to the wall as possible. Bend your knees, roll your pelvis up and place a folded blanket under your hips to support your lower back and give your buttocks a lift. If you wish, slip a small flat cushion under your head and an eye pillow over your eyes, too. Your buttocks should be touching the wall, your arms should be at your sides, palms up. Straighten your legs up against the wall. Extend your arms out to the side, palms up. After the ten minutes has passed, get out of the pose by bending your knees and rolling onto your side, then lying flat for two minutes.

# 60. ACT LIKE A GROWN-UP

Sayings, proverbs and phrases have been handed down through the generations for good reason — they express a belief, a feeling or an aspiration perfectly. We are made by our beliefs and feelings: as we believe and feel, so we are. These are the 'golden rules' that I find most meaningful. What are yours?

**Behave with integrity.** 'Integrity' means wholeness. When your actions and inner beliefs are out of accord, the resulting tension leads to anxiety and loss of will.

**Do not sit in judgement on other people.** The saying 'Live and let live' is a particularly wise one.

**When you are wrong, admit it.** There is a Buddhist saying: 'Between him who has conquered thousands of men in battle, and him who has conquered himself, it is the latter who is the greater conqueror.' Minimise self-righteousness by staying scrupulously aware of your actions.

**Don't procrastinate.** When you put off things that need to be done, you'll only end up wasting precious energy worrying about it.

**Learn to laugh at yourself.** In her autobiography, Ethel Barrymore wrote: 'You grow up the day you have the first real laugh at yourself.' You can usually find humour, even in the worst-possible situations. It's always there.

**Like yourself.** Write down all the qualities and abilities you like about yourself. Do this every time you catch yourself being self-critical.

**Have faith in yourself.** Surveys consistently find that self-confidence is an important component of happiness.

**Don't worry about what other people will think.** Consider these lines from Sadi: 'Were the diver to think of the jaws of the shark, He would never lay hands on the pearl.' In other words, anxiety about others' reactions can cripple you. We all want to be liked, but if you find you are being stopped from taking action by a little voice in your mind that says 'What will people think of me if I do that?' answer with, 'People mostly think about themselves,' and notice the effect on your attitude. The reality is that most people won't notice what you're worrying about!

# 61.  BE GLAD IT'S NOT WORSE

'Learn to wish that everything should come to pass exactly as it does.'
**Epictetus**

'Downward comparison' is an exercise favoured by psychiatrists trying to help
people learn serenity and acceptance.

When you're feeling unhappy, try thinking of someone even unluckier than
you are — not to gloat, but to gain a new perspective on your situation (and
maybe a new understanding about how well you are coping, really). In one study,
subjects were given a sentence to complete five times: either 'I'm glad I'm not a
...' or 'I wish I were a ...' Afterwards, those who reflected on their good fortune
expressed anything up to ten times more satisfaction with the way their lives
were going than the whingers did. Peace of mind comes from not wanting to
change other people or things, but simply accepting them as they are.

# 62. STAY STRONG

> 'If you have built castles in the air, your work need not be lost. That is where they should be. Now — put the foundations under them.'
> **Henri David Thoreau**

Probably the most critical aspect of feeling good about your life is to 'bullet-proof' yourself — to have a contingency plan for what will happen if things don't go according to plan.

Getting yourself on an even keel financially, and plugging up your spending 'holes' is one thing. Hopefully, you can put a plan in place to start saving, even just a little. But money means nothing if you haven't got your health. Many people find thinking about things like medical insurance very distressing — so they just don't do it. The best medical insurance is, of course, to stay healthy — get plenty of rest, eat properly, take nutritional supplements, exercise regularly, reduce stress, stop smoking or using excessive alcohol. Yet sometimes, a person can do all the right things and still get sick.

My grandfather used to say that insurance was something that you always paid out — but hoped never to have to use. It's far better for peace of mind to get medical insurance, so that you or your partner would be covered in the event of a problem. Otherwise, it could represent a major disaster in your otherwise manageable financial plan. Make a list of the major insurance companies and start ringing around to get comparisons. By preparing for any emergency in your health or home, you become more self-reliant and, ultimately, less stressed, because your survival is not dependent on week-to-week activities.

# 65. BEAT BAD CIRCULATION

Do you feel the cold very easily? And take ages to warm up again? The weather doesn't have to be cold to play havoc with your circulation. Sometimes, an office air-conditioning unit being consistently set on a fiercely cold setting is all it takes to upset your system. Here's how you can ease any discomfort.

**Wear warm clothing, and gloves in winter.** Protecting yourself from the cold and avoiding dramatic changes in temperature will alleviate the problem. Wear lots of layers of clothing: several thin layers of clothing are better than one thick layer, as air trapped between the layers warms up and acts as an insulator. Natural fibres, such as cotton, wool or silk, keep you warmer than most synthetic fabrics.

**Massage your feet and hands.** Do this using rosemary or black pepper essential oils to help stimulate blood flow. Mix two to four drops of one of these oils in 10 ml of carrier oil, such as almond.

**Stop smoking.** It causes the blood vessel walls to stiffen so they are less able to respond to a sudden change in temperature.

**Eat for warmth.** Frequent, small meals will help to maintain your energy and heat levels — and don't skip breakfast. High-energy foods include carbohydrate-rich cereals, bread, potatoes and baked beans. Hot drinks can also help to keep you warm.

**Get more exercise.** If you are prone to circulation problems, avoid sitting for long periods. Get up every so often and walk around the room. Then shake your legs, roll your shoulders and wave your arms.

# 66.  CHECK FOR CANDIDA

Overgrowth of the fungus candida in the digestive system has been associated with a whole range of seemingly unrelated problems, including irritability, tiredness, mild depression, thrush (which affects 70 per cent of women at some time), food sensitivities, flatulence, and poor digestion. It often takes hold following a period of long-term stress, lowered immunity and over-use of antibiotics. If you suspect you may have candida, these tips can make a real difference to how you feel:

**Cut back on sugar**. Candida thrives on sugar, meaning it becomes more widespread, and symptoms become more severe. Investigate natural alternatives in your health food store, such as the powdered herb stevia (claimed to be 100 times sweeter than sugar, and kilojoule-free) and supplemental forms of fructo-oligosaccharide (FOS), a sweet-tasting soluble fibre. As a bonus, FOS boosts the production of the 'good' bacteria in the gut which keep candida in check, and improve digestion.

**Use plenty of garlic**. It contains a powerful antifungal substance called allicin, which slows the spread of candida.

**Eliminate yeast-containing foods**. Remove 'yeasty' foods, such as bread, from your diet for at least a fortnight. Then gradually reinstate them and note if they cause any symptoms. If so, it may be that a yeast sensitivity is behind your candida problem — checking it out with a nutritionist is the best long-term solution.

**Take probiotics**. These helpful bacteria, notably *Lactobacillus bulgaricus* and *Lactobacillus acidophilus*, help keep your digestive system balanced. Choose from the wide array of probiotic foods and supplements available, including easy-to-take yoghurt-style desserts and drinks.

# 67.   USE A MOISTURISER EVERY SINGLE DAY

As well as causing skin cancer, sun damage causes up to 80 per cent of premature lines and wrinkles. It's vital, therefore, always to use a moisturiser that contains a sunscreen of at least SPF15. Choose one that does more than just add moisture if you want to keep your skin looking younger for longer. The three best-proven anti-ageing ingredients in skincare products are vitamin A derivatives — such as retinoic acid and retinol — which work by encouraging the top layer of skin to renew itself more quickly; vitamin C, a powerful antioxidant that helps to counteract the ageing effects of harmful molecules — known as free radicals — found in the body; and vitamin E, which speeds up cell repair.

# 68.  DRINK, DRINK, DRINK

Lack of fluids is one of the main reasons for constipation, travel-related dehydration and endurance problems during exercise. Plus, a study by Boston Women's Hospital has found that drinking eight to ten glasses of water a day helps prevent kidney stones. (Tip: if you're bored with just drinking water, eat more watery fruit and vegetables, such as melons, oranges, cucumbers, lettuces and tomatoes. Eating fruit, vegetables and clear soup can be equivalent to about three glasses of water a day.)

# 69. GO FOR SLOW-BURNING FOODS

Some carbohydrates are much better at boosting your metabolism and giving you energy than others.

Your metabolism tends to function better on foods that are low on the glycaemic index: the rate at which the body converts carbohydrates into sugar. High-glycaemic foods get broken down quickly, releasing excess sugar. But 'slow' foods — low on the index — release sugar gradually so it is used more efficiently. Rye bread, brown rice, lentils, beans and vegetables are all 'slow burning' carbohydrates while dried dates, watermelon, honey, sugar and bananas are 'quick'. To maintain healthy metabolic function, eat fresh vegetables at least twice a day and choose whole foods over refined or processed ones. About 60 to 65 per cent of your diet should come from carbohydrates.

# 70. Buy more fresh fruit and vegetables

Check the crisper — today's the day to make sure you've got these healthy essentials to hand in the kitchen. And, if you need an extra incentive, according to an American survey it seems vegetable-eaters make better lovers. Participants claim that people who eat more vegies smell and taste better, have more energy and stamina in lovemaking, and are more gentle, caring and sensitive to their partners' needs than those who eat few to no vegetables.

**Red capsicums** Contain two and a half times more vitamin C than oranges, and are one of the best sources of beta carotene.

**Onions** Provide sulphur compounds that benefit your immune system and circulation. They are also a rich source of a flavonoid called quercetin which may lower the risk of allergies — red onions have the highest amounts.

**Spinach** A great source of lutein, a carotenoid believed to protect against cataracts and other eye diseases. Also a good source of folic acid (vital for a healthy pregnancy) and vitamin C.

**Bananas** Rich in potassium, a mineral credited with reducing high blood pressure, bananas also provide vitamin B6, needed for a healthy nervous system.

**Apples** A nutritious and cleansing fruit, apples help reduce blood cholesterol levels, remove toxins from the body and are great for digestive upsets.

# 71.   SAY NO TO NEGATIVE THOUGHTS

A quick way to get out of a pessimistic frame of mind is to force yourself to think about something else.

Say you're stuck in traffic — a situation that so easily triggers a cascade of self-flagellation ('I'm always late. I'm so disorganised. I never leave on time.') Before you give in to moping and/or beating yourself up, look out the window and notice the passengers in the other cars. Make a mental note of people to invite to dinner. Or relive a favourite memory in exquisite detail, right down to the colours, smells and spoken words. The idea isn't necessarily to think 'positive' thoughts, but rather to stop the bullying ones from attacking.

# 72.  CLEAR THE AIR

Sobering thought for the day: the air in your house — and your car — could be more polluted than the air outside. Here's how to clean it up:

**Avoid drycleaning**. Apart from being expensive, the jury is still out on whether the solvent that's used by many drycleaners is cancer-causing. If you have items that simply must be drycleaned, then at least air them in the sun on a clothesline before putting them away.

**Open the windows**. A stuffy atmosphere and central heating or air conditioning drain energy levels and make you susceptible to colds and flu. Leave doors between rooms open, and open the windows. Keep heating and cooling systems on low, and consider buying energy-efficient fans, which pull in and circulate extra fresh air.

**Keep your car properly tuned**. Changing the oil before it's necessary and getting regular tyre checks both help reduce your car's emissions — which means breathing in less pollution. They also help maximise your mileage.

**Love natural timber**. Try to buy furniture made from real wood rather than modern particleboard, which releases formaldehyde, a chemical which has been linked to cancer. If possible, pull up any wall-to-wall carpets, which are a breeding ground for dust mites and which trap fumes and smells. Have polished floorboards and colourful cotton or hemp scatter rugs instead.

**Cut back on synthetics**. When choosing curtains, blinds or other soft furnishings, carefully check the materials you're using. Some polyester or plastic-backed fabrics release dangerous — and odourless — fumes when heated by sun coming through a window, or by a nearby stove or fireplace. Opt for wool, cotton, untreated canvas or linen instead.

**Don't buy artificial air fresheners**. They're expensive and unnecessary, and the can is just one more bit of non-recyclable rubbish. If you have a problem with damp or musty smells, this tried-and-tried and true alternative costs next to nothing, and it's very effective in absorbing odours: mix a few drops of essential oil into a cup of bicarbonate of soda, and leave on top of a shelf or cupboard.

# 73.   WASH SMARTER

Did you realise that part of saving money on your clothes and making them last as long as possible is in your laundry? Specifically, in your washing machine and choice of laundry detergent or soap, and in your drier. Simple choices about fabrics you buy and how you care for them can definitely have a positive impact on your finances. Try these tips, and reap the benefits:

**Wash less often**. If something has just been worn once or twice briefly, and doesn't have any obvious stains or marks, don't wash it automatically. Check out what's left in the lint-catcher of your washing machine sometime — that's part of your clothes in there! Sometimes, all a garment needs is a good airing or a brisk once-over with a clothes brush.

**Make some simple house rules**. For starters, one towel and one face washer per person, per week. This can almost halve the amount of washing you do every week, particularly if you have a family. Wash sheets every fortnight, rather than every week. Choosing a single colour for all the bedding — like white — also makes things easier, because it means they can all be washed together. And, from now on, choose clothes with an eye towards managing the wash. Read care labels and avoid anything that requires special hand-washing.

**Choose gentle detergents and soap powders**. The milder they are, the gentler they are on clothes. With underwear, in particular, hand-washing with a pure soap or soap powder will serve you better in the long run, as they will last anything up to four times longer than if they're chucked in with a dose of harsh detergent better used for cleaning work gear.

**Only use the drier in emergencies**. They really do take the life out of clothes. If, like me, you wash pretty much every day, enjoy those few minutes that it takes to hang the clothes on the line — feel the breeze and look up at the sky, enjoy the birds — before it's time to go and get on with the working day. Your clothes will smell better, too.

**Bring back aprons**. A lot of the time, perfectly good clothes get spoiled by carelessness. Put pinnies or designated play-clothes on children when they're using paints and Textas, and wear an apron yourself when you're doing housework or cooking. Reserve worn-out clothes for fabric-destroying jobs, like working on the car.

# 74. CLEAN UP YOUR KITCHEN ACT

You're in there every day, cooking and preparing meals. However, if you're like most people, you scoot in and out without really paying attention to basic hygiene. A few simple rules in the kitchen can dramatically reduce the spread of germs and bacteria and protect you from coming down with all manner of tummy bugs, as well as streamlining the flow of activity, and so making you feel a bit better organised.

**Wash your hands**. Do so before handling unwrapped foods and after handling any raw food.

**Don't dip your fingers into food**.

**Don't use the same knife or chopping board for raw and cooked meats**.

**Dry your hands on kitchen paper**. It is better than using a tea towel.

**Clean your fridge once a week**. Throw out anything that has passed its use-by date.

**Be particularly careful about leftovers**. A common cause of food poisoning is leaving cooked food out of the fridge for too long. To cool cooked food quickly before refrigeration, place it in a bowl of iced water.

**Use a nylon brush rather than a dishcloth**. If you use a dishcloth, make sure you disinfect it regularly.

# 75. Put down the pick-me-ups

Sugary foods such as lollies and chocolate only raise your blood glucose temporarily. Then the pancreas releases the hormone insulin which brings your glucose levels back down again, causing an energy dip. Stimulants such as coffee and tea have the same effect: though they do not contain sugar, they stimulate the liver and other tissues to release glucose rapidly into the bloodstream. Alcohol may liven you up for a moment as your inhibitions slip away, but too much is likely to send you to sleep. If you need help giving up or at least cutting back on these popular 'pick-me-ups', consider the following:

**Strong tea and coffee** Fresh coffee has about 150 mg of caffeine per mug, and tea about 100 mg. More than 300 mg a day can cause anxiety symptoms, headaches, nausea and diarrhoea. Tea also contains tannin, which inhibits iron absorption.

**Sugary snacks** Cakes and sweets make your blood sugar rise sharply and then fall dramatically. Too much can also trigger reactive hypoglycaemia (low blood sugar), which can leave you feeling shaky and spaced out.

**Alcohol** Drinking initially makes us feel happier, but alcohol is a depressant, which means it slows down the central nervous system. You may think it lifts your spirits, but your body treats it as a poison. The danger of relying on drink to make you feel good is that you can build up a tolerance, and need more and more to produce the same effect.

**Smoking** The stimulating effect of nicotine is short-lived. To keep up that temporary high, you would have to chain-smoke. Smoking causes cancer and heart disease.

# 76.   CHECK YOUR CHI

Qigong (pronounced chee-gong) is a 5,000-year-old Chinese practice designed to promote the flow of *chi*, the vital life force that flows throughout the body, regulating its functions.

Try this calming exercise: stand with your feet shoulder-width apart and parallel. Bend your knees to a quarter-squat position while keeping your upper body straight. Observe your breathing for a couple of breaths. Inhale and bring your arms slowly up in front of you to shoulder height with your elbows slightly bent. Exhale, stretching your arms straight out. Inhale again, bend your elbows slightly and drop your arms down slowly until your thumbs touch the sides of your legs. Exhale one more time, then stand up straight.

## 77. DON'T PUT OFF PEACE

Philosopher Thomas Fuller wrote: 'Being content does not consist in heaping up more fuel, but in taking away some fire' back in 1732 — which goes to show that the 'just as soon as . . .' bug has been around for a while.

This is the highly intrusive and destructive virus that affects pretty much everyone in the Western world: the one that teaches us not only to rank material possessions and external experiences over inner ones but which — and this is far more sinister — tells you that you can only be happy 'just as soon as' some particular thing occurs. Now, this could be something substantial that quite likely will have a positive impact on your life, like going on a much-needed holiday, or trading up to a more comfortable car. However, the trap is when the 'just as soon as . . .' bug finds its way into every thought and sentence, affecting how you feel about your furniture, your washing machine, your relationship, the way your kids are turning out, even the weather forecast for the day. If you keep putting off feeling pleased with things until something about them changes, contentment slips through your fingers like water.

Make today the first day of the rest of a simpler, more content life. Being conscious of the tenacity of the 'just as soon as . . .' bug is a good start. So is knowing — and believing in your heart (they're two different things!) — that chasing after new and different things only brings dissatisfaction. Most important, make a commitment to yourself that your peace of mind is worth everything to you. It's too important to allow it to be eroded in a perpetual cycle of want-spend-dissatisfaction. Today's a good day to start.

# 78.   CULTIVATE ACCEPTANCE

The Chinese have a wonderful proverb: 'When my heart is at peace, the world is at peace.' But that's only half the story.

Anyone can feel at peace if nothing too awful is happening to them or to their loved ones. It's easy to feel affectionate when someone's paying you lots of attention, or to be sympathetic when you don't have to actually do anything or make any changes in your own life. It's easy to be calm when it's not your home that's being stalked by trauma and fear. It's even reasonably easy to forgive if you haven't been that deeply offended. It becomes more of a challenge, however, when trying or downright terrifying things happen — but you still need to stay calm and focused and be capable of taking the appropriate action.

Coming to grips with your own hurting heart — whether it's been wounded by anxiety, dissatisfaction, loneliness, fear, or fury — is only possible if you accept and take responsibility for how you feel and what you do about it. Many things happen that you can't be responsible for: you can't change other people's opinions and actions, for instance, and you certainly can't mould the world at will to suit just you. But you can be responsible for how you think, for how you react to situations, and for how you plan to react in future. You can pinpoint unrealistic goals and expectations, and toss them out — or at least revise them. You can step back rather than go barrelling ahead. You can be still and listen. Then, and only then, can you see what's really happening, what is and is not true, and accept it.

Remember, acceptance doesn't necessarily mean rolling over and agreeing with something or someone — it just means aiming to live in harmony with that thing or person, and to rise to the occasion with deeper levels of compassion and empathy.

# 79.  HONOUR THE SABBATH

It's frighteningly easy to just keep going, day after day — working, doing, fixing, helping, tidying — without taking a break. Reports have to be written, the grocery shopping has to be done, meals have to be cooked, and the relentless list of household chores has to be tackled before you can relax. The only way to get through it all is to just keep plugging away . . .

Well, during World War II, the British government thought exactly the same thing. They were so sure they were right — and they were also under so much pressure from the war effort to increase production of uniforms, food and equipment — that they passed a law abolishing Sunday as a day of rest. Workers were told to just keep going, week in, week out, with no time off. Given the exceptional circumstances, everyone cooperated wholeheartedly. However, even though all the different workers really were working hard — no one would have thought of taking a sick day, for instance, because it would have been seen as letting the side down — productivity actually decreased, because officials found that the number of mistakes made and the resulting downtime had both increased dramatically.

The moral of the story is: make it a priority to stop spending your physical and mental energy, day after day, without a break. You need one day a week to recharge your batteries, an energy-saving day, as opposed to all the other days when you spend your energy. Consider reintroducing the ancient and extremely sane idea of the sabbath. It comes from the Jewish word *shabbat*, which means 'the seventh'. Everyone needs one, whether you're Jewish, Buddhist or atheist. Nor does it have to be Sunday — it could be Monday or Tuesday if you work on weekends, or spend them ferrying children to various activities. Or, as a minimum, you could make Saturday afternoons a special time for quiet contemplation and spiritual nourishment, through reading, prayer or meditation. Whatever time you select, be aware that you will need to be extremely firm about keeping it. Do not let duties and responsibilities intrude on your sabbath. Make it a time of rest that will sustain you through the whole of the coming week.

# 80. SAY GRACE

My favourite grace is a very simple one — the words from Ophelia to Hamlet: 'God be at your table.'

For your physical health as much as your mental one, saying a grace of some sort, religious or otherwise, makes good sense. Creating that little still, steadying space before you eat makes for a relaxed meal, which makes for good conversation as well as sound digestion. And, with so much sadness and hunger in the world, it seems only right that we be grateful for our blessings. For a brief moment, you have the chance to contemplate and offer thanks to the power that created your wondrous body, which is now ready to receive nourishment, and give thanks for the presence of those who will share it with you, as well as considering the plight of those who may have nothing to eat.

I also like the Quaker habit of a silent grace. Those gathered at the table may hold hands and bow their heads for a few moments' silent meditation before starting to eat. This is a particularly gentle and calming way to start a meal. You might want to try the Jewish idea of passing a candle when family and friends eat together. A lit candle is passed to each person in turn. They hold it and, if they want to, they have the chance to talk about something funny or special that has happened to them that day or week that they think is important and want to share. No one else is allowed to speak or interrupt while that person is holding the candle. Then it's passed on to the next person, and they do the same thing.

Nor, naturally, does saying grace have to be confined to mealtimes. Consider the words of the British author G.K. Chesterton: 'You say grace before meals. All right. But I say grace before the concert and the opera, and grace before the play and pantomime, and grace before I open a book, and grace before sketching, painting, swimming, fencing, boxing and walking, playing, dancing and grace before I dip the pen in the ink.'

# 81. BE LAVISH WITH FRAGRANCE

One of the first things you notice when you walk into a house is what it smells like, so try these sweet-smelling strategies:

**Welcome yourself home**. Place a bowl of potpourri in the hallway — the lovely smell will help you enter your home in a positive frame of mind.
**Use essential oils when cleaning**. They make rooms smell great and perk you up. Shake ten drops of your favourite essential oil on to a cotton ball and put it in the bag of your vacuum cleaner. Polish wood with lavender oil-scented furniture or floor polish. For scented drawer liners, spray lining paper with a fragrant oil spray: make your own by filling a house plant mister with purified water and adding your favourite essential oil (use about 15 drops of oil to every 125 ml of water).
**Go for natural fragrances**. Never use air fresheners, odour eaters or fake scent sprays — they smell synthetic, and many people are allergic to them.

## 82. BE KIND TO YOURSELF

'Make the most of yourself, for that is all there is of you.'
**Ralph Waldo Emerson**

No matter how hard anyone else judges you, you judge yourself the hardest.

Be kind to yourself: next time you're giving yourself a dressing-down, stop, and talk to yourself as if you were a friend. Imagine she has the same problem. Would you condemn her as you condemn yourself? You certainly wouldn't be as hard on her as you are on yourself! Instead, be reassuring — and apply the same advice you would give that friend.

If you're stuck in the loop of negative self-talk and automatically beat yourself up and expect the worst possible outcome, a good mental habit to adopt is to imagine yourself as a television interviewer. Rather than panic or come down on yourself, ask yourself some tough but realistic questions. Get the facts: what evidence do you have that this bad thing will actually happen? And, even if it does, haven't you got any plans you can put in place to anticipate the problem? What can you do to reduce the impact? This line of questioning prevents you from turning everything into a disaster by looking at the situation rationally.

# 83. KNOW WHEN TO LOSE

'The wisest, the bravest, the richest, the most beautiful — will never make a crab walk straight.'
**Aristophanes, fifth century B.C.**

Realise that you can't always 'win'. A resolution that's completely to your liking just isn't always possible. You may have to decide whether you'd rather be 'right' — or stay friends with someone. That doesn't mean giving up your opinion or beliefs — just weighing up the wisdom of expressing them, and realising that sometimes it's smarter to back off.

# 84.   DO THE RIGHT THINGS FIRST

As Frank Sinatra sang in 'My Way': 'Regrets — I've had a few — but then again, too few to mention.' My son would say, 'Get with the program, Mum.' The two adages mean the same thing: life is not a rehearsal, and you're a long time dead, so get on with it! If you woke up again today, congratulations! You have another chance. Get on with it and do the best you can. These are my best tips and ideas for instantly getting yourself back on track. Do at least one today.

Tell your partner, your kids, your parents that you love them. Hug them *hard*.

Think of something you're grateful for, then call or write to thank the person responsible.

Buy a pile of cards so you can write to friends you haven't heard from in a while, just to let them know you're thinking of them.

Keep a running list of the good things that happen in your life, no matter how small. Sometimes we forget just how fortunate we really are.

Don't overplan your weekends. Leave some time for yourself.

Join something. It helps you see the bigger picture.

Be a tourist in your own area. Discover a museum, a lookout, or a café that you have never been to before.

Raise your blinds and tie back your curtains the minute you wake up in the morning. Natural light, even on a grey day, will make you feel happier.

Open the windows for at least 15 minutes a day, even in winter. Your home or office will feel and smell fresh, and you'll think more clearly.

# 85.  OVERHAUL YOUR MEDICINE CABINET

Every home should have these remedies in the medicine cabinet.

**Aloe vera gel** Increases the rate at which burns, wounds and skin problems heal. Use for acne, burns, cuts, sunburn, itchiness, wounds, bites and stings. Soak the gel in cotton wool and dab directly onto the affected area.
**Arnica ointment** Use for back pain, bruises, muscular aches and sprains to reduce pain and swelling. (Caution: do not use on open wounds or broken skin.)
**Echinacea — tincture or tablets** Good for all infections, increasing the body's resistance to infection and speeding recovery. Use for colds, flu, digestive upsets, mouth ulcers, sore throats, thrush, cuts and grazes, catarrh and sinusitis and asthma.
**Garlic — fresh, capsules or tablets** A natural antibiotic, use for all kinds of infections, particularly for the nose, throat and chest.
**Lavender — essential oil or tea** A gentle pain reliever, lavender helps relieve headaches and migraine. One of the few essential oils that can be used neat, rub a few drops directly on insect bites, stings or burns. Add five drops to a bedtime bath to encourage sound sleep.
**Marigold (Calendula) — tincture, ointment, cream** If your skin is red, sore and angry, marigold has healing and anti-inflammatory properties. Apply tincture to cuts and grazes, and use ointment for athlete's foot and itchy skin; great for nappy rash.
**Slippery elm — powder or tablets** A wonderfully soothing herb, slippery elm can produce dramatic results in acid indigestion, gastritis, diarrhoea, constipation, bronchitis and coughs.
**Tea tree — essential oil** A potent antiseptic. Apply neat to small areas, such as pimples or around a hangnail. Dilute by adding ten drops to 5 ml of almond oil for larger areas. (Caution: keep away from eyes.)

# 86.   DO SOMETHING ABOUT THE BLUES

'In the depth of winter, I finally learned that there was in me an
invincible summer.'
**Albert Camus**

People of all income, education and ethnic groups suffer from depression and it's
hardly surprising that Prozac is the most frequently prescribed psychiatric drug
in the world. Taking a holistic view, however, means regarding depression as less
of an illness and more of a signal for change. You can either bury it deep within
you, so that ghosts keep coming back to haunt you, or you can use depression as a
profound life challenge. Holistic medicine offers a host of natural therapies for
beating the blues: regular exercise, along with balanced nutrition, bodywork and
herbal medicine, can dramatically boost mood.

    If you feel you need help in order to cope with depression, have a medical
examination before beginning any medication: physical reasons for depression
can be as wide-ranging as food and chemical allergies, hypothyroidism, candida
and hypoglycaemia. Then, find a counsellor you can trust — one with humour as
well as wisdom. A natural therapist may suggest any of the following natural
depression lifters: flower remedies (Gorse for despair, Walnut for major life
transitions, White Chestnut for compulsive thoughts); herbs (St John's wort for
mild to moderate depression and irritability; hops and skullcap for insomnia;
ginkgo for alertness); and homoeopathics (*Aurum metallicum* for severe
depression; *Ignatia* especially for women feeling depleted by stress). Seek answers
in whatever places 'call' to you and invigorate your spirit — bookstores,
community gatherings, the church, music, meditation, or the company of old
friends. And if you need professional help, ask for it.

# 87.   SOOTHE EYE STRAIN

At the end of a particularly exhausting day in 1900, Dr William Bates, a New York ophthalmologist, sat and placed his palms over his eyes. After ten minutes, he noted that his eyes were not as sore and that things in the room seemed sharper and brighter. These observations led him to develop the Bates method, a system of 'eyesight re-education' now widely taught by natural therapists who aim to improve eyesight without artificial aids. To keep your eyes in good shape, practise these exercises five to ten minutes a day:

**Palming** Sit comfortably at a table, close your eyes and rest your elbows on the table. Rub your hands together briskly for 20 seconds or so, then cup your palms over your eyes, without applying any pressure. Keep your back and neck level and don't drop your head. Do this for ten minutes twice a day. Tip: if you use a computer, rest your eyes by palming for at least one minute for every ten you estimate you are looking at the screen.

**Remembering** While palming, try to recall an object in the brightest possible colours. Bates found that remembering things in the mind's eye helped patients to see them more clearly in reality.

**Blinking** Make dozens of delicate 'butterfly blinks' for ten to 20 seconds, several times a day; as you do so, turn your head gently from left to right, and back again.

**Shifting** Pick out an object just out of your vision. Imagine your nose is a pointer, and move your head slowly and gently as you trace around the object's outline with your nose. Repeat in the opposite direction.

**Splashing** Gently splash warm water over your closed eyes 20 times, then repeat 20 times with cold water to improve circulation to the eyes. Do first thing in the morning and last thing at night.

**Swinging** Stand with feet apart and sway gently from side to side (to music, if you like), allowing your eyes to 'swing' along with your movements. This helps your eyes to become more flexible.

**Focusing** Hold one index finger at arm's length and the other about six inches away from your face. Use both eyes to focus on one, then blink and focus immediately on the other. Repeat several times a day.

# 88.   STAND TALL

How you stand and hold yourself can have a powerful effect on your mood. If you look proud and happy, you will actually feel proud and happy. And apart from giving your self-esteem a boost by looking the world in the eye, it will also make you look slimmer — instantly. Try these tips to boost body confidence:

Stand or sit upright, with your weight evenly spread.

Imagine that the top of your head is attached to the ceiling with a piece of string, and 'pull' yourself upwards, feeling yourself stretch from the lumbar (lower back) region of your spine.

Contract your abdominal muscles, sucking your tummy up underneath your rib cage. Imagine you're laced into a Victorian corset!

Let your shoulders relax downwards, getting as much distance as possible between your shoulders and your ears. Mentally run through your body and make sure you aren't holding tension in the classic places: shoulders, neck, thighs, hands. Relax your jaw by first yawning widely, then smiling.

Blink your eyes tightly shut half a dozen times, then allow your gaze to settle. Your gaze will be more direct and alert.

# 89. GET THE EXERCISE HABIT

Any type of exercise benefits your health, even if you start with just ten minutes here and there.

**Firstly, decide what you want to do.** For stress relief and flexibility, for instance, choose yoga or tai chi. To lose weight, do aerobics, a dance class or anything that raises your heart rate — work out for at least 20 minutes three times a week.

**Pick something you like.** There's no point buying an exercise bike if repetition bores you to tears. You'll give up. Health club fitness classes are a good bet because they offer maximum variety. Council-run ones are much cheaper than private clubs. And make sure the club is no more than five minutes from your workplace or home, or it'll be too easy to not go.

**Team up with a friend.** If you've got the same fitness goals, chances are you'll support each other and stick at it. Try sharing a personal trainer for the first ten sessions.

**Keep to a routine.** Choose the same workout time on the same three days a week and stick to them. Exercising in the morning is best as it gives you less time to make up excuses not to go. Lunchtime workouts are also efficient — just make sure you allow time to eat.

**Reward yourself.** When you've passed the ten-session mark, give yourself a treat — a facial, for example. Treat yourself every ten sessions.

# 90.   LISTEN TO YOUR BREATHING

For the most part, we normally take our breathing for granted. In fact, most of us breathe badly some or even all of the time, meaning we are not providing our bodies with sufficient oxygen: our stress-related symptoms therefore worsen. It takes a bit of practice, but breathing properly can become second nature. Start with doing this exercise for ten minutes, twice a day for a week, and see the difference.

**Lie flat on your back, with your knees bent up**. Place your hands side by side on your stomach, so you can feel it move in and out with your breath. To begin, breathe shallowly in through your nose, and out through your mouth. You may find it helps to say 'ahhh' as you exhale, until you have no air left. Pause and relax for a moment, and let the next breath come naturally.

**Try to think only about your breathing**. Your thoughts are bound to wander, so concentrate. If you feel light-headed, it means you're over-breathing. Cup your hands over your mouth and nose for a few breaths to reduce the loss of carbon dioxide from your system, then continue.

**Start counting**. Once you've got into a rhythm, start measuring your breath. Ideally, your out-breath should be about twice as long as the in-breath. Breathe in for four counts, out for eight, and pause.

**Apply what you've learned to breathing the rest of the time**. From now on, practise counting as you breathe when you're driving (breathe in for four steps, out for eight), at work (keep your shoulders relaxed!), walking, cleaning your teeth, or waiting for a bus.

# 91.  MAP OUT YOUR WORK LIFE

Often, in looking for a job, we lose sight of what we actually love and do best. If you feel you've hit a wall in your working life, and want to get your future on track, one way is to take a close look at your past. Try this exercise:

**Take a sheet of blank paper and, leaving an inch margin on the left, draw a horizontal line across the middle**. From left to right, mark out the years you've been working. Then draw a line down along the left-hand margin from top to bottom. Above the horizontal line, write the numbers 1 to 10 (+) going to the top of the page along the margin. Write the numbers 1 to 10 (–) going down the bottom one.

**Now you have a rough grid on which to plot all your jobs to date**. Starting with your first job in the first year to the left, plot its place on the grid. (Out of 10, was it a 3, or a 7? If you had a bad time, plot it in the minus area.) Your instinctive responses are important —work quickly, including your present job and the current year.

**Now take an extra sheet of paper and head it with the name of the first job**. What things made it satisfying or unpleasant? Note them down. Repeat this for all the different jobs. Be honest. You're the only person who will read it. What did the good jobs have in common? Which type of work was most fulfilling, and why? Which people were most significant? Where did you laugh most? Where did you get into trouble? Where did you get promoted? Why? Did you enjoy being in charge, or prefer being part of a team? Think about all the other issues, such as companionship, the atmosphere, benefits (or lack of them) and the type of product or service you were involved with. For each job, note why you left.

**Now, review your notes and start pulling together all the stray threads**. The answers to getting your future working life are in front of you: what has to be present in your work to make you feel fulfilled and proud, what challenges you, what stifles you, what sort of people and responsibilities you enjoy — and those you should avoid. Brainstorm all the possible avenues that will include more of the 'peak' experiences that you've identified, and minimise the ones that give you grief. You may be surprised by what you come up with — chances are, it will be something quite different from where you've ended up right at the moment.

## 92. THINK THINGS THROUGH

'I was thirty-seven: too old for a paper route, too young for social security, and too tired for an affair.'
**Erma Bombeck**

Don't rush into change just because you're desperate to get out of your current job. The most successful career movers are those who spend a long time carefully planning and deliberating before applying for jobs, then set targets and deadlines and keep to them.

**Contact the Careers Advisory Service near you.** It has a whole range of useful publications which deals with how to find what you really want from a job and overcome barriers to career change. Your local library may also have copies.

**Carry out an audit of your abilities, skills, qualifications and work experiences.** List your career motivations and expectations and what you like most and least about your current work. Only then can you begin to consider new job possibilities seriously.

**Look at other options.** If you know you're in the right career but feel you're in the wrong job or company, check out other companies.

**Do a SWOT check.** Eliminate jobs that wouldn't be right for you by listing your Strengths and Weaknesses relating to the job, plus Opportunities it may afford and Threats that may stand in your way (like a partner not prepared for change or a long way to travel to work).

**Think flexibly.** In the last decade, the number of self-employed people has risen dramatically, and many other new ways of working are now beginning to be accepted by employers, including flexible working hours, job sharing, working from home, and working longer hours over fewer days.

**Practise networking.** There are many organisations that can help women move on in their careers and offer women — however high or low on the management scale — an opportunity to meet like-minded professionals and gain career advice from those who've made it to the top. Contact the Careers Advisory Service in your city or state.

# 93. STOP SMOKING FOR GOOD

With a career as a natural therapist and health writer, I blush to admit I was once quite a heavy smoker. And, like all the other smokers in the world, I knew how bad it was for me and how much other people hated it, and I was fully aware of all the warnings on the packets. But I didn't take the slightest bit of notice. The simple fact is this: you have to really want to quit to become an ex-smoker, otherwise you just keep going. If you do want to stop, though, there's no reason why, in the space of a month, you can't. Start now:

WEEK 1: Decide to quit. Get rid of all your cigarettes in your home, in the office, in the car. Throw them out, don't finish off the packets! Throw away the ashtrays as well. Take vitamin C to speed up the detox process. Drink plenty of water — it gives you something to do with your mouth. Also, expect a nasty taste in your mouth: the mouth is a primary escape route for the tar in your lungs and it doesn't taste nice. Time your cravings: they usually last only a minute or two — wait, and it will pass. Persevere.

WEEK 2: If you haven't smoked for a week, you are no longer addicted to nicotine physically — but you could still be psychologically dependent. You may start resenting or envying other smokers. You may start reminiscing about smoking as something that helped you stay calm (it doesn't), or keep weight off (nup, sorry). These memories may challenge your motivation — don't let them.

WEEK 3: Expect setbacks. If you've smoked one or two cigarettes this week, it doesn't matter. Treat it as a one-off. As long as you're prepared to keep going, you have not failed. Focus on your successes. When the urge for a cigarette seems overwhelming, give yourself a mental leg-up by thinking about how well you've done so far to reinforce your strength to get past the crisis.

WEEK 4: Congratulations. You are now an ex-smoker. If possible, stay away from other smokers and ban smoking in your home. Cleaning your teeth makes you less likely to want to breathe in smoke, too. Keep busy and practise relaxation techniques like deep breathing exercises or meditation so you never pick up a cigarette because you feel stressed.

# 94. Salute the sun each morning

This well-known yoga routine is the perfect way to start your day, as it massages your internal organs as well as increasing flexibility.

1.  Stand with your feet together, big toes touching, arms by your sides. Tuck your chin in, look straight ahead and keep your shoulders relaxed.

2.  Bring your arms up over your head, inhaling slowly and deeply. As you finish, put your palms together and look back at your thumbs. Exhale as you bend over, placing your hands on the floor beside your feet. Touch your head to your knees (you may have to bend your knees slightly).

3.  Inhale deeply and stretch your right leg back to an extended lunge. Tilt your head backwards to stretch your back. Exhale and push your left leg back to join your right one.

4.  Rise on your toes, supporting yourself on your hands, keeping your arms straight. Your head, back and legs should be in a straight line. Exhale again and lower yourself to the floor.

5.  Inhale and push until your arms are straight, with hands on the floor in front of you. Bend backwards and look upwards. Then exhale and return to position 4, with your head, back and legs in a straight line, breathing slowly and deeply.

6.  Inhale and return to position 3, this time with your left leg stretched backwards. Exhale and move back into position 2, bending over with your hands on the floor. Then inhale and look backwards, as in position 2, then return to the standing position, arms by your sides.

# 95.   BE A CHILD

Poet Francis Thompson wrote that '. . . to be a child is to turn pumpkins into coaches, mice into horses and nothing into everything'. Playfulness not only recharges your imagination, but it is a great mental and physical energiser. Research shows you will be happier, more productive and more creative if you approach a task in a playful frame of mind. And it is perfectly possible to express your childish nature without making a fool of yourself! Here are some ideas:

Play a computer game where you get to blow things up (great for tension release!).

Challenge a friend to a skipping contest or set up a netball hoop on an outside wall.

Collect stuffed animals. Talk to them.

Go fly a kite.

Go camping.

Use sparklers on birthday cakes instead of candles.

Watch cloud formations. Take a walk in a park or down the beach and find an unobstructed view. Flop down and gaze — what do you see? Lions and tigers? Dragons?

Get a favourite toy or item from your childhood — a book, a picture, even a report card or certificate and put it where you can see and enjoy it.

Who said toys are only for kids, anyway? Crayons and glitter-glue are great for scrawling notes. Then there's Play-doh, jigsaws, Lego . . .

# 96. ORGANISE YOUR TIME

When the writer Henri David Thoreau decided to take time out from the rat race and live alone, he wrote: 'As you simplify your life, the laws of the Universe will be simpler, as well.' His philosophy dovetails neatly with the wide-reaching, feel-great benefits of organising your time well.

One of the best ways to start is to firstly see how much time you waste: keep a diary for a week, and jot down every single thing you do — every trip, errand, meeting, and phone call — and approximately how many minutes you've spent doing them all. (If you use a tiny notepad that slips into a pocket or handbag, it's an easy habit to adopt and you won't forget to do it.)

Next, add up how many minutes you spent on all the different things, and group them into categories — time spent on partner, family, travel, work, shopping, leisure, and so on. How much time did you spend on each group? How much time was wasted on duplicating chores or errands? And (most sobering of all) how much time did you spend on your partner, family or friends? Hmmm. The less time you spend on things you really want to do, the more frustrated, cranky, guilty, and exhausted you'll be.

Time management sounds hard, but it's a simple art. The only thing you'll find difficult to start with is looking at how you do things with different eyes: everyone tends to think that the way they do things is the only way there is to do them! Flip back to your notepad, and then take a fresh look at your daily routine tasks — the things you have to do without fail. Now, brainstorm some alternative ways of dealing with them. Learn to prioritise. Make lists, and rank the tasks according to what really is important. Where are the opportunities to double up on activities? If you love to read and spend several hours a week commuting on a train, plan to visit the library more regularly to borrow books so the time is not wasted. Leave plenty of time for the important jobs so you don't have to rush them, make mistakes, and start all over, so cannibalising time you'd thought you'd have for other tasks. And be sure to leave several free slots in your timetable every week. This way you actually factor in time for the unexpected things that occur, as well as much-needed 'downtime'.

## 97.   USE YOUR ENERGY HIGHS

'To every thing there is a season, and a time to every purpose
under the heaven.'
**Ecclesiastes 3:1**

Depression has its greatest effect when your energy levels are low. As it's not
possible to keep your energy levels on a constant even high, either, try to schedule
easier tasks for the low-energy times: I call them the 'donkey jobs', tasks like
ironing, weeding and stuffing envelopes that take very little brain power, but which
nonetheless give you a great deal of satisfaction when they're out of the way.

If you are not sure when your high and low energy times are, start writing
them down. Then, depending on what you've got planned for the day, you may be
able to schedule more demanding tasks for when your energy levels are high. You
may find this applies on a broader, seasonal basis as well: it's quite common to feel
more sluggish in winter, more energetic in summer.

# 98. DRESS CONSCIOUSLY

Besides falling short in the practicality department, most 'fashionable' clothing isn't flattering on the majority of people, let alone comfortable. If, on the other hand, you aim to consciously create a clothing style that suits your needs in terms of the activities you engage in, that fits your body type and figure, and that falls in classic styles that are pretty much always around, you'll always look good without having to think about it too much. You've got better things to think about! Besides, you'll end up with more money in your wallet, too, because you will straight away always have something to wear in your wardrobe. Start off by following these guiding principles:

> Dress for comfort, according to the weather, and for the job you're doing that day.
>
> Buy or make good quality clothes of classic style and cut.
>
> Make sure you've got the basics: lightweight knit tops, a smartly tailored shirt, A-line skirt, and a pair of pants. They should stretch, they should travel well, and they should look good with your skin tone.
>
> Recycle unused clothing by donating your used items and by buying pre-owned clothes yourselves. Other people's discards, available through thrift and secondhand stores, can be a fantastic find.

Go through your wardrobe and look at what you've got. What do you wear most often? Why? What style is it, and what's it made from? Take out anything you haven't worn in a year or more and try it on. What's wrong with it? If it needs mending, do it. If it just doesn't fit, pass it on and acknowledge the mistake. Look at everything, not just clothes — underwear, shoes, woollens, hats, accessories. What makes sense for your climate and lifestyle, and what clashes? Resolve not to follow the 'fashion nazis' — follow your own style, instead. Self-expression and simplicity can go hand in hand.

# 99. Don't be a billboard

Everyone has at least one sticking point when it comes to clothes. The thing that irritates me the most is logos.

I refuse to wear clothing with brand advertising, and I fight a (usually losing) battle with my children to instill the same values in them. I just figure the world is cluttered up with enough advertisements and exhortations to consumerism as it is without adding to it every time I pull on a t-shirt. Somewhere a team of marketing gurus are sitting around a table and deeming this logo or that shirt the Next Big Thing, and it makes me feel as if I'm being exploited. Plus I hate the idea of being just another little sheep — of handing over my hard-earned cash and being given the same image as is being handed out to hundreds of thousands of others, rather than pursuing my own.

When what we wear becomes unconscious consumption and mere image imitation, I think it compromises our self-expression and freedom of choice. I'll get off my soapbox now — but even if you don't feel as strongly as I do about the commercial implications, simply refusing to wear clothing with labels on the outside is a very effective way to reclaim your sense of personal style and give you a sense of real, inner confidence about how you look. Not to mention the fact that non-'name' clothing is almost always considerably cheaper.

# 100. SIMPLIFY YOUR GROOMING

Try this quick quiz: how many bottles or jars of moisturiser have you got in your bathroom cabinet, or on your dressing table? How many different rinses, gels, sprays, powders and lotions? Lipsticks? Bottles of nail polish? Mascara wands? Throwing out old make-up and personal care products will help you focus better on the present and open your eyes about the cost of keeping clean and well-groomed. Aim to get down to the basics of what you really need. With personal care products, that's probably shampoo, soap, moisturiser, toothpaste, and deodorant, at the most; as far as make-up goes, less really is more — a little mascara, lipstick and powder may be all you really need. Naturally, you're going to want to splash out on special occasions with perfume and eye-shadow. However, in the interests of pursuing a simpler, less expensive lifestyle, consider the following suggestions:

**Investigate making some or all of your own personal care products**. It's extremely easy to make your own lotions, oils, gels, powders and even soap and toothpaste. Apart from saving money (and being heaps of fun to do), you are avoiding all sorts of chemicals and additives that you don't need and that may be giving you grief with sensitivities and allergies, besides. **Rethink your hairstyle**. Long or very short hair seem to be the two easiest options. A style that can be air-dried rather than moussed, blow-dried and tonged, saves time and is better for your hair. **Keep your nails short**. By all means, indulge in a manicure and polish every so often, but in the meantime you'll find that rubbing a little vitamin E or jojoba oil into the nails and cuticles is all you need to add strength and lustre. **Cull your make-up box**. I like to wear make-up and think I look better with it. Having said that, I am very deliberate about what I will and won't use. Here are some questions to ask yourself: is there a neutral colour palette that goes with everything, rather than one-off lipsticks and colours? Are the products relatively free from chemicals? Have they been tested on animals? If you are going to buy into the beauty industry, make your choices conscious ones.

# 101. HAVE FRIENDS, NOT ACQUAINTANCES

'A friend is a present you give yourself.'
**Robert Louis Stevenson**

I have decided that, after myself, my husband, my mother, and my kids, I only have room in my life for a few more special people — otherwise, I am spread too thin and end up not being able to give properly of myself or to be available to those people.

Do you find you are spending lots of time with people who matter very little, and not enough with people who matter a lot? It's time to change that. It may sound very hard and clinical, but it's important to prune out people who do not contribute anything of value to your life. This is not to say that you can't be civil to the many acquaintances you make through work, sport and community interests, at your kids' school, while studying, or whatever. What it does mean is that, in order to allow a person into your inner circle of quality relationships, they need to have the same priorities as you do, as well as, say, sharing an interest or similar background. Then, when you are faced with the choice of spending time with one of your inner circle of friends, or someone outside, the choice is clear as to who has priority.

Being selective in your friendships helps you to simplify your life and enhances the quality, loyalty and level of commitment present in your long-term relationships. It doesn't mean you can't make room for lots of people in your life. And it certainly doesn't mean that you can't seek out new friends, or work to revitalise a relationship that is flagging. However, it will make you decide who comes first in terms of filling the limited time resources you have.

# 102. BE REALISTIC ABOUT ROMANCE

'The greatest enemy of the truth is very often not the lie — deliberate, contrived and dishonest — but the myth — persistent, pervasive, and unrealistic.'
**John F. Kennedy**

Put the Damsel out to pasture. Most women know the pain of having to recover from a marriage or relationship that failed to give them the emotional and physical support they had anticipated. Often, they have been expecting in some way that their relationship would be a version of the Knight coming along on a rescue mission to save them, the Damsel in Distress. This is one myth that women do not let go of easily, no matter how disappointing their first relationship. Often, after that relationship, they think 'Wrong Knight: the next one will be the right one', when the real problem is 'Wrong Myth'.

It's time to discard fantasies like these that just don't work, and adopt ones that reflect your needs for equal partnership. A romantic projection is too much for any person to carry. Whether 'falling in love' lasts for a week or six months, eventually it comes crashing down. A woman will say: 'You're not the white knight on a silver charger after all', while the man says: 'Well, you're not the princess I expected, either.'

It is, in fact, the next stage that is the wonderful opportunity for love. It is only when a romantic projection fades that a sustainable, human-sized love becomes possible. This sort of love is based on knowing a person as he or she really is, not grasping for unrealistic qualities. The Chinese philosopher Lao-tzu described this love as being like water, because it brings nourishment to all it touches. Reality is far nobler, more practical, and more long-lasting.

# 103. ACCEPT YOURSELF AS YOU ARE

The Chinese philosopher Tao-te Ching once wrote: 'Because he accepts himself, the whole world accepts him.' Self-acceptance is the number one key to happiness. Self-love and self-acceptance is hard work — it's a 24-hour business — but you really need to achieve it and believe it for happiness. Here are some strategies to think about:

**Assume you will have a happy ending**. Consciously create happy outcomes in your daily life. The wounds of childhood tell us that we're no good. Get past 'I'm not worthy of this'. A healthy self-esteem has been discouraged in our culture. Instead, try working on the idea that you will not be punished if it does all work out as you'd wish.

**Tackle self-doubt, once and for all**. Challenge all the 'what ifs' and 'yes, buts' in your mind. Don't dismiss your ideas as stupid. We are often unaware of how our negative self-talk can destroy our confidence. If you're thinking negative or derogatory things about yourself, it will influence the way you see yourself, and the way you behave. Life will feel a lot better when you learn to catch yourself doing this — and when you make a deliberate effort to stop.

**Each day, give yourself a mark out of 10 for feeling good**. Write it in your diary, or on your calendar. Look for a pattern of what makes you feel down and what makes you feel terrific. Try to do more of the things that boost your rating.

## 104. STOP COMPLAINING

'Rather light a candle than complain about darkness,' goes the proverb. You don't realise how much complaining can dominate your conversation — until you try to stop doing it! Enlist the help of a friend and agree that, for an entire week, neither of you will complain, but instead you will focus on the good things in your lives. At the beginning, you can expect quite a bit of silence!

# 105. TAKE CHARGE OF YOUR WORK

Take charge of your work rather than letting it (or your boss) take charge of you. A major study of public servants showed that the lowest-grade employees, who were less likely to have as much control over their work, had a much higher risk of heart disease and other stress-related illnesses than those in a higher grade. Here are some ideas to get you started:

**Make your work day more interesting**. If you are in a repetitive job with few other people around, you should listen to music to maintain alertness, or vary your pace or method of work. If you have boring tasks to get through, intersperse them with more interesting ones. If you find your entire job boring, volunteer for new challenges and initiate variety — ask about more work or training, offer to help colleagues, or take more interest in clients or an aspect of work that changes. **Stand up for yourself**. If you find this difficult, it may help to repeat to yourself some of your fundamental rights at work — such as 'I have the right to express my thoughts and opinions even though they may be different from those of others,' and 'I have the right to say I don't know or understand something.'

**Avoid information overload**. A survey by Reuters news agency has shown that more and more managers are falling victim to Information Fatigue Syndrome, a form of stress where people become so paralysed by fatigue and indecision that they are incapable of working. Do all of your paperwork immediately and learn how to prioritise.

## 106. LIVE WITH YOUR EYES WIDE OPEN

Breathe in the colours of mountain and sky, cityscape and landscape; know the sound of leaves rustling, the smell of soil, the texture of bark. Rub your hands all over your life, sing where and when you want to, jump and dance. Notice every glorious and tragic thing. Laugh and cry freely. Do not whine about not having enough time, but be creative with every moment. Create joy wherever you are — dress colourfully, tell jokes, pick flowers. Love every minute.

# 107. PUT FAMILY FIRST

'They do not love who do not show their love.'
**William Shakespeare**

Now, you may not think this sounds right for you. Your family might be scattered all over the world; you may be estranged from particular family members (and quite happy to leave things that way); or perhaps you don't have children, and therefore don't really think that you qualify somehow. Nevertheless, 'No man is an island', to quote John Donne, and it's important to consider where you're at with these important relationships.

With your immediate family, the basics are: treat them with respect, talk to them and explain what you're doing and how it affects them, and then give them plenty of space to get on with their own lives. With extended family, the golden rule is to try to reach out and stay in touch. Be there when you are needed, but respect their privacy. Be strong — and don't allow any family members to destroy or interfere with what you see as the integrity of your family and home. Have standards of behaviour and stick to them. Three good ideas for nurturing family relationships are:

**Communicate**. This is one area where email has enormous relevance. Pictures, photos and cartoons can all be scanned and zipped back and forth quickly. It's not a substitute for telephone conversations, but it's a great way of staying in touch.

**Create events**. Family meals, reunions, picnics — they don't have to be expensive extravaganzas, and a neutral territory like a beach or park is always better than putting the burden and cost for entertainment on one person's shoulders.

**Keep rituals going**. They might be simple — and possibly quite silly — but pass them down to the next generation with family stories. If you identify strongly with your ethnic or religious background, these areas should provide a rich palette of rituals that will add colour and continuity to your family life for years to come.

# 108. USE ESSENTIAL OILS

Aromatherapy is a wonderful way to stimulate your senses, either helping you to relax and think calmly, or give you a revitalising boost. Here are some ideas:

**Facial splash** Add a few drops of geranium or lavender oil to a bowl of warm water. Breathe deeply, then gently splash the water all over your face and neck.

**Wake-up bath** If you're feeling sluggish and can't seem to connect with anyone or anything, taking a bath to which you've added several drops of rosemary oil should do the trick. Ancient Roman soldiers used to keep rosemary sprigs in their helmets to help them stay awake and alert during battles and long watches. It's marvellous during times of stress and physical tiredness.

**Positive attitude** Juniper berries are traditionally used to flavour gin, because of their ability to stimulate the appetite, which is why a gin-and-tonic has long been a popular aperitif. However, in aromatherapy, they're classified as a detoxifying cleanser and mental stimulant. To clear your mind of worries and help you focus on the task at hand, sprinkle a few drops on a tissue and inhale the aroma.

# 109. TALK TO PEOPLE

A study in the *Harvard Business Review* says that faxes, memos and emails are replacing conversation at work and, increasingly, in our personal lives. According to the researchers who conducted the study, this can lead to misunderstanding and mistakes, not to mention isolation and loneliness.

At least once a week, go for lunch with a friend — preferably not a colleague, or you might just moan about work and indulge in office gossip. Look forward to this time out and change your routine regularly — sit in the park once a week, for instance, and check out a new café the next.

The human moment adds colour to our lives and helps us build confidence and trust at work and at play. Ignore it at your peril.

# 110. NAVIGATE MENOPAUSE NATURALLY

What do you do if you can't take HRT (hormone replacement therapy) because of your medical history or side effects, or you have ethical objections?

**Eat plenty of soy foods**. They contain phytoestrogens, which are plant substances that behave like natural oestrogen in the body, helping to lessen symptoms.

**Try homoeopathic medicine**. The three best remedies are Belladonna for hot flushes, Pulsatilla for mood swings and Sepia for vaginal dryness.

**Take herbs**. Black cohosh and red clover for hot flushes; dong quai, vitex and raspberry leaf for irregular or heavy bleeding; kava and St John's wort for nervousness and stress; motherwort for night sweats, cramps and emotional upheaval. Licorice root tea also has oestrogenic properties, and is a wonderful tonic for the menopause.

**Have a course of acupuncture**. Many women say they feel relief and balance for menopausal symptoms almost immediately.

**Focus on the right fats**. Essential fatty acids (EFAs) help balance hormones and prevent heart disease. Flaxseed is a convenient and economical option: grind a few tablespoons in a coffee mill and sprinkle the ground seeds over your cereal each day.

# III. BE FRUGAL

It's not a four-letter word! If you have the sneaking suspicion that money is ruling your life, decide that every potential purchase must be carefully considered. Is that dress, book or packet of chips going to be worth the hassle of working to acquire it. Make a once-and-for-all distinction in your mind between lifetime investment purchases, such as houses, which hopefully hold their value, and things whose value cannot be relied upon, such as clothes and restaurant meals, which become almost worthless the minute you've bought them. To get ahead financially — or at least break even — you must make more of the first sort of purchases, and less of the second.

The word 'frugal' has unfortunate connotations. As a child of parents who were brought up in the Great Depression, I am quite comfortable with staying home, making chocolate fudge, and playing Snakes and Ladders rather than going out to a movie. However, many see such adjustments in taste and lifestyle as an exercise in bleak deprivation, but that is not what living frugally — living carefully and responsibly — is about. You can still be creative, and saving money can be fun and a challenge. My kids are perfectly happy and healthy and smart in secondhand clothes. We think homemade pizza tastes better than the takeaway stuff — and it's a great deal cheaper. Starting a vegetable and herb garden has been a fun project for my boys, as well as a surprising money-saver. Here are some other ideas:

Pack lunches for school and work every day. Make them the night before if you think you'll go under in the early-morning chaos.

Ring around the insurance companies and ask about deals. It's almost guaranteed that you'll find a policy for your home, life and contents that's better than what you've got now.

Take a car-care course and learn how to change the oil and water in your car.

Buy a secondhand freezer and stock it with muffins, pasta sauce and soup you've made yourself.

Write letters and send email instead of making long-distance phone calls.

As a bonus, you'll find that non-financial aspects of your life also get a boost — your relationship gets stronger, you feel more self-reliant, and your kids grow more independent and discerning.

## 112. WRITE DOWN WHAT YOU SPEND

'Don't let your mouth write no cheque your tail can't cash.'
**Bo Diddley**

Sick of getting to the end of the week and not having a penny in your purse? Borrow one of the techniques used by the big weight-loss consultancies, and get debt under control by writing down everything you buy, big or small: petrol, coffees, chewing gum, drycleaning, fares, flowers, the lot. Do this faithfully for a whole month and you'll see exactly where your money is going — and, no matter how 'on top of things' you thought you were, there are bound to be a couple of items that will really surprise you. Just as someone who's overweight usually has no idea what they eat until they keep a diary, most of us don't have a clue when and how much we spend, or on what.

Writing down all your expenses helps you save in several ways: firstly, it makes you aware of the day-to-day, hour-to-hour act of spending money, and how often purchases are automatic, therefore registering in the 'budget' part of your brain. Secondly, it shows you where you have opportunities to cut back — or at least delay payment, such as picking up drycleaning next week if you don't absolutely have to have it this week. Finally, a nifty side effect is that, after a month, you are so sick and tired of writing things down that you really do think twice about small purchases — you might not buy that muffin because you just couldn't be bothered writing it down. And, having to think about the muffin, however briefly, might make you realise that you didn't really need it.

# 113. PAY IT OFF

> 'And is not the chief good of money the being free from the thinking of it? It seems so to me.'
> **Elizabeth Barrett Browning**

Never before have Australians owed so much money — and if even only a tiny bit of that national debt is due to you, it's safe to say that money is on your mind.

In a society that encourages us to seek empowerment through money, the absence of money and its trophies can have a devastating effect on your sense of self-worth. And the two-edged sword of debt is so often the result: two-edged because debt can be, on the one hand, sort of empowering. It allows us to do things we might otherwise be unable to do: go to university, or buy a house or a car. On the other hand, debt can be very destructive, causing emotional stress and undermining the quality of daily life. Not for nothing does the word 'mortgage' come from *mors*, the Latin for death.

The question to ask yourself is: are you willing to give up the lure of immediate gratification and acquisition, replace it with a greater appreciation of the limited time and energy available to you — and plan to use that time and energy for things other than racking up more debt? Only then can you take control of those limited amounts of time and energy you possess, and make choices as to whether you want to earn more or less money. Only then can you decide how you will handle the repayment of debts you may already have — or whether you are willing to be in debt at all. By forcing yourself to realise that it is an either/or choice between time and energy and buying possessions with money you don't actually have, this struggle with debt may help you discover values that make your life more worthwhile.

# 114. Choose raw foods

We all know the best way to stay well and get all the nutrients we need is to eat a wide variety of fresh fruits and vegetables. Problem is — we just don't do it! Nuts, seeds, fresh fruit and vegetables are all free from colours, preservatives and emulsifiers. It makes sense that if we put this type of food into our bodies, we will feel more alive. They have the advantage of being easy to digest and providing all the fibre, vitamins and minerals we need. Prolonged cooking can destroy these nutrients, so in order to reap their benefits, they must be consumed raw. To feel truly energised you should aim to include as many raw foods in your diet as possible, because good health should not be defined as the absence of disease, but as a vital, dynamic condition in which we feel positively charged and fully able to take whatever life has to throw at us. To make eating raw fruits and vegetables more exciting, all you need is a juicer and a blender. Try these delicious and revitalising 'raw recipes':

**To improve skin**, juice four carrots, two spears of asparagus, half an iceberg lettuce and a handful of spinach leaves. This drink protects against skin infections because of its high vitamin A content, plus it's full of vitamin E, which helps maintain supple skin. Drink three times a week.

**To keep up energy levels**, juice six apples, then blend with two bananas (peeled) and one tablespoon of smooth peanut butter. The fruit sugar (fructose) in the apples gives you an instant boost, while the slower-releasing energy in the bananas will keep you going all day. The peanut butter supplies protein, iron, magnesium vitamin E and folic acid. Have a glass in the morning if your day's looking chaotic.

**To beat insomnia**, juice together three apples, two oranges (peeled, with pith), 1 lemon (with peel, if thin-skinned) and two handfuls of iceberg lettuce. Iceberg lettuce contains lactones, calming substances that act as a natural sedative. Have one glass before bed.

## 115. BRUSH AWAY THE COBWEBS

This simple yoga exercise really sends a burst of energy right through your body.

1. Stand with your feet shoulder-width apart, knees relaxed, feet facing forwards, and eyes open so you can keep your balance.

2. Clasp your hands behind your back with your palms facing the floor. Slowly bring your hands up behind your back, as far as is comfortable.

3. Now, bend forwards from the waist so your back makes a right angle with your legs. Keep your head in line with your back (press your chin into your chest rather than stretching out your neck — you can strain your neck by looking upwards or forwards). See how far you can stretch your still-clasped hands above your head. Now breathe as slowly and deeply as you can and come back to a standing posture. Let your hands drop back to your sides. Repeat.

116. BEAT THE BULGE

In developed countries like Australia, anything up to 60 per cent of women are overweight, and the problem is on the increase. Excess weight is known to play a role in conditions such as heart disease, diabetes and high blood pressure. You're also less likely to exercise regularly if you're overweight. If you do have a serious amount of weight to lose:

**Get support**. Enlist the help of a group or see a counsellor who will give you advice.

**Say no to fads**. Faddy diets may restrict kilojoule intake, but they usually eliminate whole food groups from your diet, meaning you'll be short on vital vitamins and minerals — plus you'll probably get bored quickly and give up.

**Keep a food diary**. Record everything you eat for a week, so you can see where the problems lie.

**Take it slowly**. The only effective way to achieve sustained weight loss is slowly and gradually. For best results, combine cutting your fat intake with regular exercise.

**When eating out, order appetiser or entree sizes**. It's a fact that restaurant plates have grown from eight to 12 inches, on average. Smaller sized plates (what used to be considered normal) will provide a more realistic portion.

**Always have breakfast**. Increasing carbohydrate intake at breakfast helps people to lose weight because it stops you craving high-fat food later on.

**Don't ban snacks**. If you do find yourself getting hungry between meals, go for a healthy, filling snack such as a banana or rice cake — otherwise you'll be plagued by cravings for fatty or sugary foods.

**Analyse your food**. In the supermarket, always read the label before you put the food in your trolley. Many products, especially ready-made varieties, are much higher in fat and sugar than you may think. Even the genuinely low-fat meals aren't always the answer: some of them are high in salt and even if they're not, they won't contain as many nutrients as fresh food. Cooking more of your own food will give you more control over what you eat.

# PROTECT YOUR REPRODUCTIVE SYSTEM

Endometriosis, PMS, fibroids, menopausal symptoms, cancer — just a random sampling of the spectres in the back of most women's minds. Taking control of hormonal imbalances with the following steps can help minimise your risk:

**Steer clear of dairy products and meat.** Unless they're organic, you can't guarantee that they do not contain unwelcome oestrogen and bovine growth hormone, which increase your oestrogen levels, in turn aggravating problems like menstrual cramping and endometriosis.

**Learn to love phytoestrogens.** Soy and flaxseed are the best sources of this type of 'good' oestrogen that helps rebalance fluctuating hormones, and also helps reduce inflammation. Add ground flaxseeds to your meals, and eat up to 150 g of soy protein daily.

**Don't forget your fruit and veg.** In particular, broccoli — which contains fibres and phytochemicals that counter dangerous forms of oestrogen in the body — and brightly coloured fruits like mangoes, which are excellent sources of free radical-fighting antioxidants.

**Bet on B.** The B vitamins help regulate the amount of oestrogen in your body; they also reduce menstrual cramping and the symptoms of PMS. It's especially important to take B6 if you're on the Pill, because it reduces your body's levels of this vitamin.

**Herbs can help.** The herb vitex agnus-castus is a wonder for women with endometriosis or fibroids, helping to adjust oestrogen and progesterone levels in the body. For women looking for safe and effective alternatives to HRT, black cohosh (*Cimicifuga racemosa)* is excellent for countering menopausal symptoms, such as hot flashes.

# 118.   BAN WATER RETENTION

**Eat celery, parsley and asparagus.** They are natural diuretics, meaning they stimulate the kidneys to excrete more urine. They also help rebalance the body's sodium, potassium and chloride content.

**Drink about six to eight glasses of water a day (up to 1.5 litres).** It's a common mistake to drink less if you suffer from water retention, and if you don't actually feel thirsty. In fact, if you don't drink enough fluid, your body will hang on to it to guard against dehydration.

**Avoid processed foods with high levels of salt, alcohol, caffeine, wheat and dairy products.** These can all have a dehydrating effect. Try dandelion — also rich in potassium — in tea or tincturep forms. Or, sip fennel seed tea, or mix some dandelion leaves in a salad — they taste great!

# 119. COLD COMFORT

If you've woken up with a scratchy throat and a runny nose, try zapping it with one of these easy remedies.

**Buffered (non-acidic) vitamin C**
Take up to 5,000 mg daily for the duration of the cold only. Divide the dose through the day.

**A good antioxidant complex**
Look for a combination of beta carotene, vitamin A and selenium.

**Echinacea** A herb that boosts immune function: ten drops of the tincture two or three times a day.

**Zinc** Suck lozenges containing this antiviral and immune-boosting nutrient every three hours.

**Steam your head** Put five drops of eucalyptus essential oil in a bowl of hot water. Place a towel over your head and the bowl. Slowly and carefully breathe in the steam and feel it doing you good.

**Aconite** Keep this homoeopathic remedy handy: take it as soon as you feel a cold coming on.

# 120. PAY ATTENTION TO YOUR HUNGER

Overeating and undereating are two big energy-robbers. When you eat too much, you feel tired because all of your energy is diverted toward digesting your food. If you are eating more than you can contain in your cupped hands, then you're eating too much. But when you undereat, for example, during a crash diet, you also cause your body to be fatigued by depleting it of essential nutrients.

Becoming more attuned to the process of eating will help you understand when you are really hungry, as opposed to bored or upset. Experience the taste, texture and temperature of what you put in your mouth; it helps you become aware of how, when and why you nourish yourself. Do not rush when you eat: sit down, take three breaths to remind yourself to be grateful, and smile. Then, for the first bite or two, try chewing your food 15 to 20 times. Why? Because it opens you up to how you feel about this food. How does it taste? Can you feel it doing you good? Is it what you really need? If not, why not? And what should you be having instead?

# 121. GO PAST CHAMOMILE

Most of us know about the calming properties of chamomile tea, but a steaming cup of catnip, passionflower, skullcap or kava also work. Use loose tea (one teaspoon of tea per cup of boiling water) or tea bags, and steep for about ten minutes to get the full benefits of the herbs. Experiment with these tasty and healthful options:

**Peppermint** (*Mentha piperita*) Relaxes the smooth muscle in the digestive tract, reducing colic and flatulence, relieves nausea and vomiting, stimulates secretion of digestive juices and bile, and its anti-inflammatory action reduces reflex and heartburn. Excellent for feverish conditions and in respiratory conditions.

**Limeflower** (*Tilia europaea*) Induces sweating so it is great for reducing fevers and treating colds and flu. It relaxes the nervous system, treating insomnia, and reduces high blood pressure. Good for nervous headaches, digestive problems of nervous origin, and dizziness. Has a mild diuretic action, making it also useful in water retention and cystitis.

**Thyme** (*Thymus vulgaris*) Useful for respiratory and digestive infections, it works well as a mouthwash and gargle for sore throats, laryngitis, tonsillitis, and infected gums. As a hot tea, thyme induces sweating and so reduces fevers and relieves colds and flu.

**Elderflower** (*Sambucus nigra*) An excellent remedy for colds, flu, mucus, catarrh, and fevers. Hayfever, rhinitis and sinusitis respond well.

**Ginger** (*Zingiber officinale*) ) Its warming effect is beneficial in all conditions related to poor circulation: chilblains, cramp, weak digestion and cold extremities. It also relieves colic, flatulence, indigestion, morning and travel sickness.

**Lavender** (*Lavandula officinalis*) Used to ease stress, tension headaches, depression, and to strengthen the nervous system when exhausted. Useful for indigestion, insomnia, anxiety and tension.

**Meadowsweet** (*Filipendula ulmaria*) A valuable remedy for arthritis and rheumatism. Good for hyperactivity, nausea, heartburn, indigestion, gastritis, and reducing fevers.

**Licorice** (*Glycyrrhiza glabra*) ) Supports the adrenal glands during periods of stress and in eczema, asthma, hayfever and gastritis. Its soothing action in the digestive system helps to relieve colic, hyperacidity, heartburn, indigestion, and constipation. **(Warning: do not use licorice tea in large quantities if you suffer from high blood pressure.)**

# 122. Choose foods the Chinese way

The Chinese believe in 'energy eating', based on their philosophy that food is the key to relieving tiredness, fatigue and illness. Their main dietary principles are as follows:

**Have light meals**. Stopping eating before you are full is seen as a powerful way to boost flagging energy levels.
**Reduce your sugar intake**. This balances the healthy bacteria in the stomach, helping to prevent infections such as thrush.
**Eat simply**. Overloading the digestive system can make you feel sluggish.
**Balance your yin and yang**.
A deficiency in yang (responsible for warmth and activity) is believed to be caused by eating too much cold food and not enough carbohydrates. To combat this, eat roasted foods, oats, garlic, chicken and spices. Conversely a lack of yin (the Chinese word for passivity and stillness) is the result of too much junk food. To balance this, the Chinese philosophy recommends eating nuts, seafood, dairy products and raw fruit.

**Choose hot, or at least warm, foods**. Cold foods are thought to slow digestion, chill and harm the internal organs and reduce energy.
**Eat in seasonal harmony**. Chinese doctors believe that different foods, flavours and body organs correspond to each season of the year. You can help strengthen and tone your organs and maintain good health by eating seasonally appropriate foods. For instance: in spring (liver, gallbladder) eat citrus fruits, salad greens, chicken and pork; in summer (heart, small intestine) eat kale, mung beans, tomatoes, cucumbers, green capsicums; in autumn (lungs, large intestine) eat apples, sweet potatoes, onions, leeks, cabbage, celery; in winter (kidneys, bladder) eat seafood, meat, brown rice, barley, beans and root vegetables.

## 123. SHARE SOME GOOD NEWS EVERY DAY

Research shows that constantly hearing bad news broadcasts can send your mood plummeting. World events can weigh heavily on your shoulders, and remembered images of war and famine can imprint on your mind, and bring you down. To recover, for at least one day a week don't turn on the television or radio news and avoid newspapers. Buy a magazine that publishes only upbeat, entertaining features. Clip inspirational, positive photos and post them on your fridge. Make a deliberate effort to share a good news story with a friend or colleague. Similarly, try to look for others' good points, and avoid saying negative things about people.

# 124. WRITE LETTERS

'Be a lamp, or a lifeboat, or a ladder. Help someone's soul to heal.'
**Rumi**

My mother is the most wonderful letter writer. She simply sits down and tells you exactly what is going on at that moment. So you read that the white lilac near her front door needs pruning, but it looks so pretty she's going to put it off for as long as possible. And one of the cats is attacking the neighbour's dog and this time she's just going to let them sort it out. Reading one of her letters is the most evocative and intimate experience. It's as though she's just sent you a piece of herself.

Take the time to sit down and write a letter. It is a gift — not just to the recipient, who will always have something tangible to remind them of the half hour you spent thinking of them, and sharing your news — but to you as well. Even short notes, a few handwritten words on the back of a postcard, speak of a moment when we were thinking only of the other person. And 'real mail' makes a welcome change from the garbage that normally tumbles out of the letterbox!

Letter-writing is almost a form of meditation, putting you in touch with your life, and with the contents of your heart. Picking up a pen and paper and spending some time alone with your thoughts of the other person is more conducive to intimacy than email, or even the phone. That's not to say that you should disregard these other means of communication: they're obviously efficient and often necessary. Remember what they are best for — emails and the phone are great for keeping in touch, for a spontaneous joke or invitation. But there is a risk that they can make you feel isolated, one of dozens on an emailing list, just another message on an answering machine.

Letter-writing, on the other hand, is slow and deliberate. It takes time. The news that's important to you at the time, your handwriting with its natural stops and starts, loops, exclamation marks and even your doodles speak volumes. Handwritten letters are about intimacy and insights, a means of cutting through the clutter and really getting in touch with someone, attempting to understand them, and having them understand you.

As we find new and improved ways of communicating with each other, it's critical not to lose sight of one of our most basic human needs — to know and be known by another person — which pretty much sums up what letter-writing is all about.

# 125. BE SILLY

The best advice I was given when I had my kids came from my neighbour at the time: become a kid again yourself. She wasn't spruiking psycho-babble about 'getting in touch with my inner child', either. She was talking about getting closer to who you were when you were at your most authentic.

Think back to when you were a kid: what were you like? What did you wear? What did you like to do? What are your best — and worst — memories? If you've forgotten, here are some ideas to help you remember:

Re-read your favourite childhood book. Mine was the *Borrowers* series — and it's still good to read.

Look at photos of yourself as a child. Find one that you really like and frame it. Keep it where you can see it.

Get grubby. Put on some old clothes and go outside to play: dig in the dirt, roll on the grass, do forward rolls, somersaults if you can.

Hire your favourite movie from when you were small. I loved *Mary Poppins* — and I still do. Make yourself some popcorn and take a trip down memory lane.

Buy a colouring book and crayons. Scribble like you did when you were a child.

Bake cookies. Eat them warm, with a glass of cold milk.

Play some simple kids' games. Play knucklebones or elastics. Draw a hopscotch board on the pavement and see if you can remember how to do it.

Dress up.

## 126. PUT YOURSELF FIRST

In his poem, *Song of Myself*, Walt Whitman wrote: 'I celebrate myself, and sing myself. And what I assume you shall assume, for every atom belonging to me as good as belongs to you.' He understood that it's important to cherish yourself and also knew that, by doing so, he was better able to experience a sense of connection with the world, and to show love for others.

Treating yourself to the things you love isn't an indulgence — it's essential to building self-confidence, regulating your moods, and gaining a sense of power over your life. When you craft your daily to-do list, don't forget to add one utterly indulgent item just for yourself. Grab a sheet of paper and spend two minutes writing down absolutely everything that gives you pleasure. Your list can contain anything: reading trashy novels, playing with your kids, eating great food, naps, fresh air, wearing perfume, drinking jasmine tea, soaking in the tub, listening to music, making up a clean and crisp bed with sheets that have been dried in the breeze, eating Key lime pie, a vase of fresh flowers, great sex, good coffee, going to a play. They don't have to cost a lot of money or force you to buy, buy, buy. Usually the most satisfying ones are free. Then make a point of trying to do at least one thing on your list every day.

To many of us, putting yourself first sounds greedy and selfish. But self-love and self-care isn't selfish: by loving yourself, we love all. If you're happy and content, if you learn to look after yourself in real ways instead of trying to fill the void with material things, you also improve your relationships with the people closest to you and everything else you come into contact with.

## 127. VOLUNTEER FOR LIFE

'It is one of the most beautiful compensations of this life that no man can sincerely try to help another without helping himself in the process.'
**Ralph Waldo Emerson**

Being of service to others and helping the less fortunate is a concept familiar to many of the world's religions, but, unfortunately, not one readily embraced in everyday life.

It's the things we do for others, and how we improve their lives that are the most potent way of improving our own. Whether you're raising funds for a charity or washing up in a local shelter, volunteering boosts your self-esteem and gives you a sense of purpose. A study from Cornell University has found that volunteering not only helps others, but it increases the helper's self-esteem and energy levels, and gives them a sense of having more control over their lives. And if you still need more reasons for helping other people, social researchers have found that it also helps you live longer, with adults volunteering up to three hours a month being a remarkable ten times less likely to become ill or die in the five years following! Every little thing we do to benefit others helps. Here are some ideas:

Donate clothes, toys and/or food to shelters and homes in your area.

Sign up as a volunteer: there are literally hundreds of work projects, some big, some very small, from working at children's camps, to painting youth centres, or helping out at local fundraisers.

Read to groups at daycare centres, hospices, churches, schools and homeless shelters.

These are all very small contributions — but that is the whole point. Not everyone can travel to Third World countries to help out, or launch national appeals for the underprivileged. But nourishing others doesn't have to be a grand gesture. It can be a smile, a touch, a simple action that restores someone's faith in human nature — and helps inspire us. Never underestimate the effect you can have with your contribution; every action is as a great as any other.

# 128. SOLVE SNORING

If you or your partner snore, your quality of sleep will be considerably undermined. Try the following:

**Don't sleep on your back.** Put a tennis ball in a sock and sew it into the back of your nightwear to stop you rolling over on to your back.
**Lose weight if you need to.** Excess weight is thought to be a factor.
**Don't smoke, and avoid alcohol within five hours of bedtime.** Both interfere with breathing.

**If you have a cold or allergy, use a nasal decongestant.** But avoid any that contain ephedrine, as they will keep you awake.
**Take up singing.** Professional singers rarely snore — and it's thought that the reason is because singing exercises their throat muscles.

# 129. Invest with your values

'Whatever man does to the web of life, he does to himself,' said Native American leader Chief Seattle. You can take this as a reference to the impact of pollution and development on our overall wellbeing and environmental health — but the idea of connectedness doesn't stop there. It flows on to all our activities, including how we invest our money.

Imagine, for instance, that there is a company doing something that you find particularly offensive, conducting activities that run counter to your values and beliefs. Now — imagine buying shares in that company in the hopes of making a big profit. How does that make you feel? Many people feel very uncomfortable when they find themselves in this situation, whether their choice was deliberate or accidental. And few of us really believe one person's actions will have no effect on others. To paraphrase Eleanor Roosevelt, it's the only thing that ever *has* made a difference.

Fortunately, there is an alternative: you can achieve your financial goals and at the same time help make the world a better place for everyone. The rapidly growing practice of socially responsible investing — also known as 'ethical investing' — brings personal values and personal finance together in a mutually beneficial way. Nor does ethically-directed investing mean a lower return — when you look at the exponential growth achieved by health food and enviro-tech companies, in particular, in the last couple of years, you can see that this is a myth.

Once you've decided to put your money where your values are, the next step is to find the investments that will be both financially solid and in line with your values. Luckily, there are many consultants who specialise in screening companies for their social, environmental and political policies, as well as their associations with industries such as firearms, gambling, logging, nuclear power and links with oppressive regimes. Make today the day you make a difference with your money.

# 130. DEAL EFFECTIVELY WITH ENEMIES

One of my favourite quotes on this subject comes from that great thinker, Aristotle. He said: 'To be angry with the right person to the right extent and at the right time and in the right way — That is not easy.'

Apart from acknowledging his points about using your anger constructively and appropriately, I like the fact that he's also making it quite clear that there's no way we're going to get on with everyone, and that this is actually OK. Dealing effectively with someone who plain doesn't like you — or even who is actively trying to bring you down — is a challenge that everyone faces. Your only real choices are whether you bring destructive or useful feelings and behaviour to the situation.

Visualisation is a useful and powerful weapon. To begin, try to see your anger and fear as an untapped potential weapon you can wield against your enemy. If you can turn even a fraction of all that negative energy around — into feelings of certainty about what you're doing, for instance, or steely determination that no one's going to get in your way — you may find you have an opportunity to grow stronger and more confident in ways you'd never imagined.

The next step is to close your eyes and imagine your enemy sitting in front of you. Feel your anger rising up — but stop the inner voice that starts to say all the put-downs and smart comebacks that you've always wished you'd said to them. Instead, focus on the feelings of fury in your body and the image of your adversary in front of you. Yes, what they did was unfair, unkind, even cruel, and you certainly did not deserve it.

Now — imagine this person doing something quite unexpected. Imagine them apologising to you, or bending over backwards to help you. Imagine generosity and kindness flowing from your adversary to you. How do you feel about them now? And before you say, 'That's ridiculous. She would never do that!' — check why that is your reaction. Is it because you really think they are malevolent and dangerous? Or because you don't want to give up your righteous anger?

Even if you don't believe me, try this visualisation exercise. What happens is that you distance yourself from your anger. That way, when you have to deal with your enemy in person, or even just think about them in the future, you will do so from a position of greater confidence, strength and self-respect, and that reduces your enemy's control over you, and your fear of them.

# 131. REPEL NEGATIVE ENERGY

> 'Don't compromise yourself. You are all you've got.'
> **Janis Joplin**

You are more than just your physical body — we all have energy fields that extend beyond us and convey information. Think about how drained you can feel after a trip to a crowded shopping centre, or when you've had to listen to someone who's hopelessly negative. Some of us are more susceptible to absorbing this negative energy than others. Here are some practical approaches for dealing with troublesome empathy:

**Intuitive shielding** Visualise a shield of pink or white light around you.

**Self-knowledge** As someone who 'tunes in' readily to others' energy, you must also work on your own. On an energetic level, like attracts like: anger attracts anger and love attracts love. Make sure you are giving off the right signals.

**Distance** If all else fails, politely excuse yourself from the person or people who are draining your energy. Move away, out of range. Turn your back so you can't see them.

## 132. GIVE PROBLEMS BACK

Unassertive people have a habit of taking on other people's problems — for instance, a friend may come to you to 'download' if she's argued with her mother. To get out of the responsibility of solving a problem that isn't really yours, say 'I can see what you're going through — but this is between the two of you and I don't want to get caught in the middle.' Stick to it.

## 133. GET CLOSER TOGETHER

Depending on whether you're single, in a partnership, or married with children, whether you're an only child, or one of eight, 'family' can mean many different things. What I'm sure we all would like, though, is time to concentrate on what matters in our family, to learn from each other and to actually enjoy each other's company. Here are some ideas:

Teach your kids (or your little brothers or sisters, cousins, nieces and nephews) a self-sufficiency craft, like carpentry, cooking or gardening.

Find a hobby the whole family can enjoy.

Teach younger family members the importance of spending time with the older generation.

Tell each other the truth. You may think you're protecting each other by keeping things secret, but they will inevitably come out one day — and cause huge hurt to those who were kept in the dark.

Create family traditions. Carry on those traditions from childhood that you found meaningful as well as creating new ones for the next generation.

Remember that the simple activities together are always the best: going for walks, playing under the sprinkler in the backyard, making Christmas cards, baking cakes (bags I lick the bowl!), and playing Scrabble.

Work together as a family to care for those less fortunate.

Have rules. Set standards.

Don't snoop into each other's lives — you can ask, but if you don't get told, respect the other person's privacy.

Limit TV watching. Some parents swear by removing the TV altogether, but that would not be a popular option in our house. However, limiting TV on weekdays and setting limits on what you actually sit down and watch the other times will make a remarkable difference to your family life. Try it.

# 134. Give people space

Having enough space is a serious issue for many people. Personal space ranges from 'territorial' tussles over sharing the kitchen in the morning, to the general feeling that you aren't free to live your own life because everyone else's needs always come first.

**Set the rules**. Make a list of issues that are irritating you, such as not having enough time to yourself, or having to clean up mess all the time (messiness is the ultimate invasion of someone else's space). Arrange a time to discuss it all properly — don't bring it up in the middle of a row.

**Be very clear about what you want**. Many people are too afraid of saying what they really want in case they lose the relationship. Once everything is out in the open, be patient and be prepared to compromise. You probably won't get exactly what you want, but it will be pretty close, so you should end up better off than you are now.

**Share chores equally.** Women are still three times more likely to do the housework than men; as a result, it's not surprising they may be more likely than men to feel exploited and resentful.

**Enjoy being apart**. Don't feel you've failed if you or your partner wants to go off alone now and again. Having your own separate lives and interests can make you stronger together as well as apart. Think about taking a health farm holiday by yourself, or doing an evening class.

# 135. KEEP A PET

> 'Animals are such agreeable friends. They ask no questions,
> they pass no criticism.'
> **George Eliot**

Through time, animals have provided us with a great deal more than we've
provided them. They've supplied our transportation, pulled our ploughs, helped
us hunt, tracked lost children, rescued us from disasters, given us sport, aided the
handicapped, made some of us rich through bets, and been subjects for scientific
experiments. They've also been our best friends: animals don't care about the
things that usually make people beautiful, successful, attractive, and popular. If
you've lost your job, they don't care. If you're old and incontinent, they don't care.
As long as you scrounge enough food for your animal and you don't mistreat it,
it's going to be quite happy with you.

Nonjudgemental and devoted friendship is not all that animals contribute to
our lives. In the last 20 years, scientists have found many times over that keeping
a pet can make an enormous difference to our health. In one recent study of
women conducted at the State University of New York, researchers found that
those who owned a dog had lower blood pressure than those who didn't. Nursing
homes have reported extraordinary drops in death rates when patients were
allowed to have pet birds or cats. Research also shows that children who have
pets learn compassion and responsibility and have better coping skills than do
kids without pets. People with pets suffer from fewer common health problems,
such as backache and colds. Nor does it seem to matter what sort of animal you
choose: from dogs, horses and cats, through to rats, ferrets or even a hermit crab,
friendship from a pet is a wonderful thing.

**Cats** They pick up your mood and show affection in times of stress; their
behaviour makes you laugh, releasing feel-good chemicals.

**Dogs** They encourage exercise, such as brisk walking or jogging — and make
you feel more secure.

**Goldfish** Watching the motion of fish is calming and relaxing and can alleviate
stress, which is why they're often used in doctors' and dentists' surgeries.

PS: Animal shelters have an unenviable job, having to euthanase thousands of
cats and dogs a year. Get a pet from your local shelter.

# 136.   THROW A PARTY

'Live! Yes! Life is a banquet and most suckers are starving to death.'
**Patrick Dennis, 'Auntie Mame'**

Give your life a boost by holding a party. It will be stimulating to organise, and it's a buzz catching up with friends and having your home filled with warmth, light and music. Getting everything ready can be stressful, but once people begin to arrive and you hear the first person laugh, all your anxiety will wash away, and you'll know it's been worthwhile! Also, research shows that people cope better with stress when they're in the company of people they know and like.

# 137. MAKE SEX SEXIER

Many women (and men) would identify with Zsa Zsa Gabor's cool retort to an interviewer several years ago, who was trying to make her say something come-hitherish, as befitting an actress who was a sometime sex kitten: 'Personally,' she said, 'I know nothing about sex because I've always been married.'

Ouch. You've got a headache ... you're too tired. Before you know it, you haven't made love to your partner for weeks, which makes you feel tense and guilty and makes them feel ... angry? Disillusioned? Hmmph — you don't care how he feels? Going off sex for quite long periods of time is a lot more common than most people realise. Here's how to overcome your differences and restore even the most boring love life:

**Deal intelligently with rejection.** The constant refusal of one partner to make love can have a devastating effect on the other's self-esteem. Talking openly about your problems is essential to maintaining a healthy sexual and emotional relationship. Blocking lines of communication will only lead to confusion, anxiety and lack of closeness. If you don't want to make love, say so. But try to explain why; give your partner access to your feelings in a way that they aren't left thinking you've gone off them for good.

**Don't bottle up your worries.** Pillow talk is the key to resolving your difficulties.

**Track down the problem.** Try to keep a diary of when you feel most and least sexy. Women's sexuality is affected by a wide variety of moods and emotions: ask yourself questions about your monthly cycle, your diet, stress, and emotional wellbeing.

**An active lifestyle can help.** Studies have shown that women who undertake mild to moderate exercise report an increase in their capacity to feel aroused.

**Say what you want.** If you are turned off by your partner's lack of sensitivity or sexual selfishness, try to give them a guide as to what you like. Move into positions that satisfy you and voice your pleasure to make them aware of what turns you on.

# 138. PREDICT THE PREDICTABLE

Don't always expect things to go wrong — but do acknowledge that a good many situations (including pretty much anything to do with kids) are destined to try your patience and are simply not worth getting strung out about.

For instance, if someone can't find their bag/tie/homework on a school morning and scuppers your schedule — tell yourself it's happened before, will happen again, and there's nothing you can do to prevent it. It's just what happens when people live together and get on each other's nerves every so often. Change the way you think: if you're feeling overloaded by the angst and unable to cope, look in a mirror and say 'I can and I will' three times. It will send a positive message to your brain and help to make your daily tasks — including the situation you're in the middle of right now! — seem much more achievable. Fretting about predictable events is, in fact, self-induced pain.

This is just as relevant in the workplace as at home. American scientists have found that, in a stressful office environment, men and women handle themselves quite differently. They claim that men tread on people's toes to get on, but they're upfront about it. Women, however, are more underhand and motivated by insecurity. And, if betrayed, women take it personally — they feel they're being let down by friends — while men confront the backstabber and have it out with them. The researchers' conclusion? That women would do better and feel less pressure by adopting a more detached, objective approach in the office, and by making the necessary allowances in their mind for the inevitable hiccups. Learn to take things in your stride — at least some of the time.

## 139. DON'T SAY YES WHEN YOU MEAN NO

How many times have you agreed to do something, then felt resentful and put-upon? Trying to do everything is a one-way ticket to serious stress. Be clear about your limits, and stop trying to please everyone all the time.

Save time and boost your confidence by learning to say no. Think of alternative phrases you could use — such as, 'I'll let you know', 'I'll get back to you', or 'I'd prefer not to at present' — and practise them in front of the mirror every day. They will give you some breathing space and help you to avoid saying yes every time.

# 140. SET REALISTIC GOALS

People who feel good about themselves and their lives have learned the art of meeting objectives — and when they fail, of simply readjusting goals so they become more attainable. Succeeding at what you set out to do improves confidence and gives a sense of control — but you already know that! The thing that is harder to learn — and to concentrate on, even after you've learned it — is to pick goals that are achievable, or else you might end up reinforcing your feelings of idiocy all over again.

Begin with something simple, like your daily to-do list. Make chores specific and manageable — instead of 'clean out the cellar', try 'stack boxes', 'pack away tent', and so on. Put them in order of importance and tick them off as you go. And keep the list short — five things you know you can accomplish and tick off instead 20 wishes and intentions.

Next, try breaking down larger goals and problems in the same way. 'Try to achieve more balance in my life' is more likely to happen if you turn it into 'meditate every morning for 15 minutes' and 'make appointment for massage'. Same goes for vague aspirations to 'get healthy': break it down into goals of 'call organic greengrocer co-op and get on list', 'only buy low-fat dairy products from now on' and 'take ginseng'.

# 141. SIP GREEN TEA

Green tea — the kind you drink with a Chinese or Japanese meal — is packed with antioxidants which help both to eliminate toxins and to prevent the free-radical damage associated with cancer. Several studies have now found that regular drinkers of green tea have a lower risk of colon, rectal and pancreatic cancer. It seems the polyphenols in green tea block the development of tumours. Plus, drinking green tea appears to benefit women more than men.

To make, steep one teaspoon of tea leaves (or one tea bag) in two cups of boiling water for three to five minutes, and strain. Drink up to three cups of green tea a day. Get the benefit of the ingredients, by drinking your tea hot, soon after brewing. Another option is bamboo grass tea, which has a calming effect. These teas are available in health food shops or oriental grocers.

## 142. Keep a diary

> 'Life is like an onion: you peel off one layer at a time,
> and sometimes you cry.'
> **Carl Sandburg**

I don't remember who coined the phrase 'the dark night of the soul', but few of us have not experienced the utter despondency that it so aptly describes. Whether your 'dark night' is due to disease, emotional stress or some other traumatic event, one way to make it to the dawn is to put pen to paper — or fingers to keyboard — and write it all down.

Writing helps you come to grips with emotionally traumatic situations and it will nearly always point you towards a solution to a problem. This is doubly empowering — not only do you have an action plan, but you've come up with it yourself, rather than having to rely on others' advice. Working things out on paper helps you learn to trust your inner voice.

There's plenty of research to show that writing in your diary can improve your physical as well as mental wellbeing. One recent study showed that arthritis patients who wrote in a diary every day experienced a remarkable 19 per cent reduction in pain. Why? Because writing about their problem, and the accompanying pain, sleeplessness and fear they'd experienced actually reduced their bodies' constant surges of stress hormones, which in turn improved their immune systems' ability to cope.

Choose a special book for your diary — something that feels relaxed, spacious, but not threatening — and set aside maybe 20 minutes a day to write in it. Just before bed is a good time. Or, just open a private file on the computer, if that's more your style. Don't be daunted by the thought of having to write 'properly'. Think of Anne Frank's famous diary — rather than formal entries, she wrote regularly to an imaginary friend, Kitty. If letters don't appeal, try poems, or just make lists and notes about problems you're facing. If you can't come up with the right words, draw a picture instead. Same goes for grammar or spelling — don't worry about it. The point of the exercise is to get in touch with your inner self. How do you really feel? What do you really want? No one else is going to read it apart from you, so let go. Later on, maybe in a day or two, re-read what you wrote. It's extraordinary how you really do have the answers inside you all along, and they turn up on the pages of your diary, time and again.

# 143. EXPRESS YOUR DESIRES

'Love is not love until love's vulnerable.'
**Theodore Roethke**

Good sex requires honest communication. Don't expect your partner to be able to read your mind.

Unfortunately, fear, shame and embarrassment cause many men and women to go quiet in bed, simmering with resentment on the inside. Even today, old entrenched values die hard, and many women have been brought up to believe that it is the man's responsibility to 'give' sexual pleasure — and that if he didn't, for any reason, then 'good girls' didn't complain or ask for anything different. As it turns out, most partners are only too happy to oblige when they're given gentle, sensual guidance.

Be brave. Don't let your relationship fail because you find it difficult to express your desire. Ask yourself, 'What would I like to do next in my sex life?' It could be telling your partner about your sexual fantasies, writing erotica, or logging onto a tantric website together. What about visiting a local sex shop? And before you think, 'Decent people don't do that sort of thing', stop right there. They do. Decent people can and do take a healthy interest in sex. They are not ashamed of having a sex life, and they are committed to developing new intimacy with their partner — and to beating boredom! So — what's the next step for you?

# 144. PRACTISE AN OUNCE OF PREVENTION

Having worked in the health industry nearly all of my life, I have seen many nutrition trends, fad diets and foods come and go. It's easy to become cynical: one minute something's good for you, the next it's bad. A herbal supplement that's a must-have one month is taken off the shelves the next because it's made someone sick, or worse.

Always, though, it's the simplest changes that really go a long way towards keeping you healthy. For instance, the famous Harvard University Nurses' study (which tracks the health habits of nearly 100,000 women every year) has just announced (surprise, surprise) that those women who ate a high-fibre diet and walked briskly for 30 minutes every day had a whopping 80 per cent lower risk of heart disease than those who didn't. So, here are my three top daily dietary Do's. As well as being the smartest habits to adopt, they're also the easiest, and they'll cut your budget, too:

**Shun meat**. Replace animal products (including dairy foods) with fruits, vegetables, wholegrains, and legumes. Meat may raise your levels of cholesterol and of oestrogens, which is implicated in cancer. Plant foods, on the other hand, are chock-full of healing nutrients and phytochemicals. Wheat bran, in particular, is a must for lowering the risk of breast cancer. Eating 10 g or more a day has been found to significantly lower blood oestrogen levels after just six weeks. If vegetarianism is too daunting a change, just omit animal products for two days a week.

**Eat soy foods**. A daily serving (approximately 25 g) of soy protein can help lower your cholesterol, reduce your risk of heart disease and possibly some forms of cancer, and minimise menopausal symptoms such as hot flashes and night sweats. Can't or won't cook? Just pour soymilk on your cereal instead of ordinary milk — or try spreading tempeh on your sandwich at lunch rather than butter or margarine. Easy, painless and very tasty.

**Add flaxseeds**. Flaxseeds are rich in a type of omega-3 fatty acid, which helps lower your risk of heart disease and breast cancer. Buy the seeds from your health food store in bulk, and grind about half a cup at a time, storing the powder in an airtight glass jar. Sprinkle a tablespoon on your morning cereal or add to soups and stews; or, buy flaxseed oil and use it in salads.

# 145. Stay Younger Longer

In 1954, Denham Harman conceived the free-radical theory of ageing, probably the best-known anti-ageing theory today.

He theorised that ageing occurs because of cumulative damage caused by the chemical reactivity of free radicals. Free radicals are atoms or molecules that are highly unstable because they've either gained or lost an electron. They wreak havoc on the cells of the body because they are forever trying to either snatch an electron to complete their shell or dump an extra one. The most destructive are oxygen radicals. Our bodies can repair this damage to a point: it's one of the jobs of the immune system. But the ability to repair damage declines with age. Eventually the oxygen radicals cause the entire body to 'rust' and disintegrate, like an old car.

The solution? Take antioxidants to prevent free-radical damage and slow the ageing process. On the most basic level, that means eating lots of fresh fruits, vegetables and high-quality raw oils. For extra nutritional insurance, dietary supplements are in order, ranging from the old standby vitamins A, C, and E to newer miracle workers, such as pine bark extract, lycopene, and grapeseed extract.

# 146. Do lunch

No matter what else you do during the day, don't skip eating in the middle of the day. A lack of food will drain your energy levels. Your body will use adrenaline and stress to maintain the correct level of blood sugar instead of giving you much-needed energy. Going without food can also make you irritable and aggressive.

Eat the right foods for lunch and you will feel bright, alert and full of energy. Eat the wrong things, and you will feel awful, cranky and aggressive. If you have a mentally challenging task ahead, eat sardines or anchovies — they contain brain-boosting nutrients. Non-fish fans can sprinkle meals with lecithin granules (available from health food shops), which are also good for mental performance. When faced with physically demanding tasks, eat complex carbohydrates such as wholegrains, fruit and pulses, for sustained energy, as well as a small portion of protein, such as fish or nuts. To improve your memory, choose foods high in thiamine such as wheatgerm, bran, nuts or fortified cereals; for extra energy, eat protein foods like prawns, fish, scallops, turkey and low-fat milk or yoghurt. And ditch the lunchtime downers. These are all energy-zappers:

**Having a liquid lunch.** Alcohol is a depressant, and it will deplete your energy.

**Running errands for other people.** Their gratitude won't compensate for the resentment you'll feel.

**Eating a heavy meal.** All your energy will be diverted to digesting it, leaving you feeling sleepy.

**Scheduling a potentially stressful personal or work meeting for your lunch hour.** If you come back feeling angry or frustrated, you won't be in a good frame of mind to tackle the afternoon's tasks.

# 147. HAVE A GLASS OF RED

Drinking to excess is dangerous and stupid, affecting both your health and others' safety. However, drinking in moderation shouldn't compromise a healthy lifestyle — quite the opposite, in fact, especially if you fancy a drop of merlot or cabernet sauvignon.

Red wine could be considered a 'superfood' due to its supply of flavonoids, antioxidants believed to help protect against heart attacks and cancer. A very encouraging London study shows that one glass gives protective antioxidant activity equal to seven glasses of fresh orange juice. Other statistics even reveal that drinking one standard drink (a small glass of wine, or a pub measure of spirits) a day may reduce the tendency of the blood to form clots and is even associated with a longer life.

Anyway, as French scientist Louis Pasteur observed: 'A meal without wine is like a day without sunshine.' Absolutely!

# 148. LET GO OF NEGATIVE ENERGY

According to the Chinese system of chi kung, gently and rhythmically tapping various acupressure points on the body creates a vibrational wave that travels deep into the tissues, balancing the flow of energy, and stimulating the circulation and flow of lymph. These are the classic 'Three Taps', said to clear negative energy and help the body and mind work in harmony to counter stress:

**Head and Neck** Clench your hands into fists, leaving your thumbs running along the outside against your index fingers. Start by tapping briskly up and down from the base of your neck to the top of your head, and back again. Then, using your knuckles, go up and down the back of your neck from the tops of your shoulders to the bottom of your skull. Finish by tapping vigorously over the top of the head and down to the forehead, then back up and over again.

**Kidneys and Adrenals** Using the back of your fists (where your fingers are tucked in) to rhythmically tap the left and right kidneys: do one side, from top to bottom, bottom to top, then the other, then repeat. Your kidneys are just above your waist at the back of your stomach on either side of your spine. Tap each area for two minutes.

**Thymus** Using the middle row of the knuckles of one hand, rhythmically tap the centre of your chest to the beat of one heavy tap followed by two lighter ones. Keep time in your mind, or softly say out loud: 'ONE, two, three, ONE, two, three.' Tap for approximately two minutes.

# 149. RE-CREATE RECREATION

Why is it that now, when we have more choices than we could possibly view, listen to, read or do when it comes to entertainment and leisure activities, are we more stressed than in living memory?

We are swamped by video and computer games, TV channels, movies, sports parks, theme parks and entertainment centres, which are all open nearly all the time. In fact, this 'recreation' gives us very little time or incentive to actually 're-create' ourselves — to renew, refresh, rest — which is where the word came from in the first place. It may be that staying home and reading — or doing absolutely nothing at all — helps us to better recreate ourselves than does participating in the multimillion dollar industry which seeks to capture your cash.

It's also sobering to consider who and what is behind the entertainment business. Big companies are not squeamish about flogging their products on television, in movies, or even through sponsorship programs for school events. The next time you see a soft drink, food packet or brand of clothing on a sitcom remember: it didn't get there by accident! Then there are the messages inherent in the 'entertainment'. The subject of the effect of TV and movie violence on children has been endlessly debated, and continues to be an area of concern. However, I think other messages communicated, including boredom, nihilism, teenage angst and restlessness, and the idea that endless spending solves all problems, are just as dangerous, if not more so, to the human spirit.

That's not to say that there aren't plenty of wonderful documentaries and quality movies and television programs around. The key is to be more deliberate about what we allow into our lives as entertainment. If we're watching, listening, reading without any thought at all about the value or effect of what we're taking in, we are amusing ourselves all the way to spiritual and mental death.

Consider making up a list of 'homemade' entertainment and cheap (even free!) thrills. Consider picnics or camping, making music or crafts, exercising or gardening, and reading or writing. Old-fashioned hobbies, games and activities are inexpensive, easy to pursue, and fun for everyone.

# 150. BE A SAVVY SHOPPER

Want to get the best ingredients for your efforts and money, as well as live simply and 'lightly' on the earth? You can save a lot of money by taking advantage of the following budget-cutting opportunities.

**Watch for in-store specials**. To maximise savings, pick up the in-store flyer or pamphlet before you shop. Come equipped with a shopping list and stock up on savings by buying enough sale items for several meals.
**Buy in bulk or by the case**. Buy flour, legumes, nuts and spices from bulk-buy bins (you save because you do your own packaging). To buy products by the case, contact the store manager for details.
**Explore local options**. Even if you live in the city or suburbs, it's possible to get to know growers. I live near the city, but I've found a fellow only ten minutes away who grows salad vegetables for the big supermarket chains. He sells the excess for a fraction of the price from his front porch! The advantages of buying locally are that it helps to sustain rural communities. It also means fewer (or no) after-harvest pesticides and other treatments for long-distance shipping, and less fuel spent on transportation and packing.

**Try the house brands**. Both conventional supermarkets, health food stores and pharmacies usually provide their own line of namesake house brands — everything from pasta sauce to olive oil and soap.
**Shop in season**. When you buy foods in season, they're usually cheaper and fresher. This general rule of thumb applies even more strongly to organic produce. Organic apples, for example, can be much less expensive than conventional apples when you buy them at peak season (autumn) than at any other time of the year. As winter approaches, you might want to start 'putting by' stocks of food from what was in season during summer and autumn. Consider investing in a small household freezer or drying racks to preserve summer fruits and vegetables. You'll save an absolute fortune on buying things like 'fresh' imported tomatoes in winter.

# 151. RETHINK CHILDREN'S TOYS

> 'Parents are the hardest-working members of the population. But they do it for the highest wages. Kisses.'
> **Pete Seeger, folk singer**

Where and when do the children play? If you've got children of your own, or are involved with kids in your family, you cannot have missed the way they are being targeted by marketers, especially to spend their money on entertainment and — surprise, surprise — the latest toy that goes with the TV show, electronic game or movie.

With most of these must-have toys and games, the negatives outweigh the positives: they do not strengthen the child's spirit, nor foster their creativity, and in many cases they denigrate the environment and energy supplies. Substitutes can usually be found for expensive plastic toys which are often little more than merchandising. Here are some ideas for making and inventing toys, rather than buying them. And remember, a whole lot of fun can be had with tin cans, cardboard boxes and a couple of old tyres.

Make ice-cream together.

Go fishing.

Try your hand at lassoos, weaving and basic whittling.

Play word games.

Write a play or story together, and act it out.

Start scrapbooks.

Tell stories.

Play cards.

Keep an eye out for secondhand pool and ping-pong tables, or a dartboard (if your nerves can take it).

Introduce kids to stamp collecting.

Learn magic tricks.

Play with some basic science equipment.

Discover the world in the backyard under a magnifying glass.

# 152. ORGANISE YOUR THOUGHTS

One way to remember new information is to link it to something already stored in your long-term memory. If you want to remember a list in order, for example, relate it to something familiar, such as your house. Picture each item in a room and, when you want to recall the list, simply 'walk' through the house in your mind. The weirder and more vivid and exaggerated you make the images, the better, because it will make them even more memorable!

Remember names and faces by linking a new face to someone you already know. If you meet someone called David Holmes who reminds you of John McEnroe, for instance, picture the man you've met playing tennis. Then, imagine Sherlock Holmes peering through his magnifying glass on the court. If you're still not confident, you could also imagine a David you already know sitting in the umpire's chair. It may sound complicated, but I guarantee the next time you meet him, you'll immediately think of John McEnroe, and the visual image should spring straight to mind, along with his name.

In fact, when left to its own devices, your brain will 'play' with facts and roll memories and associations around in the most extraordinary fashion (consider some of your more out-there dreams, for instance), so it can actually be more efficient to work with your capabilities in this way than to try to remember facts in rote order.

## 153. GO TO BED EARLY

Sleep is indispensable as the basis for feeling good and for experiencing clear awareness during our waking hours. More than anything else, it determines the overall quality of your day.

The average person sleeps about six and a half to seven hours a night: two hours less today than they did 100 years ago. The problem of sleep deprivation is enormous. Living in a culture of late-night television, of working long hours, of supermarkets open 24 hours a day, most of us pride ourselves on how much sleep we do *without*. To think of sleep not as 'downtime' or 'wasted time' but as 'real time' is to shift your way of thinking about every other aspect of your life. To go to bed early — even just half an hour earlier — is to give over a larger portion of your life to that vast repository of images and possibilities that lies in dreams. As well as replenishing yourself physically, it is a way of acknowledging that the world we experience during the day begins within our minds, with our state of spiritual and emotional wellbeing and the condition of our souls, which are all accessed during sleep.

# 154. GET RID OF NIGHTMARES

Half of all adults have occasional nightmares, while one per cent recall one every week. Apart from being distressing at the time, English researchers have found that, if you have them consistently, nightmares can greatly impair our ability to assess risks and potential problems in the daytime: one in five road accidents were found to occur the day after one of the drivers involved had experienced a violent nightmare.

Psychologists believe that nightmares are a symptom of repressed emotions such as fear, grief or guilt. They can also be triggered by traumatic experiences, or as a side effect of drugs, for example beta-blockers and some tranquillisers. Even supposedly innocuous over-the-counter medications, notably cough syrups and decongestants, can trigger nightmares in some people.

If there does not appear to be an obvious culprit, such as a drug or overeating late at night, try to work out what your nightmares are trying to tell you — there could be an issue you have avoided dealing with. If they are frequent, you may want to see a counsellor, who can help by working through them with you. Taking a Bach flower remedy before bed may help: these remedies work to control negative feelings, and can help you cope with underlying problems — for example, try White Chestnut for worry and tormented thoughts; and Mimulus or Rock Rose for fear. Avoid drinking liquor during the evening, as this can often trigger nightmares and restless sleep as the body attempts to burn off the excess of sugar and alcohol.

## 155. TEACH YOUR KIDS TO CARE

Instil the spirit of charity and helping others in your children by encouraging them to become active in their communities.

Ideas for simple service projects might include visiting people in a nursing home, collecting unwanted toys and clothes for the homeless, raising money via walkathons and competitions for the local hospital or childcare centre, or helping walk dogs at a nearby kennel. Or, simply make a charity box for your home and, once a week, get the kids to contribute to it. Not only will the community benefit from the pint-size charitable contribution, but children also develop greater self-esteem. No matter how little a task may seem, it adds up, and the outcome is empowering to children.

# 156. MAKE LOVE TO YOURSELF

The old proverb says: 'Love attracts love.' So often we fear pleasure and associate it with decadence and sin, while viewing pain and deprivation as somehow virtuous. Provided our pleasure does not harm ourselves or others, we should consider it healthy and healing.

Sexuality honours pleasure: it is Nature's way of letting us know what is good for us. Masturbation — self-pleasuring — can be a voyage of self-discovery and an experience of positive self-love. But there are many other ways to turn yourself on as well. Have a warm scented bath. Wrap a glittery shawl around your hips and dance wildly to music. On a warm summer night, go out and lie on the grass, letting your body commune with the earth. A good lover is a wonderful gift — but don't think that without one, you can't be sexual — or that you aren't worthy of love and sensual attention. Be open to pleasure. Welcome it into every moment of your life and embrace it as a teacher and a friend.

# 157. ENERGISE YOUR HOME

Most us know exactly what the phrase 'you could cut the air with a knife' means: that feeling you get when you walk into a room where there's been a really dreadful argument, or an accident — or even something more sinister. The Chinese believe that the ancient art of feng shui — which means, literally, 'wind' and 'water' — can unblock trapped or stale energy in a room, and that this can dramatically improve your health, happiness and even finances, as well as improving the whole atmosphere and feeling of a home. Here are some helpful ideas to get you started:

**Fix sticking doors.** If a door or window is difficult to open it will hinder the flow of energy to your home and cause career stagnation, especially if it's the front door.

**Put the toilet lid down.** Otherwise, you are flushing your money down the drain.

**If it's broken, fix it.** Faulty appliances and tools or broken furniture all drain the general flow of household energy.

**Overhead beams are a feng shui no-no.** They 'cut' the atmosphere, and so can cause fights and, if you're lying underneath one in bed, digestive problems.

**Get rid of rubbish.** Messy piles of papers, bottles and cans waiting to go out for recycling, old clothes — they all cause anything from constipation to headaches. Don't overload shelves and cupboards — they can create an oppressive atmosphere.

**Mirrors are helpful for promoting the flow of chi, or energy.** Don't hang them too low, or they can cause headaches.

**Are your front and back doors in a line?** Hang a wind chime or crystal in between to allow chi to circulate and attract luck, not to flow straight through the house and out the other side, like a river.

# 158. CLEAR OUT CLUTTER

If you're hankering for a new look for your home, but your budget doesn't stretch to a makeover, do what the Balinese do and try clearing the clutter out instead. In Bali, regular house-cleaning and clutter-clearing is seen as a purification ritual, an opportunity to repeatedly meditate on and bless the home and family.

Clutter can drain you of more energy than you might imagine possible. Although embarking upon a big annual spring-clean and chuck-out gives you a terrific feeling of achievement, it's also extremely hard work and very easy to put off. Far more sensible to adopt cleaning and clutter-clearing as a habitual practice, much as you might watch television or clean your teeth. Anything that becomes a habit is more easily done. The Balinese have this down pat — you only have to watch them perform their cleaning — they go about it in an unhurried, rhythmic and graceful way, and clearly don't resent it or regard it as time wasted.

Anything you don't love or use can be considered clutter. Old toys, chipped china, plastic containers that you've lost the lids for — give the lot to your local charitable agency. Transplant or throw away plants that are dying or dead. Repair or throw out anything that has been broken for a long time or has parts missing. Now — take a tour around the house as if you were a visitor. Write down items that immediately strike you as having no benefit in your life, things that you could easily call 'stuff'. Good places to start: wardrobes, cupboards, bulletin boards, pots 'n' pans drawers and linen presses all have a tendency to become catch-alls. Then plan a time to start sorting it all out. The trick here is to set yourself small goals and work up. What works for me is to set aside 15- or 30-minute chunks, and take one small area — say, a drawer — and just do that until it's done. Finally, do a thorough clean. Vacuum the rugs, mop the floors, wash the windows. Open the windows wide to allow sunshine and fresh air to fill your home.

Housework stops being a drudge when you realise you are sweeping out old thoughts, rigid ideas and stagnant emotions along with the dust. Aim to continually check and cull possessions. Only keep things you know are useful and necessary, or which you consider beautiful and give you pleasure. Be tidy: if it's open, shut it. If it's spilled, wipe it up. Put things away as soon as you can after you've finished with them. Be sure you put things where you can find them next time. Keep these points firmly in mind, and you'll be left with a home that looks and feels lighter, larger, brighter, fresher and more harmonious.

# 159. LIVE COLOURFULLY

Colour therapists maintain that the colours of what you wear can have an effect on how you feel and react, and on what others think of you. Use different colours to lift your mood and cheer yourself up. Try this colour code:

GO FOR

**Orange** Increases your energy and makes you feel stimulated. Wear orange when you need a creative boost. It signals vitality and originality to the wearer's brain, giving you the impetus to try something new.

**Red** The colour of passion, adventure and drama, wear red when you need a shot of confidence, say, when you're starting a new project or attempting to enthuse others.

**Blue** The most soothing of all colours, blue is a wise choice if you need to calm down or become more centred — or if the people you're going to be with do.

**Green** To regain a sense of balance, particularly if you're feeling depressed.

**Yellow** To create a cheerful, upbeat mood or atmosphere.

**Turquoise** To strengthen the immune system, improves morale and makes you feel calm and positive.

**Violet** To foster feelings of self-respect and dignity, which are often missing in people who have a poor self image.

AVOID

**Grey** This is the colour of denial. It may help you forget about your problems temporarily — but emphasises feelings of indecision and weakness in the long run.

**Brown** The colour of commitment and fortitude, this can make you feel overwhelmed by pressing tasks, resulting in negative energy.

**Black** It attracts negative energy, so avoid wearing it altogether when you're feeling down.

Colour schemes set the tone for rooms in your home, and small colour changes can make a big difference to the spirit of a room. When you're choosing wall colours, think about the everyday shades that give you pleasure. Make sure you have one item that's blue in every room; this colour is relaxing. Be daring: paint your bathroom walls an outrageous colour (purple, black, gold . . !) — this room is only little, so should only take a small can of paint — and it's easy to cover up if you change your mind. Yellow may be the ideal bathroom colour — one study found that it can actually stimulate elimination.

# 160. GIVE YOUR DESK A HEALTH CHECK

If you spend a large part of your life sitting at a desk, it makes sense to ensure that it's safe. Here's how to reduce the health risks:

**Telephone** Don't cradle the handset between your head and shoulder. If you're right-handed, put your phone on your left-hand side so you can pick it up with your left hand and write with your right hand (vice versa if you're left handed). A headset is a good idea if you use the phone a lot.

**Keyboard** To prevent wrist strain, keep your keyboard in a position that allows your hands and wrists to hover slightly above it with your wrists straight.

**Lighting** Your work area should be properly lit but without reflections or glare on your screen. Avoid directly facing windows or bright lights. Natural lighting and outside views are best for your health.

**Plants** Leafy plants are good for your health at work. Studies have found a drop in fatigue, coughing, sore throats and cold-related illnesses among employees when plants were placed on their desks. Research also shows that people suffer less anxiety and stress and recover better from mental fatigue in an environment dotted with plants. They can also counter the dry environment created by computer equipment.

**Desk** Your desk should be deep enough for your screen to be at the right distance for your eyesight and there should be enough space underneath for you to move your legs freely. Make sure there's room to keep your papers and phone at hand so you don't have to make repeated stretching movements.

**Chair** Your chair should have adjustable height and backrest. If your feet don't touch the ground, use a foot rest. It should also have five feet or castors for optimum support. Swivel chairs are best; they allow ease of movement.

**Mouse** Keep the mouse comfortably close to your body — if it's too far away you can strain your neck and shoulders. Ensure your mouse is clean so it slides easily and position your mouse pad near the edge of the desk so you don't have to stretch to use it.

# 161. ADMIT IT

Each of us has unique individual stress signals which we usually ignore — neck or shoulder pain, shallow breathing, stammering, eye strain, queasiness, loss of temper. Learn to identify yours, then acknowledge them. Don't be a martyr and carry on regardless. Instead, say out loud, 'I'm feeling stressed' when they crop up. Recognising your personal stress signals, and respecting them by taking time out, helps slow the build-up of negativity, resentment, and anxiety.

# 162. JUST SLOW DOWN

Lewis Carroll put the feeling of spinning chaos that comes from go-go-going too fast in a nutshell when he wrote of 'life becoming a spasm and history a whiz'. Sometimes you spend days just rushing from one meeting or task to the next, but no matter how hard you push yourself, you still end up feeling as if you haven't accomplished anything. As an experiment, see if you can make a conscious effort to slow down — both your thinking and your actions. If you do this, you'll be pleasantly surprised to discover that, despite your slower speed, you will become far more effective, as well as more relaxed. Try these tips when things get out of control:

**Desert a crisis** A quick and easy way to clear your head during stressful periods is to physically remove yourself. Take yourself away from the problem environment — your house, or your office, for instance — and walk around for at least five minutes.

**Drop everything** Occasionally allow yourself to do absolutely nothing. Zero. Zilch. Discard your to-do list, put away your plans, and forget about the news. Instead, look out the window and watch the world go by, or stretch out on your bed and daydream.

**Relish your privacy** Consider these exquisitely wise words from Chinese philosopher La-tzu: 'Just remain in the centre, watching. And then forget that you are there.' Take time to just be. Cutting yourself off from the world not only relaxes you, it can help you to achieve inner peace and enable you to clear your head for solving any unresolved work or emotional problems. The next time you are given a few delicious free moments — you get off work a little earlier than usual, you're alone in the house for an hour before the kids come home, you've got 30 minutes before a meeting — try not to immediately fill it with crossing things off your to-do list. Simply stop.

## 163. BE PHONE SMART

Constant phone calls can waste valuable time at home and at work, slowing down your day and making you feel as if you never get anything done. Leave your answering machine on at particularly busy times, then set aside time when you'll deal with the calls. Attaching a caller-display unit to your phone will enable you to see the number of the person ringing you — so you can pick up any urgent calls. It's also a savvy personal safety measure.

## 164. HEAL YOUR BROKEN HEART

> 'The choice may have been mistaken — the choosing was not.'
> **Steven Sondheim, from 'Move On'**

All you want to do is climb into bed, pull up the covers and cry forever. The next little while is going to be tough — but there are some natural remedies you can take to ease the classic symptoms of a broken heart.

**Homoeopathy** Trickle four drops of Rescue Remedy under your tongue to help you deal with the shock and stabilise your emotions.

**Vitamins and minerals** Take a super-stress formula to nourish your nerves. Extra calcium and magnesium help relieve tension, the essential fatty acids found in flaxseed will even out hormonally-driven mood swings, and chromium helps control sugar craving and bingeing.

**Aromatherapy** Try a few drops of peppermint oil in your bath to raise energy levels.

**Herbs** Take kava to boost your mood, St John's wort to combat depression, and valerian if you can't sleep.

**Mind/body** Write down three good things about yourself. Stick them up where you will see them. Read them out loud, at least three times a day.

**Time** It really does heal all wounds.

## 165.  MAKE NEW FRIENDS

The more diverse your circle of friends, the healthier you'll be, say researchers. Here are some 'natural' ideas on how to connect with others:

**Say 'Soy Cheese'**. Wear your feelings on your chest, and you never know who'll strike up a conversation! The cotton shirts from Wearable Vegetables feature slogans like 'Girl from Echinacea', 'Silence of the Yams' and 'Shiitake Happens' which can't help but raise a smile. Visit the site www.wearablevegetables.com for more.

**Put your hand up**. Besides introducing you to new people, putting yourself forward for charity or volunteer work makes you feel better about yourself.

**Open your mind**. Fancy making a vegetarian lasagna? Learning the lotus position? Check out the noticeboards at your local health food store for ideas on courses where you'll meet like-minded people.

**Think pink**. Crystal therapists say rose quartz has the power to encourage love and friendship. Carry a small piece in your purse, or place it on your desk.

**Stamp out shyness**. Flower essences such as Mimulus *(Mimulus guttatus)* can help you overcome nervousness and communicate better. Place up to four drops under your tongue four times a day.

# 166. GET TO THE ROOT OF HAIR LOSS

The B vitamin biotin helps combat a dry, scaly scalp and hair loss. Take daily, according to manufacturer's instructions, for at least six weeks.

Drink one cup of horsetail tea *(Equisetum arvense)* daily for the mineral content, particularly silica, which is essential for strong, healthy hair.

Massage your scalp with old-fashioned bay rum tonic at night (from your chemist), or a few drops of rosemary oil.

To stimulate the hair follicles and promote growth, use strong, strained nettle tea to rinse off shampoo.

Stand on your head once a day for 25 to 40 breaths. While it may sound crazy, this yoga exercise helps bring fresh blood to the scalp.

# 167. MAKE LIFE MORE MEANINGFUL

'We all live with the objective of being happy and fulfilled;
our lives are all so different, and yet so much the same.'
**Anne Frank**

We're all seeking meaning in our lives, trying to find a path that's richer, more real, more authentic. But if you're seeking more spiritual depth in your life, can it only be found in a church? A synagogue? A prayer circle? Or can you come across it when you're sweeping the floor, lighting candles, peeling vegetables for soup?

The truth is, you can cultivate a sense of the spiritual everywhere in daily life. Rather than try to figure out where it is, the opposite is true: there is nowhere it is *not* to be found. I think women can see the natural sense of this more than men. Throughout history, women who have wanted to learn about themselves and examine their innermost thoughts in a quest for spiritual attunement and balance have usually been changing nappies, sweeping floors, folding laundry, and raising kids at the same time. And, just as the priestesses of ancient times knew how to create and protect sacred space through the use of candles, aromas, music, food and objects of beauty, you also know, deep down, how to create a peaceful environment, where all who enter feel safe and comforted.

The beauty of this philosophical approach to making your everyday humdrum life more meaningful is that it fills boring daily routines with depth. Taking a child by the hand to guide him across a road becomes a vitally important act, encapsulating the most important job you will ever do. Cooking is less of a chore, and more a gift of nurturing and comfort, even cleaning becomes a means to an end — a bright, ordered and inviting home.

## 168. CUT BACK ON CAFFEINE

Anything over 250 mg a day — that's two or three cups of filtered coffee — and you could start to feel the effects of too much caffeine, such as nervousness and raised blood pressure. But if you brew your cuppa for one minute instead of five, you halve the caffeine content from 80 to 40 mg. Cut back very slowly over four weeks to avoid withdrawal symptoms of headache, fatigue and depression.

# 169. CHECK YOUR ENERGY CONSUMPTION

Start by taking a look at your electricity and gas bills, then at what you spend on appliances, lighting, plumbing, and housekeeping. Now, rather than getting upset: a solid first step towards feeling good about your life is to feel more in control of your outgoing expenses, and to be able to conserve more of your money, time and energy for other things. Taking these economical tips and hints on board is worth the effort:

**Use a measuring scoop for laundry and dishwasher powder** or you use twice as much as you need to.

**Buy an old-fashioned soap shaker** from a chemist or hardware store. Pop all your soap scraps in it and you'll get at least an extra bar of soap a fortnight.

**Cut the kids' hair yourself**. Buy good scissors and a razor-comb and you'll save hundreds of dollars a year. If your hair has to be professionally cut or tinted, find a cheaper hairdresser who works from home or does home visits.

**Pay as many bills electronically or via direct debit or b-pay as you can**. This neatly gets rid of all those account keeping fees and charges; plus, there's great pleasure to be had from getting a nasty two-hour job done in ten minutes! Most banks offer online bill paying, but there are also many new Internet companies offering a full range of bill-paying services.

**Put new washers on dripping taps**. A dripping backyard tap is a common money-wasting trap.

**Make your own lunch every day, without fail**. If you're working, make it the night before so you won't fall into the 'no time in the morning' trap.

**Find new uses for old things**. An old ice bucket makes a great plant pot, a framed but cracked mirror frame could be a perfect fit for a poster.

**Use old clothes for rags**. Wash them instead of using paper towels.

**Don't throw away paper that's only printed on one side**. Use it for scrap paper, kids' painting paper, or print first drafts from your computer on it.

**Use all old containers**. Jars and film containers can be used to hold paints, spices, keys and buttons. Shoe boxes are perfect for filing recipes and CDs.

**Re-use all supplies possible**. Get a second use from packaging, padded envelopes, wrapping paper and ribbon.

**Turn off the lights in rooms as you leave them**. If you are not in the room, why light up the furniture? Go to bed earlier — that way all the lights are turned off.

**Turn down the heating in winter**. Put an extra blanket on the bed and wear warmer clothes around the house.

**Close the curtains**. They'll keep the warmth in during cold weather, and the heat out during summer.

## 170. LOOK FANTASTIC

The fickle finger of fashion can play havoc with your finances — don't let yourself be conned. There are plenty of ways to dress with style for far less money than you'd expect to pay. Here are some tips to get you started:

**Make a list before you shop**. Evaluate what's in your wardrobe and only write down things you know will help you stretch what you already have. Same goes for shopping for other family members.

**Check for quality**. Whether you're buying new or secondhand, don't hand over your money until you've checked the seams and buttons, tugged and crushed the fabric to see how it wears, and read the care label.

**Always try it on**. Sizes stated can vary widely.

**Choose natural fabrics like cotton and wool**. They're more energy-efficient to produce and to wear.

**Buy the best shoes you can afford**. Ill-fitting synthetic shoes can affect your health in the short- and long-term — they're not worth it.

**Decide on colours**. Having one basic colour (mine is navy blue) makes it a lot easier to mix and match.

**Look after what you've got**. Clean your shoes when they need it, protect them from humidity and direct light, and you'll have them for longer.

**Don't get ripped off by designer labels**. A plain white t-shirt from Lowes will look the same as one from Trent Nathan — and cost anything up to $100 less!

**Swap with friends**. Do you really need a special outfit for a one-off party or wedding? Borrow something from a friend, or hire from a formal hire company.

**Go to markets and sales**. Moving sales and garage sales often provide an opportunity to pick up great clothes and accessories, especially for children.

# 171. DON'T BUY SOFT DRINKS

If you're looking for a feel-great energy buzz, don't reach for a bottled fizzy drink. Most are packed with sugar, preservatives and colourings, and some contain caffeine, which may give you a short-term rush but will leave you feeling even more tired when the effect wears off. Cheaper and healthier alternatives include:

**A vitamin-loaded smoothie.** Mix together fresh apple juice and low-fat drinking yoghurt in equal quantities; add a banana and a teaspoon each of honey and of brewer's yeast for extra energy. (Tip: any other soft fruit, fresh or tinned, such as strawberries or peaches, will do fine.)

**A banana.** To replace energy after exercise, just eat a banana and drink a glass of water.

**Blended hunks of watermelon (including pips).** The pips are rich in energy-giving nutrients such as vitamin E and zinc and essential fats, while the flesh is a great source of vitamins C, E and beta carotene, which keep you feeling on top of things.

# 172. BARBECUE SMARTER

The good news is, everyone loves a barbecue, and it can be a delicious and easy way to cook and entertain. The bad news is that you need to be wary of the potentially carcinogenic heterocyclic amines (HCAs) which form if food gets badly charred. These tips to keep your food free from HCAs work equally well whether you're barbecuing seafood, chicken, vegetables or meat.

Precook or parboil food to reduce the time it spends on the barbecue.

Add minced or mashed fruit to hamburger mix before forming into patties. The antioxidants in fruit help counteract HCAs. Try mashed pawpaw and banana, or grated carrot: they actually make for a moister, more flavoursome hamburger.

Marinating meat in any kind of liquid, especially vinegar- or citrus juice-based recipes, can help prevent HCAs.

Pierce several vitamin E capsules and squirt the contents into mince meat mixtures before making hamburgers and cooking. Vitamin E may reduce HCA formation.

# 173. MAKE GREAT SALAD DRESSINGS

'Eating is not merely a material pleasure. Eating gives spectacular
joy to life.'
**Elsa Schiaparelli**

It's not good enough to think: 'I'll just have a salad', if what you're putting on top
of it is cancelling out any health benefits. By learning which oils are better for you
than others, and experimenting with healing herbs and spices, you can increase
the health value of your salad dressings and decrease the kilojoules on offer,
without compromising on flavour. Here are some tips:

**Choose oils that provide something
besides kilojoules.** Sesame, grapeseed,
walnut and olive oils are all rich in
antioxidants, which help prevent heart
disease and some types of cancer, as well
as being elegantly flavoursome. Flaxseed
oil is another light-tasting option which
has the bonus of helping to lower
cholesterol with its high content of
omega-3 fatty acids. Canola oil is another
heart-healthy option, at a budget price.
**Use a low-acid vinegar**, such as
balsamic or rice wine vinegar. They are
very moreish and don't need as much oil
to tame their tang. Or, use citrus juices
— fresh lime, orange or lemon, or a
blend of all three — instead of vinegar.
**Be lavish with seasonings**, and reap
the health benefits. The fresher, the
better. Onions, shallots and garlic are
traditional immunity boosters; ginger
may help combat blood clots and
congestion from colds; parsley is rich
in vitamin C, iron and calcium;
rosemary, another antioxidant,
stimulates circulation.

# 174. MAKE SOUP

'Cooking is like love. It should be entered into with abandon, or not at all.'
**Harriet van Horne**

Money may not buy happiness, but it certainly makes grocery shopping less stressful. It's a challenge to feed a family when you're broke. One of the best foods for hard times is soup. Apart from being delicious and nourishing, cheaper cuts of meat or vegetable scraps can be turned into a hearty broth or stock without too much trouble.

It doesn't have to be a cold day for me to be inspired to haul out my big soup pot. In winter, corn chowder, and creamy potato fennel with Parmesan croutons are two of my favourites; in summer, I can afford to be extravagant with avocados, which make a silky, sophisticated chilled soup, and when I have an abundance of tomatoes and basil, I make gazpacho. But the staple I make nearly every week all through the year is this tonic soup that not only tastes terrific, but has the added benefit of potent immune-strengthening herbs: ginger, garlic, onions and shiitake mushrooms.

**Tonic Soup**
  2.5cm (1 inch) fresh ginger, slivered
  1/2 cup (4 fl oz) basmati rice
  1/2 cup shiitake mushrooms, sliced
  1/4 teaspoon sea salt
  6 cups (3 pints) vegetable or chicken stock
  6 cloves garlic, minced
  1/2 cup onions, chopped
  1/2 cup carrots, sliced into half-moons
  1/2 cup red capsicum, chopped
  2 tablespoons (1 1/2 fl oz) olive oil
  1/4 cup (2 fl oz) light miso
  1/4 cup parsley, minced

Simmer ginger, rice, shiitake mushrooms, sea salt, and stock in a heavy covered pot for one hour. In a frypan, sauté the garlic, onions, carrots, and capsicum in olive oil for a few minutes. Add vegies to soup pot, cover, and simmer for a further 30 minutes. Add miso and parsley to soup, stir, and let stand, covered, for a few minutes before serving.

# 175. SING IN THE RAIN

Spitting? Pouring? Or just a grey drizzle? Pull on your rainhat and button up your coat, open a big umbrella — and out you go.

Walking in the rain is one of my favourite pleasures. Veiled by rain (cry, and who's there to see?), muffled up in your coat (sing as loud as you like! Remember Gene Kelly scampering through puddles?), you have the parks and pavements to yourself. You're exuberant, as free as Christopher Robin to splash and paddle and stamp. You're playing hooky, getting away with something, an illicit treat. And, apart from being fun, it's a surprisingly sensual experience, sending wet prunus petals to stick to your shoes and hands, cooling your face, filling your ears with swooshy noises as cars go by. Breathe deeply: rain releases deep earthy scents of soil and grass and mulched up leaves. Enjoy the solitariness of it all, listen to memories whisper of times past that you haven't thought of for ages. Many sensations are called forth by rain. Then come inside, put all your wet things in the bathroom to drip, put on slippers, and make yourself a steaming pot of tea to drink as you gaze out the streaming windows.

# 176. STOP EXERCISING EXCUSES

Exercise only works if you actually do it regularly. Here are the most popular avoidance tactics — which one is yours?!?

**I haven't got time**. Exercising doesn't have to take much time. In fact, small bursts of exercise are better for you than long hauls, particularly if you're not used to it. Trick yourself: sneak exercise into your life when you least expect it. Jog on the spot while you open your mail or wait for the kettle to boil. Do knee bends and stretches while you clean your teeth. Do star jumps or ride on a stationary bike while watching TV. Do progressive stretching exercises while you're lying in bed before you go to sleep.

**I look terrible.** If you're concerned about being surrounded by perfect bodies at the gym, in the pool, or on the tennis court, don't be. For one thing, there really aren't too many that will look any better than you. And even if they do, you'll soon find out that they're too busy to give a thought to what you look like because they're busy concentrating on their own program. If you really can't scrape up the courage to walk in the door, team up with a friend and go together.

**It's too cold/hot.** Dress according to the weather: if it's cold, wear a fleecy tracksuit and a beanie. If it's boiling hot, wear a hat and glasses and take a big bottle of water. Better still, do your exercise in the shade or in air conditioning. If the weather's just too bad to go out, stay home — but put on an exercise video and work out to that.

**It will cost me money.** Some gyms and health clubs are ridiculously expensive, but there are many with far saner prices: check out the government- or council-run ones in your area. While you're at it, ask about their payment deals and options. Sometimes there are special off-peak rates first thing in the morning or late in the evening, which might actually suit you better, anyway. Nor does it have to be a gym — economical alternatives include getting together with friends to hire a tennis or netball court once a week, or buying a set of light weights and a couple of good exercise videos to work with at home.

**I feel sick.** If it's just a headache or sore throat, a light exercise session or brisk walk may actually do the trick by boosting your immune system and your spirits. Of course, if you really are under the weather, just go to bed and rest until you're well again.

## 177. GET INTO GEAR

Before starting any fitness plan, big or small, make sure your gear is up to scratch. A baggy old leotard or uncomfortable walking shoes are just more excuses to put it off. Follow this checklist:

**Wear something comfortable that you don't mind being seen in**. Cotton leggings, leotards or shorts and a bra top are all fine. Look for a breathable fabric (check the label).

**Avoid wearing t-shirts for classes**. Whether it's aerobics or yoga, your instructor needs to see your body line and whether you're moving correctly. But take a T-shirt or sloppy joe along to the class to keep you warm before and after.

**Always wear socks to avoid blisters**. For any activity that requires shoes, put on some socks. (They will also make your runners last longer.)

**Take care when buying running shoes**. Check that they flex at the toe where your foot naturally bends and ensure that they have plenty of cushioning on the toe — as this is where you put most of your weight.

**Buy a sports bra if your breasts bounce uncomfortably**. A sports bra with wide shoulder straps and an 'action' back for support is a good investment.

# 178. WORK OUT SAFELY

If you're a relative newcomer to fitness, and you're planning on joining a class, here's how to improve your odds of sticking to your plan — and enjoying it!

Make sure you're exercising on a properly sprung floor, to ease the impact on your joints.

If you're taking up walking or jogging, avoid hard surfaces. Seek out nice grassy areas near you, or synthetic running tracks.

Check that your instructor is properly qualified and warn him or her in advance about any injury.

Don't try too hard in a class to begin with. It's not a competition, and you can easily over-exert yourself.

Choose non-weightbearing exercise, such as swimming, if you're at risk of osteoarthritis.

Never use a bandage or support without first getting a professionally qualified osteopath, your GP or a physiotherapist to check out your injury or weakness.

Drink plenty of water when exercising, as dehydration can put extra stress on the joints.

# 179. REDUCE YOUR BREAST CANCER RISK

Although it's now one in eight women who will get breast cancer in their lifetime, you can reduce your chances:

**Watch the foods you eat**. Food affects your levels of oestrogen, an excess of which may contribute to cancer. Base your diet on wholegrains, legumes, fruits and cruciferous vegetables, such as broccoli. The fibre in these foods helps you metabolise and excrete oestrogen.

**Avoid conventional dairy products and meats**. These may contain pesticides and bovine growth hormone. Buy organic wherever possible.

**Pick the right fats**. A high intake of saturated fat (found in meat and dairy products and oils such as coconut) may elevate blood levels of oestrogen. Replace saturated fats with mono-unsaturated fats, such as those found in olive oil. Plus, supplement with fish oils, which are an excellent source of essential omega-3 fatty acids, which protect against breast cancer. Eat two to three servings of cold-water fish such as salmon a week, or add one teaspoon of flaxseed oil to your meals daily.

**Cut back on caffeine and alcohol**. Alcohol appears to increase circulating oestrogen levels and the effect is especially dramatic in post-menopausal women who take HRT. Also consider cutting out coffee because too much caffeine may increase breast pain. Do drink green tea: it contains potent antioxidants that scavenge the free radicals that can lead to cancer.

**Break into a sweat**. For the greatest reduction in risk, do vigorous aerobic exercise — like walking briskly or running — for at least 30 minutes four times a week.

# 180. BE AT PEACE

Consider this Buddhist saying: 'The perfect disciple is one who is always stumbling — but never falls.' We all fall into traps of selfishness and delusion when we least expect it. The chance remark that wounds someone else, the careless lie, the irresistible urge to cheat — they are universal. Forgive yourself for being human. Apply to yourself the same gentle acceptance as to others. You are doing the best you can, with the tools available to you, right now. Try these strategies:

**Put it on paper.** Writing provides perspective. Divide a piece of paper into two parts. On the left side, list the things that irritate you that you may be able to change, and on the right, list the ones you can't. Change what you can, and stop fretting over what you can't.

**Create a new vocabulary for yourself.** Although there is no harm in expressing worries and problems, you want to avoid falling into the pit of constantly 'talking down'. Toward that end, create a new vocabulary for yourself where you focus on optimistic words and phrases. For example, instead of seeing a problem or obstacle, try to see an opportunity for learning and growth.

**Reward your good tries as well as your achievements.** After suffering a setback we're often not functioning at our best, so we may find we need more rewards than usual. Have a nurturing treatment, such as a relaxing facial or a soothing aromatherapy massage.

# 181. NOTICE MIRACLES

'Happiness depends on ourselves.'
**Aristotle**

It's all too easy to take life's little miracles for granted, especially when you're locked in a routine. Recharge your appreciation for all the wonderful, complex, beautiful things around you with this exercise: study an object which you see all the time — an old lamp in your bedroom, a vine in the garden, a painting in the hall or a copper bowl in the kitchen. The more familiar it is, and the more you think you already know everything there is to know about it, the better this exercise will work. Now, really look at it, concentrate on it, examine it, *re-examine* it. See all its different colours and textures, its shape, what it's made from, and think about these things. Keep right on looking at it: does its shape remind you of anything? An animal? A musical instrument? Does it have a smell? What happens when the light falls on it differently? Use the same exercise to look again at your partner's or your own body, the face of your child or a pet, and find a special new detail you have never noticed before, such as a freckle on their ear
or a crooked eyelash.

# 182. WAIT WISELY

Whether you're in a supermarket queue, lined up to get movie tickets, or at the doctor's surgery or the dentist, use the time to read, write or just daydream. Don't stand there seething and raging inwardly over the delay. Instead of feeling bored or annoyed, use this opportunity to create a mini-meditation. Breathe three times and refresh yourself.

Being aware of your surroundings can help you create a sense of more and better quality time, rather than of 'wasted' time. Isn't it wonderful to experience every minute of your life, as opposed to watching it whiz by while on your way to getting to Point A or B? Savour every precious moment, even at red lights and in traffic jams. Same goes for dealing with the stress of commuting. When you first get into the car, train or bus, take three easy breaths in and out through your nose. Count the breaths to yourself and collect yourself. Really notice where you are — and enjoy it — rather than fret about time or traffic. Is the sun shining? Is it raining? Who's next to you? Look around and pay attention to what you see. Feel the moment. Don't jump ahead of yourself, turning your thoughts to the workday ahead. There'll be plenty of time for that when you get there.

# 185. CELEBRATE THE SEASONS

> 'Live in each season as it passes: breathe the air, drink the drink, taste the fruit, and open yourself to the influences of each.'
> **Henri David Thoreau**

Spring, summer, autumn and winter. Marking the turning of time is a magical way to honour love and friendship between people as well as to simply embrace the beauty of life itself. Try these ideas for marking the passing of the seasons:

IN SPRING
Read the Sunday papers in the local park.
Toss a Frisbee with a friend, human or dog.
File your foot calluses, slather on moisturiser, and go to bed wearing socks.
Pick flowers for your bathroom.
Watch at least one sunrise and one sunset.

IN SUMMER
Zap fresh herbs in the microwave for one to three minutes to preserve them for winter.
Build sandcastles at the beach.
Eat cherry tomatoes.
Freeze bananas, blueberries and strawberries and keep them to make instant smoothies.
Close your eyes, riffle through a cookbook, then stop. Prepare that dish.
Look up at a clear night sky and take a deep breath.

IN AUTUMN
Walk through drifts of leaves, listening to them crunch underfoot.
Simmer a cinnamon stick, a teaspoon of cloves and an orange peel in some water to scent your home.
Visit a grandparent (yours, or someone else's).
Bake a pie.
Start a book you've been meaning to read that's been sitting on the shelf.

IN WINTER
Dine by candlelight.
Get some seeds or crumbs and go and feed the birds.
Shoot a roll of black and white film around your neighbourhood.
Sprinkle cinnamon or ginger on your porridge to warm the cockles of your heart.
Light a fire.
Wear soft, hand-knitted woollen mittens. They contain moisturising lanolin.

# 186. PLAN ATTAINABLE GOALS

'Whether you think you will succeed or not — you're right.'
**Henry Ford**

If you are working towards something, whether it's big or small, short-, medium-
or long-term, you will gain a sense of purpose and direction, which in turn leads
to happiness and contentment. Drifting aimlessly, being unsettled and unable to
focus on a task feels dreadful, and it's the quickest way on earth to feel depressed
and useless. Take charge and find meaning in your life. Get out there and do
something that makes you feel you've really accomplished a goal, such as running
the local fund-raising marathon, taking a computer course or learning a language
— and resolve to really appreciate your friends and family.

## 187. Be mindful

'Learn to be silent.'
**Pythagoras**

It is nearly 100 years since the American writer James Agee defined the objective of the new Western society as: 'Motion with the least possible interruption.' His phrase is all the more shocking when you consider that he came up with it before the impact of the First and Second World Wars, nuclear power, computers, genetic technology, pollution and the arms race on our lives had even been considered.

Our lives now are far speedier than they were in 1904, racing past us in a blur. To be safe, happy and fulfilled, it's imperative to slow down, take stock. Realise that there's no point in tearing wildly after ever-changing prizes. You already have what it is you are seeking, and what you really need. It's been in you all the time.

One of my favourite exercises for re-focusing your mind and putting the brakes on a life that seems to be hurtling along out of control is also the simplest. It comes from the Vietnamese Zen Master, Thich Nhat Hanh, and involves taming that demanding terror — the telephone. He teaches the simple idea of not snatching up the phone on the first ring, or the second, or even the third. Instead, take those few moments to breathe deeply, in and out, at least twice, taking the time to really feel the beating of your own heart. Listen to your heart's rhythm, observe the rhythm of your breathing, and then visualise yourself coming back to a position of balance. *Now* you can pick up the receiver.

As simple and quick as this exercise seems, just doing it routinely can have a powerful effect on how you feel about time. Time is no longer a god to be obeyed, you are in charge of how you spend your time. Plus it puts a physical plug in your tendency to race ahead, and so stops you from making as many mistakes and from missing out on important details in your life.

# 188. TRY DO-IT-YOURSELF SHIATSU

Shiatsu massage, which is said to act on the subtle electromagnetic forces of the body, has been practised in Japan for centuries. These simple exercises can help most common conditions. Here's what to do:

**Stress** Hunch and drop your shoulders twice, then rotate them. Rub your head briskly, and tap it all over with your fingertips. Tug your hair and then release. Finally, squeeze all around your jawline.

**Low energy** Take a handful of pebbles, roll them around in your palm and squeeze them. Open and close your hand several times, then squeeze the pebbles between your fingers.

**Insomnia** Lie on your back, slide your fingers under your neck and apply gentle pressure. Tighten your whole body, from the tips of your toes to your scalp. Release each part in turn.

# 189. GOOF OFF

'Life is far too important to ever talk seriously about.'
**Oscar Wilde**

When I contemplate my life, with biros in the washing machine, endless lists, and two lemme-at-him-gimme-my-switchblade little boys, I prefer to believe that I am not abnormally stressed — that all over the world, there are women who, in similar circumstances, are not relaxing. There are plenty of times when you just don't have time to make a soothing cup of kava tea, when you can't bliss out to Handel's *Water Music* because someone has got the Backstreet Boys turned up to *there* and when you just can't go and have a nice, steamy bath because you've run out of hot water!

I've got a tension tactic I'll share with you which is just perfect for those moments when you need relief *immediately*: get a yo-yo. I keep one in the kitchen drawer for when I'm feeling stressed out, and another one next to my computer for when my brain turns to blancmange. Apart from being fun, some quite serious research exists to show that playing with one boosts creative thinking, coordination, and helps both sides of your brain work together.

# 190. SNACK SMARTER

If you're ravenous, reduce the risk of making stupid food choices by keeping healthy, tasty snacks on hand. Eating wholefoods little and often is the key to keeping energy levels up through the day. The alternative is the all-too-familiar boom-bust-boom effect of eating sugary, processed foods, and then having blood sugar levels slump shortly afterwards, so necessitating another 'fix' for your fatigue as the day wears on. By eating wholesome snacks regularly, you maintain the correct, sustained levels of glucose in your blood, which is your body's main source of energy. Here are some ideas that are satisfying, taste good, and offer health benefits:

**Banana chips** A great pick-me-up, they're rich in carbohydrates, iron and magnesium, with natural sugars to give your body a boost.

**Toasted sunflower seeds** Dust with chilli powder, cumin and coriander.

**Brazil nuts** If you've been avoiding nuts because of their high fat content, a new Harvard study has found this doesn't seem to apply with brazils. Researchers found that women who ate them regularly had a 32 per cent lower risk of heart attack than those who didn't. Just three a day can supply enough of the mineral selenium to help protect against cancer and heart disease.

**Rice crackers** Spread with peanut butter, tahini or low-fat savoury spreads like tzatziki and tapenade.

**Dried apricots** Keep them on standby as a snack if you've got a sweet tooth. They're a good source of fibre, potassium, iron and beta carotene. Make sure they've been air-dried, not sulphur-dried, as sulphites have been linked with different forms of cancer.

# 191. BUILD YOUR BONES

Osteoporosis, or brittle bone disease, develops most rapidly in the first five to tens years after the menopause, when total bone density can decrease by between one and five per cent a year. So, take action — it's never too late to start protecting yourself against osteoporosis, and the sooner you do, the sooner you'll benefit.

**Increase calcium intake**. Include plenty of calcium-rich products in your diet, such as dairy products, dark green leafy vegetables and wholegrains. This doesn't mean you can't stick to a low-fat diet: skim and semi-skim dairy products include the same amount of calcium as the full-fat variety. Consider taking a calcium supplement daily.

**Increase magnesium, too**. Researchers in California have discovered that magnesium supplements can reduce your risk for osteoporosis by dramatically slowing the rate at which bone is broken down in the body. Excellent sources of magnesium include nuts, beans, wholegrains, and bananas.

**Exercise regularly**. This builds up the strength of bones by stimulating bone-building cells to create new bone and strengthen existing bone. To strengthen bones, exercise needs to be weight-bearing. Brisk walking is the minimum. Better still, do aerobic exercise with mild impact, such as playing tennis or weight training in a gym.

**Don't smoke**. Smoking reduces bone mass by 25 per cent. Smokers, together with those who drink to excess, have the highest risk of osteoporosis.

# 192.  RELIEVE HOT FLUSHES

A single hot flush, which sweeps through your upper body to your face, reddening your skin, may pass in a few seconds or last up to 15 minutes. The most effective remedies are those that boost levels of oestrogen.

**Eat the right plants**. Phytoestrogens — naturally occurring plant oestrogens, found in more than 200 plants — are probably the most effective natural alternative to HRT and have been proven to help relieve hot flushes, night sweats, headaches and concentration problems. Soya and soy products, organic linseed and the herb red clover are especially high in phytoestrogens. You can also buy bread containing soy flour and linseeds at the supermarket.

**Think alternative**. Sarsaparilla and the Chinese herbs dong quai and schizandra have phytoestrogenic qualities. And wild yam cream (available from health food stores) is said to be good for night sweats as well as irritability. Drinking aloe vera juice last thing at night will help cool your system and prevent hot flushes while cleansing your digestion.

**Cut out caffeine, alcohol and spicy foods**. Although they don't cause hot flushes, they can make the problem worse. Alcohol also leaches calcium from your body. Instead of coffee, try rosehip tea — it's caffeine-free and is rich in cell-renewing antioxidants.

# 193. WORK OUT AT WORK

Office work can be hell on your back and shoulders. You sit all day, balancing the phone on your shoulder, twisting from filing cabinet to computer and back again. Sound familiar? Try this yoga exercise:

**One Elbow Up, One Down**

1. Sit up straight in a chair.

2. Keep your shoulders low.

3. Stretch your right arm straight up over your head, then bend the elbow so that your palm touches your back in between your shoulder blades.

4. Stretch your left arm behind you, placing your hand in the middle of your back, palm out.

5. If you can, clasp your hands together. If that's not possible, hold a sock or towel in your right hand and grasp it with your left.

6. Now stretch up through your right elbow while stretching down through the left.

7. Hold for 20 seconds.

8. Repeat on the other side.

# 194. Never skip breakfast

A strong coffee may feel great for a morning lift-off — but unless you have a good breakfast, it's often followed by an energy nose-dive. Hearty wholegrains, natural juices and fruit will supply much-needed vitamins, minerals and fibre, and give you steady energy till lunchtime. Several studies have also shown that eating in the morning improves memory and concentration throughout the day. One study found that people who ate cereal reported a more positive mood, had better recall and felt calmer after a series of tests than those who did not eat breakfast.

**Check the packaging**. Nutritional values should be listed so you can check levels of kilojoules, fat, sugar, fibre and carbohydrate. Choose cereals with the least sugar and fat and the most fibre. Cereals high in fibre are excellent for helping to prevent constipation. All cereals provide carbohydrates for energy, but some have a lower glycaemic index than others — important for diabetics.

**Consider popular additives**. B vitamins, iron and calcium are sometimes added. Soy and linseed are used for their phytoestrogenic benefits. Choose the least processed cereals, like rolled oats, puffed brown rice and corn, or untoasted muesli.

**Experiment with different wholegrains**. Spelt, for example, is the oldest known grain. Mix 'n' match your own muesli, using puffed wheat and oat flakes, plus sun-dried pawpaw, and spices like cinnamon.

**Add flavour and nutrition with dried fruit and nuts**. For added convenience, grind a couple of handfuls in the food processor, store in an airtight jar, and sprinkle over cereal or yoghurt.

**Think about flavourful liquids**. You may be used to eating cereal or porridge made with water, which makes it bland. Organic juices (apple, cranberry, blackcurrant) or milks (rice, almond, oat and soy) complement the flavour of most wholegrains and add sweetness. Oat and rice milks have a faint flavour of the grain they are made from and are an excellent choice in cereals using the same grain. Soy milk has a rich flavour that works well in any cereals with nuts. Add a dash of apple cider for warmth and sweetness.

**A drizzle of maple syrup or honey** makes every cereal more inviting.

**Try whole-fruit spreads or organic honey**. Instead of your usual jam, spread these on hearty wholegrain toast or crispbread for all-morning energy. Prefer something savoury? Try tahini or a vegetable-derived yeast spread.

# 195. EAT THE FIVE SUPER-FOODS

There's plenty of evidence to show our immune systems may be compromised by lack of nutrients and stress. However, the good news is that many tasty and inexpensive foods are highly protective. Add them to your diet!

**Onions and garlic** These help boost natural immunity and aid circulation. Red onions are a particularly good source of the antioxidant called quercetin, which may guard against cancer. Garlic, used as a cure-all for centuries, helps fight colds and flu, and lowers blood pressure.

**Cabbage** A source of phytochemicals (plant chemicals), known as glucosinalates and indoles, which reduce the risk of bowel cancer. Studies have also found that indoles reduce levels of oestrogen derivatives that stimulate breast tumours.

**Tomatoes** The richest dietary source of lycopene, an antioxidant which research suggests can protect against cancer. Studies have shown that people who regularly eat tomato-based foods can reduce their risk of developing cancer by up to 40 per cent or more, especially cancers of the prostate, lung and stomach.

**Sardines** An excellent source of omega-3 fatty acids and calcium. Omega-3s boost bone density, reduce inflammation, and keep the heart healthy. Eating oily fish is also important during pregnancy because the oils play a vital role in foetal brain development.

**Brazil nuts** An excellent source of selenium, an important antioxidant. A US study found that patients who took 200 mcg of selenium daily (equal to four Brazil nuts) experienced 50 per cent fewer cancer deaths than those who didn't.

# 196. CATCH THE NUTRIENT THIEVES

Here are some simple ways to make sure your food doesn't go to waste.

**Don't boil vegetables for too long**. The water steals away vitamins B and C. Instead, lightly boil or steam them. An exception is carrots, which should be boiled lightly in order to break down the cell walls, which makes it easier for your system to absorb the cancer-fighting beta carotene they contain.

**Don't drink tea straight after dinner**. It slows the absorption of calcium and magnesium. Wait at least an hour after eating before putting on the kettle.

**Don't peel fruit**. The skins are a valuable source of dietary fibre. Scrub fruit thoroughly and, wherever possible, eat the skins.

**Store oils in a dark place**. Sunlight destroys vitamin E, found in vegetable oil, which gives you energy and boosts your immune system. Instead of displaying them on a counter top, keep oils in a cold, dark place. If you buy in bulk, pour some oil into a small bottle for current use and keep the larger bottle somewhere dark.

# 197. HUG YOURSELF

Acupressure is an old-but-new massage technique — knowledge of the different acu-points is centuries old, but awareness of how easy and useful it is relatively recent.

Try this yourself next time you feel your neck and shoulders becoming stiff and sore: place your fingers at the base of your neck where it meets your shoulders. Press for 15 seconds, take a deep breath in, and breathe out. Move your fingers half an inch outwards, then repeat. Move your fingers another half-inch outwards and repeat. Then give yourself a big hug to stretch your back, swap your hands over and hug yourself again.

# 198. OVERHAUL YOUR DESK

Clutter is depressing. It saps your energy, because it reminds you of all the things that need to be done, fixed, or finished. Try the following ideas to make your workspace creative and inspirational, and to recharge your mind.

**Be selective**. Only keep on your desk the projects you are working on right now. Put everything else away.

**Sort mail immediately**. Decide straight away what you're going to do with it: throw it out? File it? Pass it on? Same goes for email messages. Whether they're paper or electronic, having different piles of incoming requests means you don't know where to start and your energy is scattered.

**Filing means filing**. It doesn't mean putting it in piles on the floor. Review your files regularly, and toss out things that have become irrelevant.

**Have a plan**. No matter how chaotic your job, try to schedule activities around your personality and behaviour. For example, are you prone to mid-afternoon slump? Then, make that the time for routine jobs like follow-up phone calls, rather than demanding tasks that require 100 per cent of your creativity.

**Boost energy levels**. Burning lemon or eucalyptus oil in an aromatherapy burner is psychically clearing and stimulating. Flowers, postcards, photos of family or friends will all brighten up the place and inspire you.

**Plan 'stretch breaks'**. These are particularly necessary if you spend a lot of time at your desk. Without fail, get up every hour and move around to refresh yourself.

**Use feng shui principles**. Your desk should be facing a door or window, and you should have a solid wall behind you. Make sure your computer is as far back towards the centre of the desk as possible: this is the area connected with success. The left-hand side of your desk represents intellect, so that's where you should store work-related books and magazines to do with your work. Place something beautiful — a shell, a pretty stone — on the right-hand side; this side reminds you of the spiritual and aesthetic things in life. And, if possible, introduce plenty of curved shapes and surfaces, such as vases, pots or lamps, because they improve the flow of energy.

# 199. FLUSH OUT CYSTITIS

Probably the best food cure for cystitis is cranberries, which contain hippuric acid to flush harmful bacteria out of the urinary tract. Drinking cranberry juice can also help to prevent an attack. Steer clear of salty foods, alcohol and large amounts of orange juice. You could also try a cranberry extract supplement. Garlic capsules can also help because they are a potent antibacterial agent. If you can't buy sugar-free cranberry juice, make your own by diluting 3 ml of cranberry tincture in water. Drinking a mixture of bicarbonate of soda and water will make your urine less acidic and slow the rate at which infection-causing bacteria multiply. It also helps make urination less painful.

# 200. DON'T LET THINGS FESTER

It's an arguable fact that sticks and stones can break your bones, but harsh words can hurt even more. Research shows that arguing with your nearest and dearest makes you more vulnerable to a range of viral infections and lowers your immune system. Most pointedly, women showed more damage than men, presumably because they are also very good at stashing resentments and worries away to brood about later. So, when a major problem looms, take steps to handle it then and there.

**Know the right time to talk about it**. People tend to talk about their problems with money, their sex life, their children and their future when they're in a bad mood — which can make everything seem far worse than it is. If you plan to talk when you're feeling calm and well, however, the problem can look quite different.

**Get emotional**. If you think you've got due cause, allow yourself to get good and angry first of all. Repress your feelings, and you're just heading for more difficulties.

**Take time to cool off**. Your first reaction might be, 'I'm fed up with you — I'm leaving.' But, before you say anything you might regret, you need to work out if the relationship is worth saving.

**Listen**. You need to hear from the other person their perspective about what led to the problem — then you can plan what to do, hopefully together.

**Don't forgive too easily**. The other person must prove they want things to change, too, otherwise you're setting yourself up as a doormat.

**Move on**. Work out what went wrong, lay the past to rest, and start again.

# 201. KEEP YOUR FEET SWEET

Proper foot care is essential to healthy, painless feet, and should be as much a part of your daily routine as brushing your teeth. When you consider that the average person takes around 5,000 steps a day (and that women are usually doing this in high heels!), it's no wonder that foot problems such as hard skin, corns and bunions are so common. Follow these tips for feel-good foot health:

Wash your feet every day in warm soapy water, but don't soak them as this might destroy natural oils. Dry thoroughly, especially between the toes.

Moisturise your feet if the skin is dry, avoiding between the toes.

Apply a little foot powder to keep feet dry.

Remove hard skin gently with a pumice stone. If the affected area is over a joint or bone, you should see a podiatrist.

Trim your nails regularly, using proper nail clippers. Cut straight across, not too short, and not down at the corners, as this can lead to ingrowing nails.

Finally, always wear the right shoes for what you're doing — whether it's a particular sport or going to work. Avoid wearing high heels too many days in a row — they can deform the foot and give you bad posture.

## 202. BE AWARE OF YOUR BOWEL MOVEMENTS

They are an excellent indicator of how well you digest your food and can point to more serious disorders, such as bowel cancer, the second biggest cause of deaths from cancer in Australia. Signs that require a visit to the GP include any change in bowel habit that lasts for more than a few days, any blood or black matter in your stools, abdominal pain, or difficulty controlling bowel movements.

# 203. LOOK AFTER YOUR HEART

Incorporate these nutritional prevention tactics in your diet:

**Cut your fat intake**. Choose vegetable oils such as sunflower, olive or canola and grill or bake foods. Eat less saturated fat (dairy products and fatty meats). Use low-fat products and spreads high in polyunsaturates or monounsaturated fat.

**Eat at least five portions of fruit and vegetables each day**. They contain antioxidants — the vital vitamins A, C and E, which help to neutralise unwanted body by-products. Fruit and vegetables also contain fibre, which helps the digestive system to function efficiently, protecting against bowel disease.

**Eat oily fish**. Oily fish — such as salmon, tuna, pilchards, trout and mackerel — contain fatty acids that help protect against heart disease. Eat two portions a week.

**Consume red foods**. Try to include more coloured fruit and vegetables in your diet — tomatoes, watermelon and pink grapefruit, for instance, contain lycopene, a type of antioxidant that has been shown to help protect against heart disease. Strawberries are powerful antioxidants and rich in soluble fibre, which helps get rid of cholesterol. Even tomato sauce contains small amounts. Cooking actually makes the lycopene more effective — try grilled tomatoes, for example.

# 204. FILL A JUG WITH WATER

One in seven offices is too dry, according to research into humidity levels in the buildings of major companies. Dryness in the air at work can raise stress and reduce concentration, making you more prone to colds and flu. After losing just two per cent of our body's optimal water content, your energy levels drop by a massive 20 per cent, making you feel lethargic and less alert. So, make sure you keep drinking plenty of water throughout the day. Don't make the mistake of upping your fluid intake by drinking other beverages such as coffee, tea, cola and alcohol — these are actually dehydrating. Stick instead to water, fruit juice or herbal tea. Try setting yourself targets, spreading out your consumption of water across the day. Keep a jug of water on your desk and then aim to drink a glass an hour. While you're at it, get into the habit of placing two pieces of fruit on your desk when you arrive. Eat them before you go home.

# 205. STOP TAKING THE PILL

If you're taking the Pill for reasons other than contraception, consider these natural alternatives:

**Headaches?**

Foods rich in omega-3 fats (such as salmon and flaxseed) block the release of series 2 prostaglandins prior to menstruation, which can trigger migraines. Soy products contain phytoestrogens that your body can use to regulate hormones.

Calcium and magnesium help prevent blood vessel spasms, which lead to migraines.

Feverfew's active ingredient helps dilate blood vessels. Tablets, capsules and tea are available in health food stores.

**Acne?**

Calendula soap has antimicrobial properties. Apply one drop of tea tree oil to blemishes.

Facial steams deep-cleanse skin. Boil two teaspoons each of dried lavender, licorice root and chamomile — all herbs with anti-inflammatory properties — in 500 ml water. Take it off the stove, tent your head with a towel and steam for 15 minutes.

Zinc helps heal skin; B6 balances hormones.

**Cramps and heavy bleeding?**

Ginger tea brings better blood flow and more oxygen to the uterus. Drink as often as you like.

Vitex agnus castus is a herb that's particularly good for irregular and heavy periods. Tablets, capsules and tea are all available in health food stores.

Vitamin E may help with excessive clotting; also, get your iron levels checked by your doctor.

## 206. MAKE A DATE FOR YOUR PAP SMEAR

Cervical cancer is one of the most easily treatable forms of cancer as it can be detected at a stage when cells are pre-cancerous. Make sure the appointment for your test isn't during your period. In fact, if you have your test in the middle of your menstrual cycle, your doctor will be able to collect more endocervical cells — the more sensitive inner cells which can carry a new, rarer and less treatable strain of cervical cancer. You'll feel reassured if you get a negative result. And, if it's positive, your doctor can act on it fast.

# 207. TAKE UP KNITTING

Looking for a hobby that will unleash your creativity, reduce stress and put you in touch with your inner self all at once? Pick up a pair of knitting needles and some wool. I love to knit, and often recommend it to people who are working on computers all day. Why? Knitting is like meditation: it's very repetitive and focused — like breathing, or counting rosary beads. Plus you're working with your hands, with colour and texture, and you see results of your work immediately!

## 208. LEARN A SIMPLE MEDITATION

> 'A quiet mind cureth all.'
> **Robert Burns**

Quiet meditation stills the mind, combats stress and mentally prepares you for whatever lies ahead. Here's how:

Sit in any position that feels comfortable and close your eyes. Keep your head upright, your shoulders relaxed. Start to breathe steadily and deeply. Don't try to force your breathing — just pay attention to it.

Now, start your mantra by intoning a deep 'Ohhhh' sound that comes from the back of your mouth and throat. Bring the sound forwards in your mouth, opening your mouth wider, as the sound shifts into a slightly higher-pitched 'Ahhhh'. Finally, close your lips and hum the sound 'Mmmm'. Feel it vibrate on your lips.

Repeat up to ten times.

# 209. MAKE PEACE WITH THE DARK TIMES

Theodore Roosevelt wrote: 'It's not having been in the dark house, but having left it, that counts.'

We have all been there, to those 'dark houses'; we've all passed through those 'dark nights of the soul'. But, in the West, we are not always taught very well how to cope with grief, suffering, bereavement, betrayal, hardship, panic, or terror. Too often, overwhelming anguish is buried deep within, and not resolved — only to haunt the imagination ever since. Try not to deny the darkness — it has much to teach you. Facing the pain gives you a power that opens your heart in a new way and makes you appreciate the light — and helps you to understand that life is unimaginably precious.

# 210. COLLECT PRAYER BEADS

You want to get in touch with your spiritual side, but you don't identify with any one particular religion, nor do you feel an affiliation with any one symbol or idea. Still the hankering for some sort of tool, some sort of starting point remains . . .

A simple idea that really helps you focus when you are rediscovering prayer or learning to meditate is prayer beads. Not for nothing have they been an important part of many spiritual traditions for centuries, irrespective of the seeker's level of intellect, age or cultural background: think of the Catholic rosary, or the Buddhist mala.

Traditionally, prayer beads were used to keep count of the number of prayers or mantras, or for counting one's breaths. But prayer beads are not just for praying. Nor do they have to be traditional in design. For today's spiritual seeker, creating your own prayer necklace with beautiful and symbolic beads that you have collected or been given can provide you with something meaningful and cherished. It may be that you find metaphors in what the beads represent: the colour red for energy, for example; the material — jade or amber for the wisdom of ages, or clay for honesty; or the shape — perhaps you'll find one in the shape of an animal or flower that you feel is somehow lucky for you.

Whether you believe the beads themselves somehow have power, or whether you just use them as a reminder to pray or meditate quietly by yourself every day, a prayer bead necklace can play an important role in spiritual practice.

# 211. PREPARE YOUR OWN FOOD

There is an ancient Zen parable that I like very much — not least because when I tell people they usually don't get the meaning because they're too busy . . . which is the whole point of the story. Anyway, it goes like this:

A novice at a monastery was working in the kitchen. As he looked out of the window, he saw the Grand Master, a venerable old gentleman with a long white beard and a back bent like a bow, kneeling in the dirt and pulling up vegetables. The novice ran to help up the old man, but he was rebuffed. 'Why don't you let a helper do that?' asked the novice. 'Others are not myself,' replied the Master.

One of the problems with our lives today is that we are completely out of touch with meaningful work. For what is more necessary, more important and more life-sustaining than collecting and preparing your own food? Yet, with restaurant meals, fast food on-the-hop and frozen dinners, how many of us can say about our food that we have been present from beginning to end, for its making?

Knowing what you're eating is central to being in touch with life. If your relationship with food is a distant one, you'll probably also feel out of touch with other aspects of your life. By preparing your own meals at least once a day — even if it means using the food processor and freezer so you can plan and store ahead of time — you are reconnecting in a small and very effective way with a simpler, more intimate relationship with the world. What you're eating is not so much the point — rather, it's the idea that, in the middle of a busy day, you take time to care about the value of what you are putting into your body and, by association, into your life.

## 212.  BOOST YOUR CIRCULATION

Try doing knee bends in the mornings to energise your body.

Stand with your feet hip-distance apart and gently bend your knees, moving up and down very slowly. (Don't let your knees bend further than the front of your feet.) Repeat this 15 times.

Knee bends will help to promote blood flow around your body, particularly to the extremities such as your feet, which receive less blood overnight.

# 213.  STEER CLEAR OF PLASTICS

Over the past couple of years, we have been shocked by stories of fish changing sex because of pollution in rivers, and of female gulls nesting together, rather than taking male partners. Then there are the reports suggesting that human sperm counts are falling, by anything up to 50 per cent. Why? Exposure to synthetic chemicals in the environment, known as endocrine disrupters or 'oestrogen mimics' are one possible culprit.

Found in our water, our food and in the air we breathe, some of these chemicals, such as the pesticide DDT, have already been banned in many countries. However, that doesn't mean we're no longer being exposed to them. For instance, the finger has recently been pointed at the oestrogen-like chemicals that are found in many plastic items, such as the plastics used to make bottles for water and soft drinks, and in plastic cling-wraps. Although the jury is still out on whether there really is a link between these endocrine disrupters and our health, you can reduce your risk by doing the following:

Buy mineral water in glass bottles.

Follow a low-fat diet (oestrogens are known to accumulate in fatty tissue).

Take fatty foods (especially meat and cheese) out of their plastic wrapping and storing them in glass or china lidded bowls.

Use china or glass containers in the microwave, not plastic ones.

Wash your hands frequently. Many chemicals settle on indoor surfaces.

## 214. GET A PUSH MOWER

If the mention of a push mower makes you think of the rusty contraption that your grandfather used to drag around the backyard on a Saturday afternoon, now's the time to take another look. Apart from being very fashionable, the modern steel-trimmed push mowers have a whole list of advantages compared with stinky power ones.

**It's a lot cheaper**. (And it's far less likely to ever break down.)

**It's better for the environment**. Apart from cutting down on the not inconsiderable smog and fumes that are given off by the power mower's engine, you also save your neighbours the god-awful roar of the typical one.

**It's great exercise**. You burn fat as you cut your lawn!

**It actually makes for a better-looking, softer-feeling lawn**. The blades cleanly slice the tips of the grass, like scissors, leaving a pretty, silky effect. Power mowers tend to rip the tops off grass blades, giving a shaggy, uneven appearance. Plus, if they're set too low, they actually encourage the growth of weeds at the expense of grass.

## 215.   BUY A POOPER-SCOOPER

As a keen walker, I have plenty of opportunities to be amazed — and infuriated
— by people who do not clean up after their pets. When you clean up after your
dog or cat, you are doing more than just removing an unsightly mess: you're
helping to counter illness. Pet faeces deposited on beaches, or in playgrounds and
gardens are a significant health risk, especially for children. Be a responsible pet
owner: follow 'pooper-scooper' laws to the letter, control fleas and ticks, and give
immediate medical attention to any bite, no matter how small.

# 216. Keep yourself sharp

Go to the top of the class and increase your brain power with these tips:

**Give your mind a workout.** Crosswords, number puzzles and mental arithmetic keep your mind agile.
**Background music** can help you remember better, according to Texas research — but it has to be the same music each time to provide a 'context' for the memory. It's thought this works by stimulating the regions of the cerebral cortex involved in learning.
**Eat brain foods** that are rich in lecithin, vitamin C and the B group vitamins. These nutrients support the production of acetylcholine, the most abundant neurotransmitter in the brain and the main carrier of thought and memory (studies show that Alzheimer's patients are low in acetylcholine). Lecithin is found in soya, eggs, wheatgerm, peanuts, peanut butter, liver and ham; the B vitamins in liver, kidneys, nuts, pulses, red meat, milk and yoghurt; and vitamin C in vegetables and citrus fruits. Fish, particularly salmon, mackerel and sardines, has long been dubbed 'brain food', because it's rich in essential fatty acids. For the ultimate brain lunch, have a salmon sandwich with lettuce or another green leafy vegetable and orange juice or soya milk.

**Try dietary supplements.** St John's wort can help lift mild depression and improve concentration. Ginkgo biloba increases the flow of oxygen to your brain, improving peripheral circulation. Studies have shown that a daily supplement of ginkgo results in improved information-processing and short-term memory. Some studies suggest a supplement of co-enzyme Q10 will help increase the energy-generating capacity of your brain's nerve cells.
**Perform circulation-boosting exercises.** Most aerobic exercise, such as walking and cycling, will improve blood flow to the brain.
**Chew!** Believe it or not, chewing may be the key to preserving your memory as you get older, according to Japanese research. Scientists have found that chewing increases activity in the part of the brain responsible for new memories and learning.
**Nix the nightcap.** Drinking alcohol before you go to sleep can greatly reduce time spent in REM sleep, which Canadian researchers say is necessary for processing memories. Just 0.6 g of ethanol per kilogram of body weight (a little over two beers for the average woman) can halve the normal amount of REM sleep.

# 217. STAND STILL

It's a terrible feeling, the feeling of being unsettled. Worrying about nameless somethings, feeling off-balance, out of whack, being caught up in a swirling mass of 'what ifs', 'if onlys' and 'shoulds'. There will be moments when you feel as though you are going quite mad.

In a culture which values clear-thinking, decision-making and certainty, not being able to see clearly is a lonely and frightening place to be. It's tempting to try to take control. As children, we were taught the difference between right and wrong so, when confronted with confusion, we try to divide issues up into 'good' and 'bad', so as to get everything back on track as quickly as possible — preferably before anyone notices that you haven't been handling things as well as you should.

A far more difficult option — but one which is far better for your mental and spiritual health — is to stand still with your confusion (or sit down, or take it for a walk) and embrace it, with an attitude of expectation that all will turn out for the good. Ask yourself questions — the more uncomfortable they make you, and the stronger your 'shut-down' reflex, the more likely you are to be on the right track! See where the confusion takes you, see what pops into your mind. Be patient with the fact that you do not know what is happening to you. Relax, and do not deny your state. No, you don't 'feel fine, thank you' — but you are moving towards that state via a detour that's trying to tell you something.

Instead, be aware — and clear a space in your life for whatever idea or choice it is that is trying to get through.

## 218. DOODLE

Scribbling shapes and pictures while you're on the phone, cross-hatching and shading all over your text books and diaries, or drawing the same image — a star, a bat, a heart — over and over on everything from shopping lists to receipts is a habit to be encouraged.

Psychologists say doodling is far from being idle or lazy — in fact, it increases concentration, and boosts memory and your ability to absorb information in both the short- and long-term. In one study, people were divided into two groups, and asked to listen to audio tapes that were designed to be monotonous and boring. One set of volunteers was asked simply to listen to the tapes and jot down target words whenever they heard them. The other group was also told to note the target words — but were instructed to doodle on a second piece of paper at the same time. The result was quite dramatic, with the people who doodled while listening to the tape being able to remember up to three times as many target words as the ones who didn't.

# 219. BE REALISTIC

You'd be foolish if you gave yourself just one day to train for a marathon, wouldn't you? Or thought you could drop a dress size in a weekend? The same logic applies to trying to live a sane, happy and healthy life. Whether you're trying to take nutritional changes on board, get a better attitude, adopt an exercise plan, make meditation a part of your life, or whatever, these disciplines require that you practise regularly — not just try once, then give up in a huff. Be patient with yourself.

If you feel depressed or upset, and think you've failed, step back and see when, and in what context, those feelings occur. Are you tired? Comparing yourself to others? Cross or frustrated about something else altogether? Even if you do not notice any obvious improvements in, say, your weight loss or assertiveness plan, it does not mean that they are not happening. The fact that you've started at all means improvements will be occurring at an energetic level, and will eventually cause positive mental, spiritual, and even physical changes. You may be a lot closer to your goal than you realise.

# 220. Communicate better

It may not be the other person's fault that they don't understand you — it could be yours. These three simple steps go a long way to improving your understanding of each other.

**Try saying something a different way**. If the other person is just not getting it — no matter how often you repeat something, or how loudly — try putting it another way. Re-group, and re-phrase your statement or request. Use neutral language, and avoid starting off with 'I want' or 'I think'. It may be that the other person thinks you are being overly critical, or they may simply shut down if they think you are angry with them. If you're still not getting anywhere, put the issue aside for the time being — and ask what it is they hear when you speak.

**Brush up your body language**. It's almost impossible to make real contact and to communicate properly if you do not have, at the bare minimum, eye contact. Do not attempt to have important discussions over the telephone — it's only when you can see the other person that you can gauge their reaction in 100 subtle ways. Use a soft, non-judgemental expression when you do make eye contact. Staring them down is bound to be counter-productive. Same goes for how you use

your body. Fidgeting, hunching your shoulders defensively and folding your arms all send negative signals to the person you're trying to speak with. Practise 'talking' to others while watching yourself in the mirror. Note your expression, how your eyes move, and how you stand and hold yourself. You'll be very surprised to see the difference between how you think you present to others, and what you actually look like.

**Don't interrupt**. Plain bad manners is often behind bad communication. If you are not interested in what someone else has to say, it is easy to become distracted, look away and either stop listening or try to talk over the top of them. Be attentive to the other person, and don't interrupt. If a discussion is getting heated, try, at all costs, not to allow things to degenerate into a slanging match. Instead, take turns talking: this not only slows down the interaction and reduces tension, it also sets up a structure in which you listen to each other and respond calmly.

# 221.  GET YOUR HEALTH CHECKS DONE

'Never go to a doctor whose houseplants have died.'
**Erma Bombeck**

Regular health checks can detect signs of disease even before you notice the symptoms. You can then take action to prevent a major health problem, perhaps just by making a few lifestyle changes. Here's a very basic list of essential checkups. Make the appointment today. They're not painful, and you're worth it.

**Chlamydia test** Often causes no symptoms in women but if it spreads to the Fallopian tubes it can lead to ectopic pregnancy, pelvic pain or even infertility.

**Pap smear** Reveals abnormal cell changes that could develop into cervical cancer. Prevents many thousands of deaths a year.

**Obesity checks** Even if you're the right weight but often feel tired or out of breath, a body-fat test will reveal the proportion of fat in your body.

**Eye test** As well as identifying sight problems, an eye test can reveal high blood pressure, glaucoma and diabetes at an early, treatable age.

**Blood pressure** High blood pressure rarely produces symptoms, but can make you prone to heart attacks, strokes and kidney failure.

**Diabetes test** Nearly 40 per cent of people have some damage by the time of diagnosis. Far smarter to get tested before.

**Thyroid test** To test thyroid gland activity, which controls the rate at which body cells use energy.

**Cholesterol check** Too-high levels of low-density lipoprotein (LDL) in the blood can increase the risk of heart disease.

**Bone density checks** To check for osteoporosis (brittle bone disease), which affects one in three women.

PS: Consider some of the newer state-of-the-art laboratory tests which a good natural therapist should suggest, too. Problems such as parasites, amino acid imbalances and heavy-metal toxicity are becoming more common.

## 222. Avoid hell on heels

Constantly wearing shoes with a heel over one and a half inches high can cause health problems. Wearers expose themselves to a higher risk of arthritis and disc disease as high heels increase the curvature of the spine, compressing the vertebrae and putting a strain on all the muscle groups. The worst culprits include stilettos (the narrow heel forces your muscles to work too hard), wedges (they put pressure on your spine and make you prone to tripping up), and mules (unless they've got decent support to the sides of the foot, they force your foot forward, ramming your toes into the front of the shoe). If you want to wear these shoes at work, at least try wearing walking shoes or trainers for the journey there and back.

## 223. FIND YOUR OWN SPACE

> 'What you are today comes from your thoughts of yesterday, and your present thoughts build your life of tomorrow. Your life is the creation of your mind.'
> **Buddha**

For centuries, people have sought refuge from everyday life. In so-called primitive societies, isolation was, very sensibly, a common part of rites of passage such as puberty and bereavement. Going away by oneself was also part of more regular rhythms — for instance, during menstruation women would take time out for reflection.

Make sure you spend an hour away from the rest of your family at least once a week in a relaxing part of your home. Ideally, create a quiet area in your spare room, cellar or attic. If you haven't got the space, at least find a corner to make your own. If there is a window available, make that the focal point of your corner. Be still: look out and gaze at the view, or just close your eyes to meditate quietly. Surround yourself with soothing sounds, such as chimes, soft music or a bubbling fountain. Choose flowers, sentimental or religious objects or art that you find beautiful and place them where you can see them. Speak to your senses: burn your favourite incense or oil nearby. Practise breathing in and out: let the fresh air in, and the stale air out. Use this time to regain your balance and sanity, to collect yourself.

# 224. KEEP A CRYSTAL

... by your bed or on your desk, particularly if you have a computer. Crystal healers claim they work by clearing blocked chakras (energy points) in your body. Holding the crystal you've chosen, imagine a positive energy beam of white light from the top of your head to the ends of your toes and fingers; breathe deeply. Although you may be drawn to a particular crystal, some conditions are said to respond particularly well to specific stones. Try:

**Amethyst** For its calming, soothing and cleansing properties; to ease headaches; to aid sleep.

**Aquamarine** For emotional and intellectual stability; peace of mind.

**Azurite** Opens the mind and the soul to higher levels, awakens psychic possibilities. Encourages inner vision, inspiration and creativity.

**Bloodstone** A 'strength stone' and powerful healer for both the physical and non-physical body. Revitalises, renews and promotes inner balance.

**Citrine** Lifts depression and makes you feel better about yourself.

**Fluorite** A 'mind stone' on all levels, excellent for improving concentration and study, and for encouraging a higher understanding of the world. A wonderful stone to assist meditation.

**Moonstone** To calm racing thoughts, heighten intuition and give you useful dreams.

**Malachite** Enhances psychic awareness and ability to communicate with the higher self; also helpful for joint aches and for giving courage to cope with pain.

**Rhodonite** One of the heart stones; its loving energies inspire self-esteem and confidence.

**Rose quartz** To help you cope with relationship problems.

**Sodalite** Enhances communication and creative expression; encourages clarity of ideas, allowing you to recognise what is true and right.

**Tiger's eye** To help you see a problem more clearly; encourages logical thinking.

**Topaz** A wonderful stone for encouraging individuality and a sense of trust in one's ability. Also good for expanding awareness to higher levels.

**Tourmaline** One of the special stones of the New Age, this is the stone of protection. It wards off fear and negativity and protects on all levels.

# 225. REVAMP YOUR BEDROOM FOR ROMANCE

Use the principles of feng shui to create a more peaceful and loving atmosphere:

**Avoid hard, shiny, angular objects.** Soft materials and furnishings are more relaxing and conducive to sensuality; curved lines stimulate harmony. Choose round or oval frames for mirrors.

**Light a few candles.** This adds the element of fire, which in feng shui terms means passion.

**Don't sleep under a slanting ceiling.** This may cause a bad temper and rows.

**Clear away the clutter.** Stand in your bedroom and check out the area in the far-right corner. This corresponds to the House of Marriage. If it's cluttered, your love life is likely to be a mess, too.

**Take a look at your pictures.** They are symbolic, so make sure you don't have solitary people or stark landscapes. Go for couples or groups or romantic scenes.

**Avoid having anything in the bedroom that is to do with your work.**

**Make sure you can see the door as you lie in bed.** You'll feel more secure. But, if your bed is right behind the door, screen it with plants or a piece of low furniture.

## 226. GO OUTSIDE

Lack of energy is one of the main characteristics of SAD, seasonal affective disorder or 'winter depression'. Experts think this is due to disturbed levels of melatonin, a hormone secreted by the pineal gland in the brain, which helps regulate the body clock. Melatonin levels are regulated by light and darkness (high levels produced at night help us feel sleepy) so sunshine really can boost energy — one reason why most of us feel so much more energetic on holiday. Try to get out into the daylight as often as you can, especially at lunchtime when the sun is strongest. In winter you can help lift your mood by decorating your house in light-reflecting colours and using 'daylight' bulbs.

# 227. BREATHE PROPERLY

Breathing from your diaphragm oxygenates your blood, which helps you relax almost instantly. Shallow chest breathing, by contrast, can cause your heart to beat faster and your muscles to tense up, exacerbating feelings of stress.

To breathe deeply, begin by putting your hand on your abdomen just below the navel. Inhale slowly through your nose to a count of five, and watch your hand move out as your belly expands. Concentrate on filling your lungs to their full capacity. Hold the breath for a few seconds, then slowly exhale to the count of five. Repeat several times. Once you've gained control over your breathing, a feeling of calm should follow.

# 228. RELINQUISH CONTROL

The silly thing about wanting everything under control, all of the time, is that the more compulsive and rigid you are, the more out of control you become. On the other hand, the more flexible and accepting you are, the more you experience genuine power by being able to deal with change and challenge.

**Be realistic**. You do have the ability to control things — within reason. You are not, however, all-powerful and all-knowing.

**Don't catastrophise**. When things do go wrong, focus on ways to put all — or at least a bit — of it right again, rather than think that everything is going to collapse.

**Delegate**. Doing everything yourself does not save time, no matter how incompetent you regard your family or colleagues as being. In the long run, it will always be more efficient to teach someone else. Consider the exasperated mother who, every morning, ties her child's shoelaces because they can't or won't. No matter how long it takes them to learn, or how many times they get it wrong, it's still going to be better for the child to learn to tie the shoelaces than for the mother to do it indefinitely. Grit your teeth when others get it wrong, and keep encouraging what they get right.

**Loosen up**. Sticking to a rigid routine of doing things a certain way at a certain time is not healthy. It borders on compulsive behaviour, and the more you do it, the more you risk becoming irrational and closed off from life. Recognise inflexibility and rituals for the time-consuming monsters they really are. If this sounds like how you approach your household and work chores — change the order in which you do things.

**Welcome mistakes**. So, something went wrong. Perhaps you could have prevented it, but probably you couldn't. Whether you made the mistake or someone else did, try to see it as an opportunity to learn something new. Pretty much every invention in the last 200 years — the chocolate chip cookie, nylon pantyhose, and the ballpoint pen, just to name a few — is the result of a 'mistake'.

**Chill out**. If your way of getting things done is to come down hard on others — or on yourself — it's time to rethink. No one has the power to upset you apart from you. And being a bully, and making people afraid of you does not give you power over them.

# 229. EAT FOR BEAUTIFUL SKIN

Forget expensive lotions and potions — you can improve the quality of your skin just by changing what you put in your mouth. Here's how:

**Eat foods containing essential fatty acids (EFAs).** These literally feed and moisturise dry, thirsty skin from the inside. Tasty examples include almonds, Brazil nuts, vegetable oils, tuna, salmon, sesame and pumpkin seeds. An easy habit to adopt is to sprinkle powdered, toasted flaxseeds over your morning cereal every day — they're exceptionally rich in EFAs.
**Eat more fruit and vegetables.** You should aim to eat at least five portions per day. Fruit and vegetables contain antioxidants — especially vitamins A, C and E — and these all help your skin look better.
**Drink plenty of water.** Six to eight glasses a day is the minimum for keeping skin cells plump and moist, so skin appears softer, more supple and younger looking. Stressful situations tend to be dehydrating, so drink extra water when you're under physical or mental pressure.
**Stock up on bran flakes.** Fibre keeps your digestive system working efficiently. A sluggish system can be a cause of cellulite as well as constipation, which is not only uncomfortable and inconvenient, but nearly always causes pimples.
**Limit your alcohol intake.** Skin conditions such as rosacea, hives, flushing and itching are all aggravated by alcohol, because it increases the circulation of blood to the skin's surface, which makes the skin feel warmer.

## 230. GET SERIOUS ABOUT PAMPERING

Sylvia Plath said it all about baths when she wrote: 'There must be quite a few things a hot bath won't cure — but I don't know many of them.'

We all need a sanctuary, a place where we can flee from the stresses of everyday living whenever we need to relax and recuperate. And what better place for some serious pampering than the bathroom? Water strongly appeals to our senses as it's one of the therapeutic forces of nature. The sound of waves lapping on a shore, a waterfall, even the sound of rain on the roof arouses the senses. Feeling water on your body — whether soaking yourself in it, or enjoying the sensation of it beating against your skin — can heal and invigorate. Think for a moment of how many sacred rituals in which water plays a part; it's used to bless and anoint. Here's how to start:

**Start your session early**. You don't want to rush. Choose a time when you know you won't be disturbed. Stop for a moment before you enter the water, and become aware of your feelings. Drop your hands and just stand there; breathe in and out a few times. Don't have the water too hot or it will make you drowsy.

**Add reviving essential oil to the water**. Up to five drops will clear your head and stimulate your senses. Try clary sage, lemon or basil.

**Temperature and duration are critical**. If the water's too hot, it will dehydrate your skin. Your bathwater should be tepid, and shouldn't produce steam. And 25 minutes is long enough. After that, your skin becomes prune-like.

**Try a Japanese-style *nuka* bath**. Wrap a few handfuls of fresh rice bran in a large, square piece of cloth and drop it in the bath. The vitamin-rich oils of the rice will cleanse your skin thoroughly, leaving it glowing and silky smooth.

**Change into a fluffy towelling robe**. Make sure you have plenty of clean towels and everything else you need close at hand, including a bottle of water in case you get thirsty.

## 231. TREAT YOUR FACE

Is your skin feeling sapped of moisture from winds and air conditioning? A hydrating facial will help. You can use a store-bought exfoliant and mask containing AHAs (alpha-hydroxy acids), or concoct an economical alternative from ingredients on hand. Try a natural fruit-acid exfoliating paste made from one tablespoon each orange juice and bicarbonate of soda (the citrus acid loosens dead skin cells while the bicarb's mild abrasives slough them away).

Wash your face to remove dirt, oil and make-up. Rinse thoroughly, pat dry.

Gently massage orange juice paste over skin in small circles, avoiding eye area. Leave on for five to ten minutes.

Follow with a moisturising mask suitable for all skin types: combine half a ripe avocado, a two-inch long slice of cucumber, and a tablespoon of yoghurt in a blender until smooth. Spread over your face, lie back, and close your eyes for 20 minutes — but not until you've put on some soothing music. Then rinse off and follow with your usual moisturiser.

## 232. RESCUE YOUR HAIR

Chlorine, salt water, sun and wind, hair driers and hot rollers are not nice to your hair. They break down the hair, steal moisture, and leave you with a dry, tangled mess. Try these solutions to hair horror stories:

**(Don't) go green**. Bleached hair can take on a nasty green hue if you swim regularly in chlorinated pools. To bring it back to a more normal colour try ... tomato sauce! Massage two table-spoonsful through freshly washed hair, comb through and leave for half an hour. Rinse well, then shampoo and condition as usual. The pink tones of the tomato sauce will neutralise the ghostly green look.

**The trouble with tangles**. This is a real problem if your hair has been chemically treated or permed, especially after shampooing. For a nifty home remedy, pour some lemonade into a plastic pump spray bottle and spray generously all over hair; leave for five minutes, then shampoo and condition as usual. The citric acid in the lemonade helps smooth the roughened hair cuticle, making it more manageable.

**The final straw**. To repair parched, flyaway, miserable hair, mash together an over-ripe banana and a really mushy avocado (rotten to the point of being black is best) plus a tablespoon each of fresh lemon juice and mayonnaise. Massage the whole lot into dry hair and leave for half an hour, then rinse it out (under a tap in the backyard, to avoid clogging the pipes!), then shampoo and condition as usual. Bananas and avocados are full of nutrients that feed and nurse damaged hair, mayonnaise is an excellent conditioner and the lemon juice helps restore the scalp's pH balance.

## 233. GO BEYOND BRUSHING

Do you have fillings, crowns, bleeding and/or receding gums, or missing teeth? If so, join the club. You are one of the estimated three-quarters of Australians who have dental or gum problems. Clearly, preventive care is important. Most dentists recommend brushing, flossing, twice-a-year cleanings, and regular checkups. But holistic dentists say quite a lot more can be done.

**Eat whole, fresh foods**. Limit your consumption of sugary foods, which create acids that attack tooth enamel and encourage decay.

**Avoid soft drinks**. They upset your body's calcium/phosphorus balance, causing a weakening of bones and teeth.

**Chew your food well**. This stimulates the flow of saliva in your mouth, which can neutralise destructive food acids.

**Avoid drugs**. A common side effect of more than 100 drugs — from cold tablets to migraine medication — is a decrease in the amount of saliva in the mouth, causing a condition known as 'dry mouth'.

**Use a product that stops plaque**. Gels and mouth rinses should do the trick.

**Take vitamin and mineral supplements**: they may help as well. Gum disease is a form of scurvy, the classic vitamin C deficiency.

**Ask for composite fillings, rather than mercury amalgam ones**. A growing body of damning evidence exists about the toxic effects of mercury, and mercury amalgam fillings have already been banned in Sweden, Germany and Austria.

# 234. WATCH YOUR BACK

One in five of us will suffer back pain that will lead to time off work. Common causes of back pain are gardening, do-it-yourself projects, hauling groceries, vacuuming and caring for children. There are three rules for being back-friendly: (a) keep your back as straight as possible; (b) do not carry out any one activity for an extended period of time; and (c) do things at a comfortable pace. Here are some more tips to keep back pain at bay:

**For sewing, ironing or do-it-yourself work,** make sure you have a quality, adjustable workbench, table or board. This should help you avoid bending over.

**For vacuuming,** use an upright model as they don't need to be dragged. Keep it close to your body and make short sweeping movements rather than stretching.

**When gardening,** plant low-maintenance shrubs and perennials. Choose plants for ground cover to minimise weeding. Always warm up and stretch before gardening.

**When caring for children,** never carry a baby on one hip, as this places strain on the spine. Kneel down to distressed toddlers rather than picking them up and adjust the height of cots and other baby equipment so you don't have to bend.

**For working at your desk,** buy a ball chair. These stylish ergonomic 'chairs' are designed to prevent back problems. By allowing the hips to stretch and relax and the knees to rest below the hips, the spine is supported in its natural S-shape (regular chairs force you into one position, which is an unnatural state for the body). Sitting on the ball is thought to improve posture and stimulate the back muscles. The balls can also be used for stretching and exercising — and fun!

# 235. TAKE A WEIGHT OFF YOUR MIND

The key to staying the shape and weight you want to be is learning not to think about food when you're not actually hungry. Try these smart psychological strategies:

**Write down what you eat**. Once you become aware of your habits and patterns, changing them becomes easier.

**Visualise the person you want to be**. This will help you stick to your healthy eating regime. To fix an image in your mind, you need to conjure it up at least 20 times.

**Every time you eat, give yourself a hunger score from one to ten**. Chances are you'll score five or below, which means you're not really hungry — so resist.

**Go for a walk**. Exercise helps you control your appetite, increases energy and boosts the delivery of nutrients to your body.

**Before you shop, write a list and make sure you're feeling full**. By planning ahead, you can avoid being tempted by fatty, sugary snacks.

**Don't eat on the run**. Sitting down to eat will make you more aware of starting and finishing.

**Do something else**. Being active will take your mind off eating — so why not write a letter, plan a party, go window-shopping, or watch a video?

## 236. HAVE A MAKEOVER

'Beauty is how you feel inside and it reflects in your eyes. It is not something physical,' says Sophia Loren. She's right, of course, beauty is only skin deep (though there's a lot to be said for her glorious cheekbones, almond-shaped eyes and dazzling smile). However, most of us are improved by a well made-up face and beautifully styled hair. You don't have to be vain or self-absorbed to be interested in the way you look — if you are confident about how you present yourself to others, it will do wonders for your self-esteem and that true inner beauty that Sophia Loren was referring to.

Spend one hour this month getting a professional makeover. On a strict budget? Check out your local *Yellow Pages* — many beauty salons offer them for free or at least at a substantial discount so that their junior/or trainee consultants get plenty of practice. You'll learn to accentuate your good features and there's an added psychological bonus if you tend to be envious of other people's looks: as you begin to appreciate your own appearance, you will stop wanting to look like other people. Don't let your makeover stop there. When you get home, give your cosmetic drawer a new look, too. Discard things that are past their prime, or in colours that don't flatter you.

And another really good idea — consider having a 'fantasy photo' done of yourself. There are many photographers who specialise in this sort of work, and who have a talent for making you feel comfortable — and look gorgeous — so they can bring out your real personality.

# 237. DRINK UP THE HEALTHY WAY

For a fast blast in liquid form, a nutrient-packed drink makes an excellent breakfast alternative. Process two small bananas, a glass of skim milk and for added sweetness, a teaspoon of honey. If you need to stock up on energy for an exercise class or before a walk, mix half a litre of fruit juice with the same amount of water, then add half a teaspoon of salt. The salt speeds up the absorption of water along with the natural sugars from the fruit juice, giving an instant boost.

And make sure you get those eight glasses of water a day. People generally don't drink enough. Research at Harvard University shows that a two per cent drop in your body's water supplies can reduce energy levels by a fifth. Don't wait until you feel thirsty, because that's a sign your body is already dehydrated. Avoid coffee, tea and cola as they are diuretics, meaning they only increase the flow of urine, and so will further dehydrate you and increase your need for water.

# 238. GET A BETTER BOTTOM

Do this five-minute routine three times a week and expect results in a month. The exercises specifically work on your thigh and bottom muscles.

**Knee bends** Stand with your feet shoulder-width apart and your toes pointing forward. Place your hands on your thighs and contract your abdomen. Bend your knees as you lower your buttocks, keeping your knees above your ankles. Don't take your hips below knee level. Return to starting position. Repeat ten times.

**Lunges** Stand with one foot in front of the other, keeping your weight in the middle. Keep your front foot flat and your rear foot on its toes. Hold your abdominals in, stand tall, and bend both your knees as you lower your body. Return to starting position. Repeat ten times on each leg.

**Inner thigh stretch** Stand with your feet wide apart, place your hands on your hips and point your feet slightly outwards. Take your weight over to one side, bending one knee, until you feel a stretch in the inner part of your opposite leg. Hold for 30 seconds, then return to the starting position. Repeat, taking your weight over to the other side. Do ten times.

## 239. DO SOMETHING SCARY

Whenever I'm scared about taking something to the next stage, or about doing something I haven't done before, I think of what Amelia Earhart had to say on crossing the Atlantic: 'Of course I realised there was danger. Obviously I faced the possibility of not returning. But, once I'd thought about it, there wasn't really any good reason to think about it again.'

A short, intense burst of excitement can actually make you more resilient and able to cope better with prolonged stress and tension. Have a day off work and organise to spend it doing something you've always wanted to do — but make it a challenge which makes you just a little bit nervous, something that expands your boundaries! Book a flight in a hot-air balloon, go on a roller-coaster ride or a parachute jump, or plan a day at the races with friends. Learn how to rally-drive, or go on an ocean trip where you can see whales and dolphins.

Taking time out to do something new, exciting and a little bit scary can set off the biological fight-or-flight response, flooding the body with stress hormones. But once the ride or jump is over, the hormonal changes are rapidly reversed and anxiety is replaced by elation. Research from the University of Nebraska confirms this idea, showing that the 'rush' you get from intermittent physiological arousal resulting in a short-term stress response can be as effective in beating stress as repeated exercise.

# 240. TRY A TONIC

Chinese herbalists say that ginger and cardamom are 'restoratives', which means they enliven your metabolism by creating heat and energy. Try my Metabolic Tonic to stimulate the circulation — it's particularly recommended for that gotta-cold-coming-on feeling.

**Metabolic Tonic**
>  5 cinnamon sticks, broken in half
>  2 x 1 cm (1/2 inch) slices of fresh ginger
>  ½ teaspoon cardamom seeds
>  ½ teaspoon whole cloves
>  3 cups (1½ pints) water

Combine all the ingredients, and simmer until the tonic reduces slightly. Strain and drink hot, adding honey if you wish.

# 241. SLEEP WELL

'Sleep, that knits up the ravell'd sleeve of care . . .'
**William Shakespeare**

Get plenty of sleep or your happiness rating will suffer. Most people need a good six to eight hours sleep a night to feel in the best of moods. Have a regular bedtime and keep the bedroom for sleep and lovemaking only (so there are no reminders of work!). Avoid alcohol and chocolate late at night — both contain enough caffeine to disturb your sleep. Watching TV or reading the paper before bed can overstimulate. Instead have a relaxing bath with a few drops of lavender essential oil and do some stretching exercises. Finally, before you turn in, consciously empty your mind of worries. Imagine your problems are a big white balloon, watch it ascend and then cut the string and let all your worries float away.

**Try yoga.** Yoga calms the nervous system. If you're unable to sleep, try this pose: sit cross-legged on the floor in front of a chair, bend forward from the hips and place your crossed arms on a folded blanket on the seat of the chair. Rest your head on your crossed arms. Stay in this position ten minutes or longer, taking slow, deep breaths through your nose. Meditating in the yoga Corpse pose — lying flat on your back with arms and legs splayed to either side — may also relax you.

**Herbs can help.** Sip a herbal tea. Choose from lime flower, passionflower, valerian, lemon balm, fennel, rosehips, hops or chamomile. Take St John's wort tablets if insomnia is linked with mild to moderate depression — but be aware that this herb might increase your sensitivity to sunlight.

**Use visualisation.** When you're worrying about something, your body produces more of the stress hormone adrenaline, which makes you alert and blocks the action of the growth hormone, so you wake up unrefreshed. Block these thoughts by thinking of a pleasant, restful scene, or picture yourself going down in a lift. The lower you go, the deeper you fall into relaxation and sleep. Repeat a meaningless word over and over in your head. If you still can't drop off, go into another room and do something relaxing, like light reading, until you feel sleepy.

**Don't go to bed angry.** Feeling cross or resentful is far more likely to keep you awake than anxiety. Either address the problem beforehand or work out a strategy for dealing with it — then put it firmly to one side until morning.

# 242.  EAT MORE PROTEIN

Protein is broken down by the body into amino acids — used for repairing wear and tear and creating energy. Because it takes longer to be absorbed by the body than carbohydrates, protein is the best type of food to eat when you want long-term stamina. Indeed, eating too little protein can result in poor concentration, fatigue and irritability. Although lean meat is a rich source, it's a good idea to obtain protein from other foods such as fish, eggs, skim milk, wholegrains, pulses, tofu, fruit and vegetables.

# 243. TAKE A SCENTED JOURNEY

Get clever with essential oils. Choose aromas for certain purposes —
invigorating, calming, uplifting — depending on what you are doing at that time.

**Wake-up call** Refreshing and balancing fragrances that are recommended for sniffing or using in the shower when waking up in the morning include tangerine, orange, bergamot, eucalyptus, lemon, and lime. **A calm commute** In the car, try dotting a few drops of lavender oil on the dashboard, or mist a lavender spray around the interior — it will energise you without being too stimulating. Rosemary is good for concentration. **On the job** If you are feeling anxious, burn geranium in a vaporiser on your desk to promote peacefulness. Peppermint is a good choice to energise. Rosemary will help you concentrate and frankincense will enhance your creativity.

**Clearing bad vibes** If you've had an argument with your partner or a work colleague and you want to improve the atmosphere, try putting two drops of pine essential oil on to a tissue and leave it lying nearby so you can breathe in the scent. Pine helps foster forgiveness and fairness. **The afternoon slump** If your blood sugar plummets after lunch, breathe in invigorating tea tree. **Homeward bound** Cinnamon is a nice relaxing and refreshing fragrance for going home. **Back at the ranch** Instead of a glass of wine, why not unwind with a vanilla-scented candle? Rose is also a lovely 'welcome home' scent to use in a burner or potpourri near the front door.

# 244. LISTEN TO YOUR BODY

Just as with food, some types of exercise are more beneficial than others. Traditional aerobics sessions can actually sap energy by overstressing the body, depressing its immune system and laying it open to infection. Gentler exercise such as yoga and t'ai chi (the word *chi* means energy) are more invigorating, because they work on the mind as well as the body.

Learn to listen to your body when you exercise to make sure you are not using too much or too little energy. Swedish researchers have found that we each have an accurate 'internal barometer' that tells us if we are exercising to the right intensity. With cardiovascular/fat-burning exercise you should work at a level you find challenging — but not so hard that you are uncomfortable. Monitor your pulse (ask the trainer at your gym or exercise class, or your GP how to do this).

The fitter you are, the longer you can keep going without your muscles tiring. If you find yourself feeling weak, it is a sign that you are dehydrated or running low on energy stores. Injury is more likely in these circumstances, so stop and rest. Make sure you always drink plenty of water, or a fitness drink, before, during and after a workout.

# 245. THINK BEFORE YOU SPEAK

Detox your emotions before bringing a bad day at work home with you. Negativity can create a chain reaction of distress that moves through a home and gives rise to anxiety, depression and other health and behavioural symptoms in susceptible household members — especially children.

Give your partner and your kids a break. Everyone messes up now and again. If a friend spilled a glass of wine, you'd probably laugh it off: 'Don't worry about it, it's nothing.' Now — think about how you'd react if your child did it. Most people would become angry out of all proportion, which is exactly the kind of reaction that can eventually destroy relationships.

Negative emotions are a fact of life, and, like other forms of pollution, low levels or infrequent exposure will not have a long-term toxic effect. But if you're bringing home work-related stress more than seven or eight days a month, that's enough to have a toxic effect, according to researchers at the University of Arizona. Instead, blow off steam before getting home. Go to the gym on the way, or even just pick up groceries and run a few chores to put a buffer between 'home-time' and 'work-time'. If that doesn't work, at least let household members know *why* you're grouchy. When there's a logical reason and other people know the source, they're less likely to be affected and, hopefully, give you a bit of breathing space to get over it.

# 246. DON'T ACCEPT EVERY INVITATION

When you think about getting rid of clutter in your life, you probably think first of clearing out drawers and wardrobes. However, it should also mean making an effort to junk negative influences from other people, including dysfunctional relationships, and people who use you. This sort of 'baggage' is not only unnecessary, but is dangerous to your self-esteem and confidence. Getting rid of it will help you to regain control over your relationships, and to get what you want by leaving more room for the positive influences in your life to flourish.

Try to spend time only with people who really matter to you, people you like and who value you. Maintaining a relationship out of a sense of duty will only make you feel hemmed in. People who don't appreciate you are unlikely to change. If you're involved in a relationship that is damaging your self-esteem, try to make it work. Arrange a time to talk to the person in question, prepare what you want to say and tell them how they're making you feel. You may want to go away for a while to give them time to think. But if they still always put you down, you should consider ending the relationship.

# 247. AVOID 'ANXIOUS BRAIN'

As a scatter-brained child with a finger in many pies, I would be extremely irritated when my mother would nag me with the old saying: 'One thing at a time, and that done well, is a good philosophy, as many will tell.' The scatter-brained child went on to become a frenetically multi-tasking woman — and she found that there are few things that feed anxiety better than doing too many things at once! So — repeat after me:

**Do just one thing at a time.** Read the mail *or* listen to the radio *or* make dinner — not all three at once.

**Fix things when they break.** Dripping washers, doors that stick, appliances that don't work. Either pay someone to come and help, or learn how to do it yourself. Slow down, read instructions, follow directions.

**One day a week, don't wear a watch.** If you're late, there's not a damn thing you can do about it, and constantly checking the time doesn't make you get there any faster.

**When driving, turn the radio off.** It's extraordinary the thoughts that roll in when you haven't got a background of constant noise and chatter, even just on a ten minute drive.

# 248.  SIT PERFECTLY STILL

This exercise is a good stress-buster if you're a person who rushes about like a headless chook all day, and is so busy being busy that you feel you can't afford time to relax. It only takes five minutes.

Sit comfortably, preferably in a quiet, darkened room, either on a chair or cross-legged on a cushion on the floor. Let your hands rest loosely in your lap and shut your eyes. If they keep fluttering open, persevere: close your eyes firmly and feel yourself breathing. Think of something pleasant.

Shift and move your shoulders and torso, getting the feel of where you need to soften your posture so you can breathe more easily. Keep your eyes closed. Sway softly forward and back, allowing your spine and neck to loosen up, feeling where you need to stretch to adjust any tightness. Enjoy the feeling of having absolutely nothing to do for five minutes.

Make an effort to do it frequently. The clever thing about this deceptively simple technique is that, if you make a point of sitting still and not tearing about and thinking about your work, your body forgets to tense up. So, if you practise sitting still for a few minutes at a time regularly, then your body and brain are also getting regular messages that these short bursts of stillness help you to cope.

# 249. GO FOR A WALK WITH A CHILD

'Hold a child's face with both your hands.'
**Nigerian proverb**

Here's a short list of things to discuss: why fallen blossoms look like snow, how many shades of green can be counted along the way, and whether or not it's good manners to run a stick along the fence. You can peer, politely of course, into the neighbour's windows as you stroll by. You can watch for cats taking sunbaths, other children, delicious-looking kitchens, lovebirds in cages, and vases of flowers.

Home again. Take whatever you've gathered, fill a jar with water, and display your finds in a window. Now it's your turn to sit inside and watch the world go by.

## 250. DRINK REALLY GOOD COFFEE

Did you know that, in the fifteenth century, Turkish women could legally divorce husbands who failed to provide them with enough coffee? A fine thing, too. And before you point to all the other places in this book where I've recommended cutting back on coffee — don't. We all know that too much coffee can trigger anxiety and tummy upsets, even the jitters. I'm not talking about drinking cup after cup of the horrid freeze-dried powdered stuff that masquerades as coffee. But drinking moderate amounts of excellent quality coffee — especially the organic varieties that Australia is rapidly becoming well-known and respected for — can be a satisfying treat. There's even some evidence that the health news isn't all bad, either: for one thing, coffee can improve mental alertness; and for another, it stimulates the action of a chemical messenger called cholecystokinin, which causes the gall bladder to release bile into the small intestine, so aiding digestion.

My dad used to make what he called a 'sort-of Irish coffee', which I pass on to you now. He's right — it's not Irish coffee — but it's rich, strong, smooth as an Irish accent, and very fortifying for dishevelled, harried mothers on a cold wintery day, when the kitchen is filled with wet washing and cross, noisy children with runny noses and someone's flushed a plastic truck down the toilet.

**Dad's Irish Coffee**
    1 egg yolk
    2 tablespoons (1¼ fl oz) whisky
    1 tablespoon (½ fl oz) condensed milk
    1 tablespoon (½ fl oz) cream
    2 cups good espresso coffee
    coffee crystals, to taste

Whisk the egg yolk with the whisky, condensed milk and cream, then stir into hot coffee. Pour into tall glass or mug and add coffee crystals, to taste.

## 251. BE PRUDENT

The popularity of get-rich-and-get-out-of-debt-quick schemes, sweepstakes and lotteries suggests that we've lost an understanding of the necessary connection between time and money. Every good (and solvent) businessperson understands the connection: the more time it takes to produce a given amount of services and products, the higher the unit cost and the lower the profit. Likewise, every employee understands the relationship between time and money: wages are received for hours worked, with overtime for extra hours.

Do not be waylaid by charlatans in very good suits proffering apparently easy solutions to money troubles. Seek professional advice in putting together a secure, goal-oriented financial plan that also allows you to save, and stick to it. Sure, one in a million people will get rich via the lottery or that amazing book deal. That doesn't mean the other 999,999 are destined to be broke — we just need to follow a different path. The best answer is still the tried-and-true — and boring — one: that true financial power and personal satisfaction accrues from making smart, thrifty choices year in, year out.

## 252. Plan for the future

I'm not trying to be cutesy here. It's been my observation — and experience — that getting stuck in a rut of bad financial habits can usually be traced back to a painful relationship with money, maybe not right now, but something that's happened and is affecting you still. Are you unable to achieve financial freedom and security? Possibly avoiding financial responsibilities, such as taxes, budgets and bills? Feel caught in the rat race? If this sounds like you, you're not alone. There is a way out, and no, it doesn't involve robbing a bank! You need to find a balance in your relationship to money and understand how you feel about it better. Only on that basis can you set financial goals.

For most of us, attitudes and beliefs to money begin early in childhood when parents pass on their own (often unstated) attitudes. The pain that often goes with your feelings about money — emotions such as envy, greed, frustration, despair, fear and humiliation — also often date from this time. Do a bit of soul-searching and ask yourself: what are the belief systems that are keeping you locked in this cycle? Were you, for instance, brought up to 'live for today: who knows what tomorrow will bring'? If so, this could explain an out-of-control credit card. For that matter, early exposure to an extremely strict, penny-pinching household, where money was a rare commodity, something that had to be wheedled into being, could also result in a 'Who gives a damn, let's cut loose' attitude later on. Once you have a better understanding of what money really means to you, then — and only then — can you move forward and plan for your financial future.

As a first step, it's important to differentiate between goals and fantasies. A fantasy could be your idea to chuck it all in and head north to grow avocados. Fantasies are usually impractical and unrealistic, and they can be quite dangerous, because the only guaranteed outcome is disappointment and resentment when they don't happen. Too many fantasies can mean nothing ever seems to work out as you'd planned, and you don't try any more because you only expect failure. Goals, on the other hand, are practical and achievable, the kind of objective that you can reach within a single lifetime. They can also be quite small and subject to a time plan: pay off the credit card over a year, for instance, or save for a beach holiday next summer with friends. And once you've identified them you'll be ready to assess your resources, save carefully, budget wisely and invest for growth.

## 253. DON'T PRETEND

'If you have any enterprise before you, try it in your old clothes,' wrote Henri David Thoreau. On first reading, this quote doesn't sound right. Surely, if you've been invited to a special party or are taking a trip, then buying something new is justified?

But, on second reading, Thoreau is actually saying something quite different. He's not saying that you should respond to change and opportunity by dressing shabbily, or denying yourself. What he is saying is that you can't buy ability off the rack and just put it on. Before starting any new endeavour or task, you need to look inwards and consider whether you can do it with the skills you have right now, and without roping in any outside props to make you look or feel more confident. That's why clothes are a particularly emotive example in this context: not just because they make you look good, but because of what they symbolise — prestige, power, beauty, money. So, before you buy something new, look inwards to consider who you really are, what stage in your life you are at, and, by association, what really suits you. Don't see Thoreau's cryptic comment as a literal suggestion to wear old clothes, but as a reminder to dress honestly, and not to pretend to be something you're not. Changing the external — covering up the way things look — is never a satisfactory way of solving problems.

# 254. EAT OUT HEALTHILY

Out at a restaurant, or indulging in a takeaway meal, we're nearly four times more likely to pig out on 'sugar-fried-salt', which is nutritionists' shorthand for foods that are bad for you. We're also more than twice as likely to drink too much booze, according to the *British Journal of Health Psychology*. However, no one's saying that you have to sacrifice fun and convenience. Follow these guidelines and you can have both:

**Italian**. Choose pasta with tomato-based sauce, rather than a high-fat cheese or cream sauce. For pizza, choose ham or prawns and avoid pepperoni, sausage or bacon. If possible, blot the top of the pizza with a paper towel first — this saves up to five grams of fat per slice!
*Traps to avoid:* garlic bread, stuffed-crust pizza, and adding extra cheese.

**Chinese**. Ask for plain boiled or steamed rice, rather than fried. Pick stir-fried dishes, rather than deep-fried ones.
*Traps to avoid:* crispy-skinned duck or chicken.

**Indian**. As with Chinese food, order plain boiled rice. Tandoori dishes are your best bet, because they're cooked without added fat. They also taste wonderful. Vegetable curries are much lower in fat than meat-based ones.
*Traps to avoid:* poppadums, pilau rice and naan bread — they're all loaded with fat.

# 255. GET TO KNOW YOUR BREASTS

Although we know a lot more about breast cancer than we did five years ago, we're also far more anxious about it. Regular breast checking will reassure you that your breasts are healthy. The aim is to become familiar with your breasts and their structure so you can tell if something seems wrong. Looking at them is just as important as feeling them. To look: stand with your arms by your sides in front of a mirror and study each breast in turn. Raise your arms above your head and look again. To feel: keep your fingers together and gently press with the flat of your fingers, moving over the whole breast. Feel every part of your breast including up towards the collarbone, into the armpit and behind the nipple. Remember, nine out of ten lumps aren't cancerous, but if you're worried, visit your GP and, while you're there, pick up a breast-care leaflet.

# 256. Don't wear a tight bra

The jury is still out on whether wearing a too-tight or wired bra may constrict your lymph flow (part of your circulatory system) and, over time, cause a build-up of toxins in the breast tissue, possibly causing health problems, notably cancer.

One provocative American study from the early 1990s found a significant correlation between wearing a tight bra for more than 12 hours a day — including actually sleeping in a bra or in other constricting undergarments — and getting breast cancer. Other studies have failed to reproduce the findings. However, going bra-less for at least 12 hours a day, and wearing a soft, non-wired bra are two easy changes to make in your life, which may have a long-reaching and positive impact on your health. And if you have already had breast cancer, consider having a massage technique known as manual lymphatic drainage, which helps keep the lymph fluid flowing, removing waste products like excess hormones, even if you have had one or more lymph nodes removed.

## 257. FOLLOW YOUR HUNCHES

'Let me listen to Me, and not to Them.'
**Gertrude Stein**

Logic and reason are not always the best way to solve life's problems. To develop your intuition:

Set aside half an hour each day to just mooch — potter in the garden, or take a bath. It's when your brain is relaxed you're most likely to come up with solutions.

Try to trust your inner voice — often your unconscious mind may have taken in information you're not really aware of.

Avoid any situation you're uncomfortable about.

# 258. LEARN YOGIC BREATHING

This breathing technique is very soothing and relaxing, particularly on hot summer days when you feel cranky and irritable.

> Sit comfortably in a quiet spot. Put your hands flat on your thighs and shut your eyes.
>
> Roll your tongue up into a tube, letting the curled tip protrude slightly out of your half-pursed lips. Breathe in slowly and deeply through the gap in your tongue. You will feel the cool air rush on your tongue. Now breathe out the same way, in and out, slowly and deeply. Continue for a few minutes.
>
> Slowly, return to normal breathing. Open your eyes and gradually become aware of your surroundings. Continue to sit quietly for a few moments more, and sense how the energy has shifted in your body and how you feel more refreshed and focused.

# 259. LOVE YOUR WORK

'The trouble with being in the rat race is that, even if you win,
you're still a rat.'
**Lily Tomlin**

Feel trapped? Hate what you do? Spend most of your time fantasising about a
dream job? It's no surprise that books like *Do What You Love and the Money Will
Follow* were wildly successful, because most of us certainly don't love our work.

However, although the 'do what you love' part is good advice, there is a flaw:
the assumption that money/success/happiness will only follow when you've
figured out that one perfect happy-ever-after occupation that's tailor-made for
you. Certainly some people are gifted with knowing precisely what it is that they
want to do for the rest of their lives, and it conveniently happens to be something
they are qualified in and are marvellous at doing. But, statistically, the rest of us
are very likely to have three, five — maybe even more — distinct *career* changes,
let alone *job* changes. So, a better approach is to find something that you love —
or at least like — about whatever work it is that you're doing right now, no matter
what the situation.

Not surprisingly, this idea is difficult to get used to, and can certainly provoke
cynicism: ('She's telling me that if I'm a single parent, working the 5 am shift in a
chicken-gutting factory, that I'm supposed to find something good in my work?
Phooey!') Naturally, if a situation is intolerable, plan to leave. But, in the
meantime, it's better for your mental and physical health to adjust your
perspective. It makes more sense to find something positive and worthwhile
about the work that you're doing now. It could be a couple of routine chores that
you get satisfaction from finishing off, chatting with a friend you've made there, a
pleasant view from where you sit — or even just a nice bus driver on your route.
The money may follow, or it may not. Doesn't matter. You'll feel more relaxed and
better adjusted, which is a much better frame of mind to be reviewing possible
career or job changes in.

# 260. BE OF SERVICE

'Life was not meant to be easy, but take courage — it can be delightful.'
**George Bernard Shaw**

The main reasons we work are to create an income for ourselves and our families, and to be with other people. This is true — but it's a half-truth. If these are the only reasons you are working, then you are cheating yourself and others. Work needs to nourish your soul and, in even the smallest of ways, nourish the community.

Think of the difference between, say, a doctor who is just turning up at work to make money and rub shoulders with peers, and one who feels genuine respect and awe for the mystery of the life he serves, and possibly saves. Or the difference between the mother who knows the value of her efforts in raising her child, and the one who sees it as useless, unpaid drudgery. Or the cashier, or the hairdresser, or the builder: you get the idea.

In India, there is an annual festival day on which everyone blesses the instruments and tools they use for work. Dentists bless their drills, dancers bless their cymbals, and tailors bless their sewing machines. This is a simple but powerful way of bringing home the message that *everyone's* work is a form of spiritual practice, an opportunity for personal growth and to serve others, and to open our own eyes to our good fortune in being able to contribute to our world in any way at all.

# 261. GET WET

If there's a swimming pool close to your office or home, you should be able to squeeze in 20 minutes worth of lengths, shower, change and still have time left over in your lunch hour. Swimming is great aerobic activity, easy on the joints and good for overall toning and cardiovascular fitness.

Afterwards, try a mini hydrotherapy session by varying the temperature when you take your shower — this enhances circulation. The golden rule when varying temperature is always to finish with cold; so, start with warm water, switch to cold for one minute, then back to warm, then cold again.

Other water therapy options are spas and floatation tanks — available in many leisure centres. Relaxing in a floatation tank can be great for creative problem solving.

# 262. CHOOSE CRUELTY-FREE

Worried that your cosmetics may have been treated on animals? Check out your local branch of Beauty Without Cruelty or The Anti-Vivisection Society. They will have a guide to cruelty-free companies and products, including a list of companies that do and do not test on animals. They can also help you with lists of animal-derived ingredients, alternatives to animal testing, and suggestions on how you can help end the use of animals in product testing.

# 263. WORK TO LIVE, DON'T LIVE TO WORK

These ideas and tips may seem obvious — but it's frightening how easily we let them slip, and allow work worries to get all out of proportion:

Start and finish one project each day.

Show your co-workers that you appreciate their help.

Go home at a reasonable hour. You only live once — do you really want to spend that much of your life at work?

Keep a cherished personal item and photos of loved ones on your desk.

Buy a bud vase and always find time to pop a single flower or sprig of greenery into it.

Make sure that you get out of the office at least once a day to breathe fresh air.

Socialise at lunch.

Don't gossip. Studies show that people associate the negative details of gossip with the gossiper, not with the gossipee.

If you work at home, set up a separate office and keep the door closed when you're not working. Don't accept calls, emails or faxes after hours.

Take pride in what you do.

Use up your holiday leave and any days in lieu. You'll bring more to your job if you don't get over-tired.

Don't go to work when you're sick; stay home and rest. When you do go back, you'll feel much better and be a lot more productive.

Bake a treat for your co-workers.

# 264. LIFT WEIGHTS

You don't have to be built like a contender for the world wrestling titles, but if you have a few muscles to start with, you're going to be able to burn more kilojoules than your podgier friends — even if you're just sitting still or lying in bed. Every muscle you have has to burn kilojoules every day in order to sustain itself. Body fat, on the other hand, is lazy — it burns almost nothing. Lifting weights has a triple benefit: it tones your body and keeps you supple, helps strengthen bones and, by building muscles, it helps you get rid of extra kilojoules every week before you even have to think about doing other sorts of exercise. The best place to start learning about weights is at the gym, where a fitness instructor can devise a safe program for you, including free weight lifting, and taking small weights with you on your regular walk.

# 265. TAKE A CHANCE ON DANCE

'To love oneself is the beginning of a lifelong romance.'
**Oscar Wilde**

Dancing is a great way to meet people, even if you're shy, and to let you express yourself creatively, and, naturally, it's great exercise, helping to improve stamina and strength as well as suppleness. All in all, you can't beat dancing for generating happiness, enthusiasm about life, and just plain fun.

Things have come a long way since the agonies of learning ballroom dancing with a pimply, sweaty-handed boy who cared even less about the waltz and fox-trot than you did. There are dozens of different types of dance classes to choose from, including adrenalin-pumping jive and rock 'n' roll, the foot-stomping flamenco, and — for a can't be beaten good time, even if you've got two left feet — line dancing, based on American country music. Here are some more ideas:

**Latin American salsa** Salsa is all in the foot while the Lambada is all in the hips, and involves moving the whole body. Both are ve-e-e-e-ry sexy.

**Jazz ballet** An ideal introduction to dance, and particularly good for body conditioning and flexibility. Excellent as a creative outlet.

**Belly dancing** A wonderful way to tone the waist, hips and abdominal areas. It's used in the Middle East to make childbirth less painful — the pregnant woman dances with friends and relatives to encourage labour, so it's no surprise the same movements have a beneficial effect on everything from lower back problems to period pain. A great way of getting in touch with your femininity.

# 266. CHOOSE SLOW FOOD

Food is one of the easiest areas in which to take charge of your life and make changes — and that's incredibly empowering. Rethinking food from 'fast' to 'slow', for example, can make a huge difference. 'Slow' food is cheaper, healthier and often quicker to prepare, and much of it you can grow, if you want to. 'Slow' food also allows you to become more hospitable and generous. Having food prepared ahead of time makes it easier to spontaneously ask friends to dinner, or give something to a sick neighbour. Here are some ideas to get you started:

**Cook from scratch**. Many fast foods that seem to be a saving really aren't. You may think cooking from scratch takes longer, but it actually doesn't, and it's definitely cheaper than prepared foods. And you have control over what goes in, which includes your own loving energy. Consider the *total* cost of food in terms of money, time and energy.

**Make one-dish wonders**. Taking fresh ingredients and eating them raw or lightly cooked in one pot, wok or bowl saves on cooking time and means more nutrition is passed on to you. All you need is a basic carbohydrate, such as rice or pasta, a few ingredients, like prawns or chicken combined with fresh vegetables, and a bit of flavour from garlic, spices and herbs.

**Get out the crock pot**. Everyone's got one gathering dust in a cupboard somewhere. If you don't you can probably pick one up secondhand at a garage sale. Slow cooking in a crock pot means there's minimum clean-up and the meal is being cooked while you're doing something else. It also makes use of less expensive cuts of meat and all the juices and nutrients are kept in.

**Cook once a month**. If you want 'fast' food without cost and poor nutrition, bulk cooking makes the most of money, time and energy. It capitalises on seasonal sales and an overabundance in the garden. The basic idea is to plan a series of menus, shop once, and then cook all the meals and freeze them. Typically, if you're cooking for a family of four for a month, this will take two full days of shopping, preparation and cooking — a big saving when you compare it with the alternative of frequent shopping and cooking every day.

**Eat slowly**. When it comes to actually eating, slow down here, too. Don't just stuff food into your mouth without thinking. Eat at the table with a pretty plate or a favourite ceramic or wooden bowl. Commune with yourself, the food and the people sharing the meal with you. Put on some soothing music. Chew properly.

# 267. GIVE TO OTHERS

'The only gift is a portion of yourself.'
**Ralph Waldo Emerson**

You don't have to be a millionaire to be able to give money to others. Charitable institutions around the world all agree that well over 75 per cent of the money donated to them every year comes from households earning the average wage, or lower. Anyone can help the world become a better place, regardless of income or social class. By giving to charity you get a real sense of power over your own life, as well as the rush of knowing you've given someone else the opportunity to improve their lives. You get a sense of real connection to the greater community.

Giving is also a practical and satisfying way of expressing yourself and your feelings. So, whether your dollars are few or many, if you'd like to make a difference with them, the first thing is to give some thought to finding a cause that dovetails with your vision and belief systems. What are your key issues? It could be animals, gun control, care of the aged, indigenous culture, children's education, domestic violence, electoral reform, hunger — what means the most to you? The difficult part will probably be settling on just one, for now, that you can put your heart into.

The next step is figuring out how much you can actually afford to give to the charity of your choice. And before you go skidding down that mental slippery dip that says, automatically: 'I'm broke — I can't afford it', consider that, if you earn *any* money at all, then you're that much further ahead than the one billion people in the world who earn precisely *no* money.

It can also be fun — and effective — to pool your dollars with those who have the same ideas or goals. There's nothing that says that you can't just call friends and invite them to share in the process, and in the excitement and satisfaction of giving, too.

Finally, if other priorities mean you really can't afford to donate cash at the moment, that doesn't mean you still can't be of help. Now you can fight hunger with a click of your mouse. Visit the United Nations World Food Program's The Hunger Site (www.thehungersite.org), hit the button labelled 'Donate Free Food', and the site's sponsors will donate half a cent to buy food for people in 80 countries. That may not sound much, but each contribution translates into as much as two and a quarter cups of rice or another staple food. There are often more than 200,000 contributions a day.

# 268. RECAPTURE JOY IN YOUR LIFE

> 'How do I know when my youth is all spent?
> My get up and go has got up and went
> But in spite of it all, I'm able to grin
> And think of the places my get up has been.'
> **Traditional**

Too often, we view life as a serious and difficult activity. Nothing could be further from the truth! Loving your life is easy because it's simply tuning into what's already inside you: your feelings of love, hope, caring, passion, interest and enthusiasm. Remind yourself to loosen up, be creative, and make sure you cherish every moment. Here are some ideas:

Create a 'Memories Box', filled with souvenirs of your life.

Go for a walk on the first day of spring — even if it's pouring.

Shop for Christmas tree ornaments.

Read the Sunday papers.

Hire a classic sports car for the day.

Take a wine-tasting course.

Do you love murder mysteries? Thrill yourself 'to death' by signing up for a 'Murder Mystery' weekend. Check your phone book for organisations that run them.

Go skinny-dipping.

Choose favourite songs and record them on a tape to listen to in the car.

Explore antique shops and markets to find furniture and other stuff for your house.

Splurge on a day of top-to-toe beauty treatments at a local salon.

Hire a horse-drawn carriage and go for a drive through the city.

# 269. CREATE A COMMUNITY

The way I grew up, there were gates cut into back fences so that the kids could run in and out of each other's backyards as they pleased. We tore up and down the pavements, climbed trees and sailed dolls down the drains in newspaper boats. It takes more of an effort to create a sense of community these days, especially if you live in a city — but it's possible. Here are some ideas:

**Approach your neighbours**. Do it one at a time if that's more your style. Ask them over and get to know them. **Shop locally**. Our local fruit market and health food store are two unofficial community centres where like-minded people seem to gather. Sometimes a bookshop or café can serve the same purpose.
**Go along to local community celebrations** — Celtic day, Christmas fireworks, the Spring Fair.
**Form co-operatives**. Practical ideas include a cooking co-op (you get to cook less and plus you get to share the fellowship of preparing meals with others), a garden co-op, or a 'skills co-op', like the one we have at our local school. Everyone pools skills and services like home repairs, computer expertise, childcare, sewing and barbering. Names and phone numbers are circulated and people use those services to channel work and money back into the community.

**Share tools**. Think about sharing bulky and expensive items like lawnmowers, luggage, kids' outdoor play equipment, even household appliances with neighbours once you've got to know them. Benefits include saved money, less time spent shopping and maintaining things, and less need for storage space.
**See if there's a carpool nearby**. If not, start one.
**Go online**. People online can be extraordinarily generous with information and ideas. Witness the time I was trying to scrape up information for a school project on llamas, of all things (due in the next day, naturally!). I got on to a llama farm in the United States who sent me heaps of information plus photos of the cutest llamas for us to download and colour in. Online communities shouldn't be a substitute for face-to-face contact with others, but I really think they have a place in enriching our lives.

# 270. LIVE IN THE REAL WORLD

Try this quick quiz: flip through a selection of magazines and newspapers and ask yourself how many faces you recognise. Chances are, it'll run to dozens, if not hundreds. You'll probably know who some of them are married to, what their kids' names are, and what new projects they're involved in. Now: walk up your street and back down again. How many of your neighbours do you know? Any? Do you know where they grew up? Went to school? How many kids they have? What they do for a living?

It's a scary thought that we can know so much about a world that's not real, and so little about one that is. Celebrities, film stars, models and politicians take up space in our lives that they don't really deserve, space that should be inhabited by family, friends, neighbours, work acquaintances, even household objects, pets, parks and shops that are a part of our immediate world. Starting today, swap the 15 or 30 minutes you spend each day looking at the TV news or flipping through the paper for a walk around your neighbourhood, or a leisurely call to a friend or family member. You'll be amazed how quickly your life will feel earthed and balanced once again.

# 271. GO FOR A PICNIC

One of the best presents I have ever been given was a picnic set; I've used it so often. When there's warm sunshine and a fresh breeze, we pack up and set off — even if it's just to the park opposite. You don't need much — maybe some hard-boiled eggs and pickles, or just fresh bread and a dip or cold cuts. Think of the tasty tidbits Rat and Mole had at their picnic in *Wind in the Willows*. If you've got a few minutes to spare, spread slices of crusty French bread with plenty of butter, then use any of these nifty fillings to make delicious picnic fare. Season well with parsley and pepper.

Cream cheese topped with thinly sliced pastrami, plus slices of tomato and a sprig of basil.

Shredded lettuce with school prawns and finely diced cucumber, tossed in mayonnaise and sprinkled with freshly snipped dill.

Slices of camembert and smoked salmon, topped with caviar or finely chopped capers and pepper.

Thinly sliced cold roast beef with a thin layer of horseradish and topped with snipped chives.

Mash hard-boiled eggs while still warm, with butter and a little cream, salt and pepper to taste, and some chopped tarragon.

Roast pork with lightly cooked shredded cabbage or minced red-skinned apple.

## 272. Try biofeedback

Enthusiasts of biofeedback say that, by learning to control how your body responds to stress, anxiety and tension, you can prevent ailments, and even treat existing diseases. A recent study published in the journal *Psychotherapy and Psychosomatics* (June 1999) showed that just six weekly treatments were able to lower the blood pressure of the volunteers participating in the study.

There are several different types of biofeedback machines: the thing they all have in common is that the therapist will connect you (via electrodes placed on your skin, and sometimes you will be connected by earphones or special glasses as well) to a machine that measures and charts your muscle tension, brain activity, heart rate and breathing patterns. Different types of stimuli are then introduced — typically, this entails being asked to talk, read or draw something about a particular issue or problem. Meanwhile, the therapist carefully watches the readings and analyses them for changes in your physical responses. You are then taught how to control these physical responses with your thoughts and cues, and again your responses are measured. After a series of sessions, you will be able to adjust how your nervous system reacts.

## 273. DON'T GIVE IN TO ROAD RAGE

'Every normal person must be tempted, at times, to spit on his hands, hoist the black flag, and begin slitting throats.'
**H.L. Mencken**

There's no doubt wasting time in traffic leaves you cranky, with a stiff neck and skyrocketing blood pressure. Try this yoga pose to help you calm down and get rid of anger while behind the wheel (not to mention take the driver of the car next to you by surprise!).

Sit up straight, moving your head back in line with your spine; relax your shoulders. Breathe in through your nose. As you exhale, lean slightly forward and open your mouth and eyes as wide as you can. Stick out your tongue and make a 'Rowwrrr!' sound, like a roaring lion. At the same time, lift your hands from the steering wheel and make claws with your fingers. Relax. Repeat five times, relaxing for a moment between each roar.

## 274. Drink while you drive

You can lose as much as half a litre of water an hour when you're driving around the city, even if it's not a hot day. This dehydration triggers emotional changes, which can easily lead to road rage. Have a couple of glasses of water before you set off and fit a bottle holder in your car so you keep yourself topped up when you're on the go.

## 275. SLASH YOUR EXPENSES

Sick and tired of watching your money get frittered away? Well, do something about it! Get tough, and try the following experiment for a week: spend half of what you do now. Before you panic and say you can't possibly cut everything in half, consider the following very effective money savers:

Don't use the clothes drier.

Put off getting your hair cut.

Don't eat out or get any takeaway meals.

Cut petrol costs by grouping errands, walking, car-pooling, or staying home.

Use up the contents of the pantry and fridge rather than tossing them out at the end of the week.

Use half as much toothpaste and shampoo as you normally would.

Turn off the lights.

Even if you don't last the week, if you're serious about de-junking and de-stressing your life, it's important to realise the point: little steps like this make a whole lot of difference towards debt-proofing your life. Without debt, you can save — and with savings, you can create choices for yourself.

# 276. Make your own clothes

It's not hard, especially with today's really easy patterns and detailed instructions. If you haven't got a clue where to start, take a few lessons. They're offered by most adult-education programs and fabric shops. Or ask a friend who does sew to help you get started.

Making your own clothes — even just a few simple tops and kids' clothes — is a marvellously satisfying hobby, and you will save yourself a very great deal of money. I also believe that, if we made more of our own clothes, we'd treat them better and wear them longer!

At the very least, learn to mend. If you know how to repair a seam, replace a button, and patch a rip, you'll stretch your clothing dollars by a mile, and have more left over to spend on other things, or to save.

# 277. CLEAN OUT YOUR HANDBAG

Making sure you've got exactly what you need wherever you go can make the difference between feeling in control of your life, or not. Most of us tote around bags that are best described as 'big, black holes', full of all sorts of clutter and grot. Start by chucking out tissues, theatre stubs and lolly wrappers, and try using this checklist as a guide:

**Moisturiser, containing SPF15+** Sunlight is the major cause of wrinkles.

**Fragrance stick** To give you a boost of energy.

**A notebook, diary, or electronic organiser**

**A good book** Reading keeps your brain toned — use every opportunity to whip through another couple of pages.

**A clean handkerchief instead of tissues** More stylish, less expensive, and better for the environment.

**Mini toothbrush and toothpaste** Having these will mean you can always have a fresh mouth.

**Healthy snack** A fruit bar or banana will perk you up during energy slumps.

**Up-to-date make-up** Throw out old mascara and foundation as it can get dirty and cause skin problems.

## 278. LEARN HOW TO SAUNTER

> 'Everything that happens to you is your teacher. The secret is to sit at the feet of your own life and be taught by it.'
> **Mahatma Gandhi**

Stroll, meander, saunter — all gentle, easy words that lilt off the tongue. But 'saunter' is a bit special. Do you know where it came from?

In medieval Europe, there was once a Christian custom known as 'sainting', which involved naming and blessing certain holy or magical places in the name of various saints. Rocks, stone cairns, caves, cliffs, lookouts, springs — very often, places that had held spiritual significance since the times of the ancient Romans and Druids — were all 'sainted'. Even birds and animals were blessed as belonging to particular saints. 'Saunter' is derived from 'saint' and even though the meaning has changed a little over the ages, remembering its roots can make the act of sauntering even more special.

It's a beautiful idea that's even more relevant today, I feel. Every time you take a walk, take a saunter instead. As you walk, do so with reverence and respect for nature. Take notice of all the many blessings that come your way in your hurried life — a bird singing, leaves rustling in a tree overhead, a weed struggling valiantly through the path, the breeze in your hair. Listen to your spirit and to the Spirit all around you. Be open to the messages from the matrix that supports all life.

# 279. CREATE ORDER

It's not just the big issues, like getting your finances under control and getting rid of clutter that sap your energy and make you think you just can't cope. It's the water-on-the-stone style of chaos and irritation on the home front that makes you insecure and confused. Try these routines and rituals to bring a little more harmony into your home:

**Mealtimes** Try to have your meals at a reasonably regular time. Plan to make at least one a week (or more, your choice) an opportunity to cook something special, and enjoy the company of family and friends. Planning menus for the week, using slow-cooking or bulk-cooking techniques, will make mealtimes go a little more smoothly.

**Mornings** Are your mornings a drama of unironed clothes, mislaid papers and bags, and hurling yourself out the door without time for breakfast? It's time to get organised. All these things can be attended to the night before, meaning you don't have to get up too early or to rush.

**Coming home** As you walk through the front door, be aware that you're switching from the outer to the inner world. Hang up your coat, tidy away your bag, take off your shoes — then put on your slippers or walk barefoot. This is a mental signal that you've left work behind.

**Chores** Have a routine when it comes to household tasks in which everyone knows what they're supposed to contribute.

# 280. TURN OFF THE TV

... especially if you're not really watching anything! Mark the programs you do want to watch, and switch them off as soon as they're over. Then you can put on a relaxation tape instead — listening to the natural sounds of wind chimes or rain will calm you down.

Watching too much TV encourages the brain to be passive. Spend at least one hour a day doing mental exercises, such as reading, playing chess, doing a crossword or playing board games to stimulate your mental agility. Being mentally active can slow the progression of memory loss that occurs with age.

Brain researchers have found that the brains of rats shrink if they are deprived of thought-provoking toys. When one group of rats was raised in a mentally impoverished environment, the part of the brain which is closely associated with memory shrank by 25 per cent! It's not a test that's likely to be repeated in human trials anytime soon (the huge media conglomerates wouldn't be queuing to fund any study along these lines?!?), but we know what the result would be anyway.

Make an effort to keep your brain active. Exercising your brain doesn't have to be intellectually demanding — just reading the paper counts. Novelty, though, is the best brain booster, so try some new life-enhancing hobbies.

## 281.   DON'T PANIC

'When written in Chinese, the word 'crisis' is composed of two characters. One represents danger, and the other represents opportunity.'
**John F. Kennedy**

Do you feel as though you are just lurching from one crisis to the next? The most important thing you can do when your life is like a pressure cooker is to learn to manage your time, and to set priorities.

You have to put yourself first. Ask yourself: is this really what I want to put my time into right now? Am I putting my time into the people and things that matter most to me? If not, why on earth not — and what am I doing about changing it?

You may find you need to cut down on the time you spend with people whose ideas and behaviour no longer fit in your life. Using time wisely also means leaving empty space for yourself — time to do absolutely nothing, so that you allow new ideas and feelings to come to the surface. That way a crisis — whatever it is — becomes an opportunity to explore life at a slower, more thoughtful pace.

# 282. LOVE YOUR BODY

It's easier to feel happy about your looks when you know you are presenting your best self to the world. As you begin to appreciate your own appearance, your envy of others disappears. Superficial changes can work very well: use make-up to enhance your best features, and invest in a good haircut. And dress to bring out your good points.

**Celebrate your body through movement**. A non-competitive, 'non-beauty' physical interest like yoga or tai chi helps you to look at your body in a more detached, less emotional way. All you are asking your body to do is learn a series of movements — not to look attractive or slim, or whatever. And, when you begin to do the movements smoothly, you feel a terrific sense of achievement. Another fun thing to try is belly dancing — as a bonus, it makes a positive asset out of a wobbly stomach! Your local community college or leisure centre is bound to offer courses.

**Indulge yourself**. The key is to do it the right way — not by shovelling mud cake in front of a soppy movie on TV, but by spoiling yourself with a treat that will make you feel good about your body. It could be as simple as a hand massage and manicure, or something more long term, such as a course of seaweed wraps to target cellulite. If you can't afford salon treatments, team up with a friend and take turns to treat each other.

**'Accentuate the positive . . . eliminate the negative'**, goes the song. Too often, people with a poor body image aren't seeing their whole body at all — they're only seeing small bits of it, say, the lumpy thighs or the floppy upper arms. As an exercise, make a list of what you consider to be figure or appearance flaws on a piece of paper. Then make a list of the things you do like about your appearance. Go back to the first list and cross out the things you can't change. Now — put a tick next to the things you can change and want to work actively on. Finally, compare the two lists and make up one or two 'compensatory' affirmations for days when you feel you might need a confidence boost. For example, 'I accept that I have a big nose, but I have really lovely eyes', or 'My hair is not my best feature, but I have very sexy feet and ankles.'

# 283. HAVE A REGULAR MASSAGE

Relieve tension and tiredness with a massage: it can stimulate and relax the muscles, improve circulation and aid digestion. Getting the blood moving faster around your body increases the flow of energising oxygen. It gets the circulation back into tight, tense areas, such as the back, neck and shoulders.

While long, slow movements can leave you relaxed enough to fall asleep, brisk techniques have a more revitalising effect. Shiatsu is a Japanese form of finger pressure massage which aims to stimulate the meridians (energy channels) of the body's 12 main organs, releasing tension and letting energy flow. Why not try some shiatsu on yourself? To stimulate energy, find the point about three inches below your knee joint, on the outer side of the leg. It's slightly tender to touch, so you should know when you've found it. This is one of the great balancers of qi (pronounced chi) — the body's vital energy, according to traditional Chinese medical theory. Press deeply with your thumb for five to ten minutes.

# 284. TAKE A WALKING MEDITATION

If the more familiar seated style of meditation doesn't seem to work for you, try something different — a walking meditation. This is a wonderful way to help cultivate stillness and calm in your daily life, helping clear your mind of clutter and so improve concentration when you return to your other tasks.

1.  Start your walk, counting the first five steps in your head as you do so: 'One, two, three, four, five . . .'
2.  With the sixth step, begin at one again, and count up to six steps.
3.  With the seventh step, begin at one again, and count up to seven steps.
4.  Continue the pattern of walking and counting in increasing numbers until you have reached ten.
5.  Now, begin all over again, counting your steps from one to five.
6.  Repeat the entire sequence as many times as you like.

If you lose track of how many steps you're up to at any point (and you most likely will), just go back to the beginning of the cycle of five steps.

# 285. Exercise while you wait

Use all your spare time while you're waiting — for a meeting, in the supermarket queue, or to pick up the kids at school — even if it's just a few minutes — to calm and energise yourself. Try these three exercises:

**Shoulder-shrugging** Sit comfortably with your arms free. Bring your shoulders right up to your ears, shrugging as hard as you can. Intensify the tension in your body as much as possible. Breathe in as you shrug upwards. Tilt your head back as far as it will go — then exhale, and let your shoulders flop down and your head come up slowly. You should feel a sense of heat in your neck — this is because you've allowed more blood to circulate through this high-tension area.

**Foot twirls** Curl your toes as tight as you can and release. Curl your entire foot down towards your heel and then stretch it upwards as far as you comfortably can. Now circle your feet slowly clockwise and anticlockwise.

**Finger stretches** Clench your hands into fists. Then release them, opening the fingers wide. Stretch your fingers and bend your hand back at right angles to your wrist. Then bend your hand down so your fingers point toward the floor. Make fists again and circle clockwise, and then anticlockwise.

## 286. FEEL SEXY

'Love is the answer. But while you're waiting for the answer, sex raises some pretty good questions.'
**Woody Allen**

Loss of sex drive is no laughing matter, especially when you get older and busier, but there's no reason why you can't have a fulfilling sex life. Apart from feeling good, regular sex is also good for your health: initially it releases the high-energy hormone adrenaline, and once it's over endorphins give you a contented afterglow. As an added incentive, researchers in Edinburgh have found that couples who make love three times a week look ten years younger than those who have sex less than twice a week. Make a date to get horizontal today!

**Make love.** Regular sex is one way to conquer vaginal dryness.

**Perform pelvic floor exercises.** Working the muscles around the vagina can increase your pleasure during sex. These are the muscles you would use to stop your flow of urine. Tighten them, hold for ten seconds, then release. Repeat this about six to eight times a day.

**Try supplements.** Studies link low sex drive in men and women to deficiencies in vitamins A, B complex, C and E, plus the minerals zinc and selenium. Women can also try the herbs wild yam and schizandra — said to increase libido by influencing progesterone production.

# 287. EAT A RAINBOW

It's not just 'eating your greens' that will keep you well. You need to eat as many differently coloured fruit and vegetables as possible, because each colour contains different nutrients that work together. So, when you visit the greengrocer this week, think outside the routine apples and bananas, and look for:

**Red** (tomatoes, ruby grapefruit, watermelons) Contains lycopene, a carotenoid that reduces the risk of breast and cervical cancer by up to 40 per cent.

**Purple** (blackberries, blackcurrants, grapes) Contains flavonoids that prevent heart disease by stopping low-density lipoprotein from building up in the arteries.

**Blue** (blueberries, bilberries) Contains anthocyanadins, powerful antioxidants that boost the production of collagen, a substance that helps the skin maintain its elasticity, and support good eyesight.

**Green** (spinach, broccoli, brussels sprouts, lettuce, cabbage) Contains glucosinolates, a vital nutrient for the prevention of cancer.

**Orange** (carrots, apricots, mangoes, pumpkins) Contains beta carotene, which boosts immunity against viral infections such as colds and flu, as well as skin conditions like acne.

**Yellow** (corn, yellow capsicums, grapefruit) Contains lutein, which helps protect the eyes from cataracts and other age-related disorders, such as macular degeneration.

# 288. STAY SANE WHILE YOU DRIVE

There's a well-known list of stressors, ranked in order of impact on your health and happiness, which includes illness, moving house, filling out tax forms, going through a divorce, and losing a loved one. Oddly, it doesn't include driving which, I think, should be right up there with the super-stressors as an unpleasant and uncomfortable thing to do to yourself. Here's how to make it a little bit better:

**Choose music with care.** It shouldn't be too aggressive, nor too sleepy. If you have to drive a long way each day to work, investigate alternatives that will make you feel your time is being spent productively, such as self-help tapes or talking books.

**Be tidy.** Throw out all the old papers, kids' toys, wrappers, takeaway food containers and plastic bags. Keep basic requirements, like a street directory and sunscreen, in the glove box. Store CDs and cassettes in a lidded box which fits neatly under a seat.

**Clean the car regularly.** Put a few drops of lemon oil in the vacuum bag to sweeten the air, and, as a finishing touch, wipe down the dash and steering wheel with a piece of cottonwool dipped in lemon or grapefruit oil.

**Keep something lucky in the car.** The Chinese have the right idea — they place holographic balls or feng shui mirrors on pieces of red ribbon from their rear view mirrors to scare off evil spirits. With all the aggression on the roads, you need as much positive energy going for you as is possible. Consider a lucky charm or symbol that means something to you — a Star of David, a Kwan Yin, a photo of a spiritual leader or an animal, or a sticker or picture from a child.

**If you can't beat em . . .** If you're stuck in traffic, roll up the windows and take advantage of the fact it's one of the few places where people can't hear you. So — if you want to sing at the top of your lungs, sigh deeply, practise your deep breathing, recite poetry or positive affirmations, or even scream — you can! Really let go, and release all that tension.

# 289. GET RID OF HAY FEVER

It's called hay fever because symptoms mainly appear during the high pollen season, which peaks in midsummer. Early morning, late afternoon and early evening are the times when you are most at risk. A bad bout is not to be taken lightly: watering eyes, constant sneezing, and a throbbing sinus headache are just some of the likely effects. Prevention tactics include:

Stay indoors when pollen counts are highest.

Keep car windows closed when driving.

Wear sunglasses to prevent pollen grains getting in your eyes.

Wash your hands before touching your eyes.

Apply a thin layer of Vaseline just inside nostrils to trap pollen.

Wash your hair and clothes frequently to get rid of pollen.

Ask someone else to mow the lawn for you.

Don't smoke and avoid smoky atmospheres.

A daily dose of one gram of vitamin C has an antihistamine effect and helps boost your immunity. A vitamin A supplement will also help reduce inflammation of the mucous membranes, and herbs such as licorice, horseradish and garlic ease irritation. Homoeopathic remedies include *Pulsatilla*, *Euphrasia* and *Arsen alb*.

# 290. Make scents

Nanna was wonderful: a tireless read-alouder, doll-clothes sewer, story-teller and walk-taker. I loved to play at her dressing table, where she kept her silver-backed brushes and a cut glass bottle of lavender water. As a special treat, if I was tired and cranky, she would pat the back of my neck with this wonderfully refreshing recipe:

**Lavender Water**
  - 200 ml (7 fl oz) boiling water
  - 3 tablespoons dried lavender
  - 150 ml (5 fl oz) rosewater
  - 1 tablespoon (3/5 fl oz) vodka
  - pinch powdered nutmeg
  - 15–20 drops lavender essential oil

Pour boiling water over dried lavender and leave to cool; strain. Combine lavender infusion with rosewater, vodka, nutmeg and essential oil; pour through coffee filter several times to get rid of resins. Transfer to a glass-stoppered bottle.

Apart from being wonderfully cooling, lavender water can be used as a mouthwash and a refreshing skin tonic, or to make a soothing compress for a tension headache. Lavender's calming effects will induce restful sleep — try sprinkling a few drops on your pillow or into an evening bath. Oh, and fleas, flies and midges all detest the smell, so you can also use lavender water as a natural insect repellent.

# 291. CHANGE THE WAY YOU THINK

'No one can make you feel inferior without your consent.'
**Eleanor Roosevelt**

Are you caught in a negative-thinking trap? By changing the way you think, you'll be more in control and your self-esteem will soar. Try these techniques:

**Avoid blaming your past**. Having thoughts like 'I'm always so stupid', or 'Why is everyone always so horrid to me?' only set the stage for more of the same. Try to cancel those thoughts and go into new situations with an open mind.

**List the advantages and disadvantages of negative thoughts and feelings**. An example of a negative thought is: 'I'll never make new friends.' This is a good trick for seeing the pointlessness of thinking this way.

**Be specific**. And, while you're making that list, check the statements themselves. Instead of a blanket statement like: 'I'm no good at that', try seeing what aspects of the activity you're a little bit good at, as well as what you're not. Play up your strengths — and work on your weaknesses.

**Remember you can't be liked all of the time**. Trying to make other people like you is often driven by a need for security. It's simple — not everyone is going to like you, so you might as well just be yourself.

**Don't expect to get everything right**. If you expect things to go perfectly, you'll inevitably be disappointed, and put yourself on the road to being a control freak. Try to accept that some things will just plain go wrong.

**Give yourself a little push**. Avoiding challenges and confrontations may be the safe way to travel, but you'll never really find out what you're capable of. Setting yourself little challenges will help build self-confidence.

**Don't be responsible for everyone else**. Let them make their mistakes and have their successes without you trying to manage things for them.

## 292. HAVE A PLAN

Doesn't matter whether it's a day plan, month plan, a year plan, or all three. You can revise them a hundred times — but you'll never get anywhere without a plan.

Consider the three critical areas: your work, your finances and your family and home life. Set goals and time limits — and then start writing down your plan.

Make things visual whenever you can. Draw up graphs, lists, charts, whatever helps you see exactly where you are and visually illustrate your progress. Post your goals where you can see them, too.

# 293. STIFFEN YOUR BACKBONE

Wanting or desiring something is not the same as having the willpower to get it! You need to train your mind and emotions to respond to the positive commands you create, and these positive thoughts must become the dominant perceptions with which your mind connects every day. Doing a 30-minute meditation once a day, for instance, and then returning to anxiety-filled thoughts the rest of the time cancels out the positive influence of the meditation. Keeping your focus in a positive direction, so you can quickly eclipse a negative thought with a positive one, takes practice. The use of a mantra or phrase you repeat silently to yourself is very effective in learning to identify and focus your willpower.

## 294. WALK EVERY DAY

'All truly great thoughts are conceived while walking,' wrote the philosopher Friedrich Nietzche. Of all the simple changes you can make to detox and de-junk your life, this would have to be the best, easiest and cheapest. So, why don't we do it? No time? — make time! You're in an area with congested air quality? Raining? Wear a waterproof jacket! Find a park! Don't feel well? A quick walk will probably make you feel better! C'mon, going for a brisk half-hour walk will help you to stay trim and boost your mood — particularly if it's sunny outside. The sun's rays can have a remarkable effect on our physical and emotional wellbeing. Without exposure to sunlight we become depressed. Even if it's not a sunny day, natural daylight will boost your mood. Don't strain yourself — build up slowly and follow these tips.

When going uphill, concentrate on tensing your bottom muscles.

Keep your knees slightly bent — don't lock up.

Flex your calf muscles to gather pace when walking uphill.

To pick up speed, move your feet faster rather than taking longer steps.

Wear supportive walking shoes.

Strike confidently with your heels as you land, toes lifted.

# 295. LISTEN TO MUSIC

Not many people know that the gentle, whimsical Hans Christian Andersen, author of dearly loved childhood favourites such as *The Ugly Duckling* and *Thumbelina*, was also a classically trained musician. Once when he was asked about how he was able to devote himself to two great talents, he said: 'Where words fail, music speaks.'

The idea that music can help heal and boost wellbeing is a very old one. The Greeks believed that flute music could ward off the plague; Cherokee Indian medicine men sang songs to cure snakebite. As recently as World War II, musicians were commissioned to play for patients suffering physical and emotional trauma. The first of many research studies into the healing power of music noted, among other things, that music evened out pulse rate and blood pressure, and reduced pain. Here's how music can improve your life:

**Control pain**. Some of the best research into music has been done on pain management. Pregnant women who listen to their favourite music during labour are 50 per cent less likely to have an anaesthetic, according to a Texan study. Try flutes, such as Japanese bamboo, or natural sounds such as ocean waves and dolphin calls.

**Manage anger**. Soft gentle music just gets on my nerves if I'm already irritated. Playing a raunchy rock number like Natalie Cole's 'Wild Women Do' or 'China Grove' by the Doobie Brothers, or turning up the volume on 'Mars' from Holst's *The Planets* helps you confront your anger and work with it.

**Enhance sleep**. Music can also be used to combat stress, and make you feel more relaxed. Research at Berlin University has found that listening to music can reduce levels of the stress hormone cortisol. Try soothing pieces, such as Beethoven's 'Pastoral', Vivaldi's string quartets or Mozart's clarinet concerto. A more contemporary choice is Harry Nilsson's 'Everybody's Talkin''.

**Improve immunity**. UK research has shown that when you listen to music you like, your body produces more immune-boosting T-cells. This helps protect you from a range of illnesses, from the common cold to heart disease and cancer. Try moody music that encourages you to explore your emotions, such as Enya, Chopin or Clannad, and inspiring, uplifting classics like Louis Armstrong's 'What a Wonderful World', Judy Garland singing 'C'mon, Get Happy' or Glen Miller's toe-tapping 'In the Mood'.

# 296. TACKLE MONDAY-ITIS

That feeling of mild dread can start on Sunday afternoon and ruin your whole weekend.

Start by finishing off your working week the previous Friday on a good note. Rather than shuffling problems from one side of the desk to the other, set aside the last hour of the day to sort them out — or at least work out how you can tackle them on Monday. This will give you a feeling of being in control.

Don't sleep in on the weekend, either — research says it compounds your chances of being in a bad mood on Monday because it makes you tireder when you do have to get up on time.

Then, on Monday morning, try listening to a different radio station or watching a different TV program — simply switching from pop to classical or the sight of a different face can give you a cheer-up.

# 297. WASTE NOT

Why is there so much waste in our society? Paper, food, power, fuel, packaging materials, just to name a few. Some of it is just unconscious. We have so much and have had it for so long that we just don't realise the extent of our abundance. We can go shopping any time of the day or night, and buy anything we want from anywhere in the world. If we're hungry, there are restaurants open; if we want entertainment, there are all-night cafés, cars and clubs. For a price, of course.

Think about how you can reduce unnecessary waste in your life. How much packaging surrounds the items you buy? Do you make frequent trips to the supermarket? Do you throw away things like vegetable and fruit peels, eggshells and coffee grounds? Do you leave the water running while you're cleaning your teeth or peeling potatoes? Do you use disposable plates or napkins? Waste is one of the first areas you can begin to control, simplify and de-junk your life. Look for alternatives that use less packaging. Buy in bulk. Use cloth napkins. Start a compost pile. When we focus on our basic needs, and prune back waste, things seem to work better.

# 298. MAKE YOUR WATER SAFER

Is bottled water any better than what comes out of your tap? That depends on what's coming out of your tap.

Water that looks brown or reddish may be caused by iron solder somewhere between your water source and your house. If the water smells or tastes unpleasant, chlorine or algae may be the culprit. Neither of these pose a substantial risk, unless they are ongoing. Far more important, particularly if you have small children and live in an older-style house, is to check for lead, once widely used as a solder. This can leach into water and cause slowed mental development in children, and kidney problems and high blood pressure in adults.

If you're concerned, call your local health department and have your water tested. If you identify any contaminants, you can buy an appropriate filter. Read the manufacturer's claims carefully to be sure it has been evaluated to remove the contaminants you're targeting, as not all devices filter all things. And remember to change filters regularly — it's a common oversight.

# 299. CONSIDER DITCHING THE CAR

Air pollution is something that affects us all. Although there have been massive improvements in air quality in the last 50 years, air pollution continues to affect human health and the natural environment. Road vehicles are major source of many pollutants, and responsible for nearly all carbon monoxide emissions — so why not think about whether you need to use the car all the time?

There are alternatives. Why not use public transport when you can, or carpool when possible — especially for the school run. Walking or cycling for shorter journeys is another option: physical exercise has obvious health benefits, and it saves you money. Walking your children to school also gives them valuable road experience for when they are older and more independent.

Of course, some journeys have to be taken in the car, but there are still greener ways to run and drive a car. Have it serviced regularly to maintain efficient running. Avoid unnecessary short trips, as a cold engine produces 60 per cent more pollution than when warm. Don't leave the vehicle idling when cold — drive away immediately but gently. Use or switch to unleaded petrol. For more practical advice, contact your local pollution information service.

# 300. Get smarter about technology

Remember — these products and services are supposed to support your life, and give you pleasure — not make your life more complicated.

**Mobile phone** Only give your mobile phone number to your partner, the kids and the babysitter; avoid giving it to work colleagues. Using the phone only for emergencies stops you from becoming a slave to it.

**Television** Cancel cable TV. Just how many re-runs can you watch, anyway? And don't splurge on a state of the art TV. An older model colour or black and white TV works just as well — but not so well as to encourage mindless hours of viewing — plus it has no remote control. It'll get you down to an hour or so a week, if that.

**E-tailing** Check out e-tailers when it comes time to buy birthday or Christmas presents. The prices are the same, if not better, than in regular retail stores, and the cost of mailing is balanced by the savings you make on time, driving and parking. Same goes for grocery shopping and banking — do them online.

# 301. EASE PMS

These seven natural solutions could work for you:

**Take a geranium bath**. Geranium oil is thought to balance hormones by acting on the adrenal glands, which are active in everything from regulating sodium levels to influencing sexual development. Add five to eight drops to a warm bath.

**Sip dandelion leaf tea**. Dandelion leaf is a natural diuretic and will help ease bloating. Steep a quarter of a cup of dried leaves (available in health food stores) in 150 ml water.

**Make magnesium a habit**. Recent clinical trials have shown that magnesium helps reduce water retention and soothe nerves. Take a 200 mg supplement daily.

**Be a child**. For lower back pain and cramping, try the yoga Child pose. Kneel on the floor, separating your knees slightly, and sit back on your heels. Place a rolled towel across the tops of your thighs, then lean forward and rest your forehead gently on the floor. Relax your arms alongside your body, palms facing the ceiling. Hold for at least 30 seconds, breathing deeply.

**Try acupuncture**. According to Chinese tradition, cramps can be caused by stagnant blood in the uterus. Acupuncture is thought to trigger several chemical reactions that increase blood flow and relieve contractions.

**Rub on natural progesterone cream**. It's available at health food stores. Apply a quarter to a half-teaspoon to the breasts twice a day as soon as your breasts start to feel tender.

**Schedule a lymphatic massage**. The lymph system helps maintain the correct fluid balance in the body. The therapist will knead your neck, groin, armpits, backs of your knees and insides of your elbows (where lymph nodes are located) with a gentle pumping motion.

# 302. BEAT FUNGAL INFECTIONS

Last summer, a friend came to me for help. She was uncomfortable wearing sandals because of an ugly toenail. It was a mass of thick flakes, a sure sign of a fungal infection. Toenail fungus is fairly common (fungi thrive in moist, dark environments such as closed shoes), and notoriously difficult to eradicate.

I suggested she apply grapefruit seed extract directly to her toenail with a tiny paint brush (like those sold in watercolour sets). It is a powerful antifungal agent available in health food stores and also through herbalists on prescription. I also encouraged her to go without shoes as often as possible and to keep her feet and toenails clean and dry. She took to drying her toes with a hair drier, making sure every bit of dampness was removed. Finally, she took the herb goldenseal to boost her immune system. Her efforts paid off, and this summer she'll be showing off her healthy toenails in sandals.

# 303. COPE BETTER

The pressure is unbearable, you're being pushed well beyond your limits — before you say or do anything you might regret, try one of these coping strategies:

**Do your maths**. Using a scale of one to ten, with one being the equivalent of a minor hassle and ten being a true catastrophe, assign a number to whatever it is that's making you feel anxious. You'll find that most problems you encounter rate somewhere in the two to six range — in other words, they're not really such a big deal.

**Don't grit your teeth**. Stress tends to settle in certain parts of our bodies, the jaw being one of them. When things get hectic, try this tip: place your index fingertips on your jaw joints, just in front of your ears; clench your teeth and inhale deeply. Hold the breath for a moment, and as you exhale say, 'Ah-h-h-h-h,' then unclench your teeth. Repeat a few times.

**Compose a mantra**. Devise an affirmation — a short, clear, positive statement that focuses on your coping abilities. Affirmations are a good way to silence the self-critical voice we all carry with us that only adds to our stress. The next time you feel as if your life is just one disaster after another, repeat ten times, 'I feel calm. I can handle this.'

**Count to ten**. Step away from the stressor and collect yourself. You can also look away for a moment during heated conversation, or put a caller on hold while you take a few calming breaths. Use your time-out to take a few deep breaths, stretch, touch your toes, or recite an affirmation.

# 304. LEARN CANDLE MEDITATION

Gazing into a candle flame is a simple, effective way of quieting thoughts and focusing your mind.

Sit quietly at a table, and place a candle in a holder in front of you. Light it.

Look steadily at the candle, and take five deep breaths, one after the other. While you are doing so, look straight at the flame — note its colour, the shape, how it moves and flickers. Then gently close your eyes.

With your eyes closed, keep the image of the candle flame in your mind's eye, still breathing in and out, and so releasing tension.

Choose the colour of your candles to enhance your mood. If you're seeking love, pink; you want to get in the mood for a celebration, orange; to encourage conversation, yellow; to restore harmony, green; you're tense and need to calm down, blue.

# 305. SEE OPPORTUNITIES

> 'Keep sowing your seeds, for you never know which one will grow —
> perhaps it all will.'
> **Ecclesiastes 11:6**

My father was a great one for seizing opportunities: 'Carpe diem, darling,' he'd say. I miss him and think of him often, particularly when I look at my older son, Edward, who is so very like him. Ed told me this great story the other day, and it's just the sort of thing that Dad would have liked, too:

There are these two Westerners working in the Saudi. They're bored, and unbeknownst to each other, they decide to get their Arab drivers to take them on a trip into the desert in their respective Cadillacs. The drivers get a bit too much into the spirit of things and the joy-ride becomes a hair-raising race. Finally, even though there are no other cars for miles and miles, the two Cadillacs manage to have a head-on collision. Luckily, no one is hurt. The two Westerners, with thunderous expressions, get out of the cars, shouting and hurling abuse at each other. But the two Arab drivers jump out, rush towards each other with open arms and shout: 'This is wonderful! Wonderful! Allah must have wanted us to meet!'

Consider the possibilities in each new situation, even if things seem as though they couldn't possibly be to your advantage.

# 306. MAKE EXTRA MONEY

Even if you're already working, you may be able to do a little extra — preferably something already linked to a hobby or interest that you enjoy. If you draw, could you sell your pictures at local market? If you like to garden, could you mow lawns or weed for someone else? If you go for a walk every day, you could even do letter-box drops.

Another idea is to find out about multi-level marketing and party plan networks. You don't have to get involved in selling if it doesn't interest you, but often products like detergent are as good as the equivalent product purchased in a supermarket — and anything up to five times cheaper. Plus you have the convenience of at-home shopping and, usually, a money-back guarantee. Find out for yourself. Same goes for kids' clothes, car supplies, knives, and kitchenware.

If you do get a pay rise at work, ignore it. Whatever it is, arrange for it to be put straight into a savings account. You didn't have it before, so hopefully you won't miss it! Another income-enhancing idea you may not have thought of is to barter your time, and your skills. If you can spare just two hours a month to do voluntary work, you can buy hugely discounted food hampers — prices start at just $10. Plus, try bartering products and services in your neighbourhood. For instance, a supply of your home-grown flowers or vegetables might get your lawns mowed, your gutters cleaned, or your car filled with petrol.

# 307. Face up to boredom

When it comes to thinking up something to say about different human moods and feelings, I invariably find that the Bard will have said it first — and usually far better than I ever could. Consider Hamlet's words on boredom: 'How weary, stale, flat and unprofitable seem to me all the uses of this world.' It's true: being bored does put you on the fast track to feeling far worse than just fed-up or under-utilised: in no time, you can find yourself in a full blue funk of depression about everyone and everything. In short, being bored can be as stressful and as risky for your mental health as being overworked.

If you're bored at work, think ahead, and plan rewards for yourself for getting through mundane tasks. A simple checklist where you can see the ticks building up can really work. You could promise yourself a cup of hot chocolate when you've finished, or save work you enjoy for later. Your rewards needn't be expensive, but the occasional impulse buy — a new magazine or a lipstick — can have a cheering effect, as long as you don't risk a blown-out credit card. It's also important to identify when you work best: if you're more alert in the morning, do the most demanding work then, and save easier tasks for later.

## 308. CHANGE NOW

If you're going to change — change now. People often say that, until they can work out what option is best for them, they feel safer not doing anything. While there's certainly a place for considered thought in making choices, postponing decisions can be dangerous. It can be wiser sometimes to start anywhere and just do something, rather than to do nothing at all. It does not have to be a big step. The important thing is to break away from the pattern of thinking and worrying about the 'what ifs' and 'if onlys', and to stop going round in circles, and that is always a good beginning.

# 309.  VISUALISE PEACE AND QUIET

'The mind is its own place. In itself it can make a heaven of Hell,
and hell of Heaven.'
**John Milton**

Visualisation is one of the ultimate stress-busting techniques, helping you to see
your way out of a stressful situation, to relax, and to improve your mood.

Practising visualisation is a little like meditation, but without the structure.
It is very easy to do, and simply involves putting yourself into a relaxed state of
mind and allowing the power of your thoughts to take you to a place of peace,
quiet and contentment. By creating this sense of inner peace, even for just
ten minutes, you completely switch off the adrenalin-charged 'fight or flight'
response, which is our age-old response to any sort of danger or worry.

Try this method: close your eyes and begin to imagine a scene that gives you
pleasure. Take your time — ten minutes is ideal. (If you're alone, so much the
better, but even if you're in a busy office, or beset by children you can still take
those ten minutes and go and sit in the bathroom. Do it. You'll feel so much
better able to cope when you re-emerge.) 'See' yourself in the picture in as much
detail as possible. It could be a place you know already — a stream, a quiet ferny
bank — or somewhere from your childhood. In your mind, touch the leaves, run
your fingers through the water, let the breeze play with your hair, hear the song of
the birds. Know that you can always come to this special place and be safe, be
calm. Then, keeping your eyes closed, bring yourself slowly back to everyday
feelings. Finally, open your eyes.

## 310. MAKE LISTS

The twentieth and twenty-first centuries do not have a monopoly on stress and confusion. Thousands of years ago, the philosopher Lao-tzu set down this succinct motto for people with difficulty getting organised: 'Deal with it before it happens.'

If you've got a list of jobs that need doing, write them down — now! Those uncompleted jobs around the house, things to do at work, people you must phone. Set yourself two — just two — and make sure you do them. Then, whatever else the day throws at you, at least you'll have achieved something. For real satisfaction, choose two of the things which keep working their way to the bottom of your list!

# 311. PUT THE KETTLE ON

There's few things as good as a good cup of tea, and few things as woeful as a lousy one. Nanna also used to say that there were few things that couldn't be cured by a good cup of tea (adding, that, if the tea didn't work by itself, to add a good shot of whisky). I think it's important to have a singing kettle. I like to listen to its rise and fall as it boils for hot cups of tea on bitterly cold days. Nanna always had a kettle on the stove. They always seemed to drink a lot of tea in my family — a cup when someone came around, a cup before going to bed. Any excuse for a cup of tea.

Heat the teapot first, by putting hot water in it for a few minutes.

Empty the water from the pot. Put in one teaspoonful of tea for each person, and one for the pot.

Pour boiling water over tea.

Let the tea stand for three to five minutes, depending on how strong you like it to be.

Pour the tea through a tea strainer into the cups. (You really can't beat good bone china - it tastes so much better than in a mug!)

Serve the tea. Offer milk or lemon according to preference. If it's afternoon tea time, tea should be accompanied by a nice slice of homemade sultana cake.

For something different, blend two tablespoons of well-dried finely shredded orange peel in to every three-quarters of a cup of regular tea for a subtle, refreshing flavour change.

## 312. CREATE YOUR OWN LUCK

'Shallow men believe in luck. Strong men believe in cause and effect.'
**Ralph Waldo Emerson**

Many people are convinced that bad luck runs in their lives — even in whole families. This means they never expect anything good to ever happen to them. Of course, this is just negative thinking, and it is a barrier to making changes in the right direction. You need to believe that something good can happen, take a few positive steps — and, inevitably, it will.

## 313. TEACH YOURSELF A LESSON

'There is nothing permanent except change.'
**Heraclitus**

'Reframing' is a basic technique favoured by psychotherapists. The idea is to find something positive in a sad or stressful situation — a job dismissal, say, or an injury or a divorce — by figuring out what you gained from the experience, what you have learned and how it has helped you — not just what you lost.

Ask yourself: 'What does getting fired tell me about myself and others?' Maybe you weren't interested in your work and you hated the travel involved. Maybe you need to work on your people skills. Even if you loved the job and you're devastated by being fired, maybe they just weren't your sort of people and something better will come up. It always does!

## 314. DIG FOR SILVER

'Two men looked out of the prison bars —
One saw mud, the other the stars.'
**Anon**

Seeing the bright side is hard if you don't know what you're looking for. A simple trick for training yourself to recognise those precious glimmers of silver is to jot down in your journal or notebook at least one positive thing that happens every day, no matter how bleak and trying that day has been. Even something as simple as making your favourite noodle salad for lunch is worth noting and appreciating. On days when something especially great happens, dog-ear the page, so you can refer to it easily when you're feeling blue.

Your thoughts have a direct influence on your moods, too. Thinking bad things about yourself can drag you down, lower your self-esteem and make you prone to depression. Here's how to counter three common negative thoughts and turn them into positive ones:

| INSTEAD OF: | SAY: |
|---|---|
| **Nothing ever works out for me.** | Life is changing all the time, and getting better every day. |
| **I'm useless, hopeless.** | I am a valuable person just as I am, and I'm getting better every day. |
| **I look terrible.** | I love and respect myself as I am. |

## 315. ENJOY LIFE

Many of us are simply too busy to enjoy ourselves. We can get over-focused on what we're supposed to be doing and how we're supposed to do it. But by being so focused on performance and achieving goals, we can lose touch with how what we are doing is actually making us *feel*. If you're goal-oriented, it's time to make enjoying life one of your goals.

**Stop rushing about**. Being in a constant hurry is not a scheduling problem. It's a state-of-mind problem. A hurried mind cannot be a happy mind because it's preoccupied by activities that are yet to be experienced rather than current enjoyable ones. Focus more on the present moment. **Don't beat yourself up**. Many of us are too concerned with 'ought to', 'should do' and 'must do' — which is tied up with judgement and self-condemnation, particularly when it comes to our bodies. Every day is a war against cellulite, greasy hair, wrinkles, love handles, sagging breasts, beer bellies, fat and pimples. The only way out of this is true self-acceptance. Happiness does not require a perfect condition.

**Have many sources of potential joy**. If you hate your job and where you live but have a great relationship with your partner, how would you feel if he or she leaves you? No one thing or person can be a reliable source of happiness; it really must come from within. However, it is healthy to diversify your sources of self-esteem: complexity is a measure of how many unique roles in your hobbies and relationships you have developed as a basis for your self-esteem. If you have high complexity, you are relatively immune to being thrown into a depression as a result of a single bad event. So try to develop as wide a circle of friends and as broad a range of interests as you can.

## 316. SMILE ON THE INSIDE

'Turn your face towards the sun, and the shadows will fall behind you.'
**Maori proverb**

Spend a few minutes a day on the Buddhist exercise known as 'the inner smile'. Have you ever noticed that Buddhas are often depicted with an enigmatic, barely-there, Mona Lisa type of smile? Rarely a broad grin, but almost always a slight upraising of the lips. It is subtle, and meant to represent more of an inner feeling than an outwards expression for the world to see.

To practise inner smiling yourself, imagine seeing something that will make you smile — but only 'feel' the smile internally. Let the smile travel down from your mind and behind your face to all your internal organs. Notice how it enhances happiness and relaxation; feel the warm glow emanating from your stomach and up, out through your arms and legs. You can do this any time — in the office, at a meeting, or on the train — and no one will be any the wiser.

We tend to think that our facial expressions are results of our true feelings, and come from the inside-out. However, the opposite is also true. Smiling on the inside — even, and especially, when you don't feel like it — creates a new intention for you to open yourself up to kindness and generosity. And naturally, between times, smile visibly as much as you can — the physical action trains your brain to act happy.

## 317. GET FRESH WITH LIMES

I love limes ... in the bath! Lime juice is less acidic than lemon juice, so it won't dry up the skin, and the sophisticated, head-clearing fragrance is the perfect pick-me-up after a gruelling day. Squeeze the juice into bathwater, and use the halves to rub your elbows and knees.

# 318.  TREAT YOUR HAIR WITH CARE

Your hair has many enemies that leave it brittle: a poor diet, stress, and hair driers. Try Nanna's beautifully rich recipe for restoring gloss to your hair. It really does work!

**Hair Glosser**
   3 tablespoons (2 fl oz) cold-pressed sweet almond oil
   3 teaspoons runny honey
   2 egg yolks
   2 teaspoons aloe gel

In a small bowl, whip together oil, honey and yolks. Add aloe, and stir to form a smooth paste. Dip an old hairbrush into the mixture and apply to clean, dry hair. Cover hair with a plastic shower cap and a warmed towel. Leave on for 30 minutes. Rinse out with warm water and allow to air dry.

# 319.   EAT CONSCIOUSLY

**Ask yourself why**. Before you scoff that packet of chips, ask yourself why you want it. Are you really hungry or are you bored, tired or frustrated? If you find you regularly crave foods for reasons other than hunger, stock up on healthier, low-fat snacks, so, if you must eat, you won't consume the wrong things.

**Slow down**. When you sit down to have your meal, turn off the TV and pay attention to what you're eating. An American study has shown that extending your mealtime by just four minutes not only gives you time to savour what you're eating, it also encourages your body to burn more fat than if you were eating at top speed.

**Deceive yourself**. Serve food on smaller plates, to give the impression that you've got a huge mound of food in front of you. This helps you convince yourself psychologically that you are satisfied after a meal.

## 320. LIGHT IT UP

Bin all fluorescent lights and, where possible, replace light bulbs with natural daylight bulbs or tubes. Make the most of the real thing by keeping all curtains well pulled back, and any blinds fully folded until you go to bed. Replace harsh overhead central lights with lamps that offer a soft, warm glow.

Try coloured light bulbs for special, mood-changing effects. Try a blue bulb to aid sleep and calm the mind (it's also good for hyperactive children); green to encourage relaxation; and orange to combat depression. Pink is very nurturing and makes a good bedroom colour, while violet, which activates the pineal gland to produce brain chemicals, has an uplifting effect.

# 321. OPEN YOUR ENERGY CHANNELS

These yoga exercises open up the body's meridians, or energy channels, and allow the free flow of blood, lymph and oxygen to the body's tissues.

Block your right nostril and exhale through your left nostril with a short blast, then quickly inhale through your left nostril. Hold the breath for one second, then repeat using the right nostril. Start slowly, then build up speed so you are taking quick, sharp breaths in and out through each nostril. With practice, you can build up to five minutes.

Bend your knees and elbows and breathe in. Breathe out. As you breathe in again, stretch over to one side with your arms straight over your head as if you are doing a waist bend. Come down again and breathe out. Repeat ten times.

Breathe in and flop your body towards your toes. Breathe out as you come up again so you completely empty your body of breath — it may help to make a sound like 'Ooooooooh' and go up on to your toes. Repeat ten times.

# 322. POLISH YOUR FACE

To feel good, you need to energise your skin with natural ingredients. Many important ones can be found at your greengrocer. Fruits and vegetables are our richest source of the vitamins and minerals needed to nourish skin. Another advantage of using fresh fruit, such as apples and lemons, is that they contain useful enzymes to digest the bacteria that live on the skin. Try the following recipe — you can make it at home, it's remarkably simple and won't cost you a fortune — as an invigorating start to the day.

**Revitalising Mask**
Energise a tired complexion with this simple recipe using pureed pineapple. Gently exfoliating, this fruit helps restore the skin's natural pH balance, as well as leaving your face feeling instantly refreshed and revitalised.

> 1 slice pineapple, peeled and puréed
> 2 tablespoons (1¼ fl oz) plain yoghurt
> 4 tablespoons (2⅔ oz) cornmeal

In a bowl, mix the pineapple purée and the yoghurt. Add cornmeal to make a thick paste. Leave for five minutes to allow the cornmeal to soften and then spread the paste over your face, avoiding the eye area. Relax for 15 minutes and rinse off with tepid water.

## 323. FIND YOUR FAITH

'I have been driven many times to my knees by the overwhelming
conviction that I had nowhere else to go. My own wisdom and that
of all those about me seemed insufficient for that day.'
**Abraham Lincoln**

Studies show that people with strong spiritual practices live longer and are better
able to overcome problems that crop up in their lives. Interestingly, it's the actual
habit of praying regularly that far outweighs the importance of attendance at a
church or synagogue as a strategy for longevity. It would appear that it is the
prayer itself which is of benefit, rather than the venue.

Not only does regular prayer benefit the individual — it has also been shown
to help friends and family. For one thing, people who pray tend to cope better
with stress and all sorts of crises that may befall a family or partnership, and so
they are better able to support those close to them. They have a greater capacity
for staying calm, and an inner calm and certainty which means they can help
direct others to behave in a more positive way. Also, prayer can be used to help
other people. Research shows that praying for someone else — which is known as
intercessory prayer — can help them feel better, even if they don't realise they're
on the receiving end of anyone's good wishes.

Using prayer in your life does not require any special skills, or even joining an
organised religious community if you don't want to. The first step is to talk to the
deity of your choice — call it spirit, God, or whatever name you feel comfortable
with — in the privacy of your own mind. Examine your thoughts and concerns
and then ask for guidance. And, if you're facing a particular challenge and need
help, try to reap the benefits of intercessory prayer. Ask your loved ones to pray
for you, to mentally wrap you in a blanket of love.

## 324. RUB IN THE TUB

If you want to turn your tub into a full-blown sanctuary of serenity, treat yourself to a little love and attention while you're there: a quick massage. Try these simple strokes:

**Ears** Using the pads of your thumb and forefinger and gentle pressure, 'walk' your fingers from your lobe all the way up and around to the top. Pull outward gently as you go. Repeat on other side.

**Hands** With the thumb of one hand in the palm of the other, start stroking upward and outward. Then press each fingertip and stroke back towards your wrist. Repeat on the other hand. Finish by bringing your hands together so your palms are touching, as in prayer.

**Feet** Cradling your foot in one hand, use the thumb and knuckles of the other to 'crawl' up and down the sole. Next, stroke your fingers in a feathery motion along the top of the foot, around your toes, then around your ankle. Repeat on the other foot.

# 325. PROTECT WATER SUPPLIES

The problems of water safety and conservation can appear so daunting as to make us feel powerless to remedy them. But there are three easy steps anyone can take to protect and conserve our precious water supplies.

**Stop using fertilisers and pesticides on your lawn**. Encourage your neighbours to do the same. Better yet, choose native plants and grasses that don't require chemicals or irrigation. **Shift your diet down the food chain**. A diet rich in meat takes at least two to three times more water to produce than a healthy, low-meat diet. Animal agriculture is also a major source of water pollution.

**Get involved**. Urge your local representative to fight for stronger water conservation and protection programs. For example, efficiency standards now exist for toilets, washing machines, taps and showerheads in most countries, but they are not always implemented by manufacturers. And fight for local zoning regulations and land-use plans in your area that protect groundwater from pollution and any nearby wetlands from being drained.

# 326. STOP SAYING 'I'M SO TIRED'

If you've missed a few hours' sleep, so be it. You might expect to feel more tired than usual, but don't dwell on it. The power of auto-suggestion means that constantly repeating how tired you are (or how tired you think you'll be when you get to the end of the busy day you're struggling through right now) will actually compound and exaggerate the physiological tiredness. In other words — you'll feel worse than you would have if you hadn't kept thinking about it.

A quick tip that helps get you going in the mornings, even if you feel wiped out is to take 'an energy shower'. As you stand in your shower, imagine that you're standing under a shower of white light. Move around under the light and feel the light as it embraces you. Then see the white light turn into the colours of the rainbow, and feel your body 'absorb' the colours as you wash and shampoo yourself. After the energy buzz, mentally turn off the shower of light as you turn off the water.

Also, try never to discuss your lack of sleep with other people. If you do, you'll always feel even more tired. Naturally, if you're consistently running down your sleep bank, it's going to harm your health, and you need to take conscious steps to catch up. However, the occasional late night will do less harm if you don't harp on about how exhausted you are.

# 327. EAT FOR ENERGY

Most of our energy comes from food. Fresh food is more healthy, so cut down on processed, convenience foods and eat plenty of fruit and vegetables. Buy them fresh, use them quickly and eat them raw or cook for the shortest time possible (stir-frying and steaming are good methods) to preserve nutrients.

For an energy boost, step up your intake of complex carbohydrates, such as potatoes and wholegrain cereals. Carbohydrate is stored in the liver and muscles in the form of glycogen. During activity, the glycogen is broken down to glucose which, along with fat, provides energy.

Wholegrain products are more nutritious than the refined varieties — but go easy on the bread. Too much wheat, yeast and gluten — the main ingredients in bread — can be hard to digest and cause allergies that in turn lead to fatigue. Alternatives include yeast-free soda breads, wholemeal pitta, sourdough loaves and wholegrain pasta. If wheat causes problems, try rye bread or biscuits, oatcakes and other starches such as brown rice, couscous, millet or oats.

The right type of fats can help to keep you alert, too. Polyunsaturated or monounsaturated fats (found in nuts, seed, corn, avocados, olives, oily fish and oils liquid at room temperature) promote good circulation, a healthy heart and blood vessels, and are necessary for brain function. Choose white meat rather than red, and cut down on dairy products.

## 328. FRESHEN UP

Simply taking five minutes to wash your hands, brush your hair or clean your teeth can make you feel refreshed and ready to tackle whatever's ahead. Stand in front of the bathroom mirror. Take three breaths in and out, relax for a moment and look into the mirror with fresh eyes. See who is really there. Now — brush your hair or teeth slowly and carefully. Be kind, reverential, even. Take it slowly, and really watch what you are doing. Pay attention to how you feel. Enjoy the feeling of clean teeth, soft hair. Give yourself a little smile. Today will be a good day.

# 329. BE A FIGHTER

> 'Self-pity is our worst enemy. If we yield to it, we can never do anything wise in this world.'
> **Helen Keller**

At the first sign of trouble, you often hear people complain, 'Why me? What did I do to deserve this?'

The trouble is, feeling like a victim only increases feelings of stress and helplessness. Instead, focus on being proactive. If your train gets cancelled, don't go into a lather of worry and self-pity. Get on the next one. If your neighbours are noisy or messy in their habits, don't suffer in silence. Call the council and ask what can be done to make things more comfortable.

## 330. SAY YES TO PRESSURE

Acupressure stimulates the same points as acupuncture, but with fingers instead of needles. Try pressing on the following three points:

**The Third Eye**, located between the eyebrows, in the indentation where the bridge of the nose meets the forehead.

**The Heavenly Pillar**, on the back of the neck slightly below the base of the skull, about half an inch to the left or right of the spine.

**The Heavenly Rejuvenation**, half an inch below the top of each shoulder, midway between the base of the neck and the outside of the shoulder blade.

Breathe deeply and apply firm, steady pressure on each point for two to three minutes. The pressure should cause a mild aching sensation, but not pain.

# 331. TAKE VITAMIN B

Essential for maintaining the nervous system and healthy red blood cells, and for creating optimum vitality, B group vitamins should form a vital part of your diet. The richest food sources of these vitamins are yeast, cereal, wheatgerm, fresh fruit and vegetables. However, most people don't get enough B vitamins from their daily diet alone and, being water-soluble, these nutrients can't be stored in the body. So if you are feeling tired and run-down and don't eat plenty of the above foods, a supplement may be the answer. To feel any real advantages, take a combined B complex supplement, rather than just one or two of the vitamins individually.

## 332. GO ON A RETREAT

'Sometimes, too much of a good thing can be wonderful.'
**Mae West**

Not on a holiday, a retreat. Even if the budget does not stretch to visiting one of the sacred retreats in magical places like Bali or Kaua'i in Hawaii, your local Buddhist temple, yoga group or Christian church will be able to give you information about different spiritual retreats they offer. The opportunity to settle in for a week's — or weekend's — meditation and quiet thought is deeply restful, helping to slow you down, and find inner calm and mindfulness. Best of all is the silent retreat. The silence is a balm, as though someone has turned off the chatter in your brain. In the absence of other voices, your own thoughts become more pronounced and you gain greater insight into your actions.

# 333. DO A GOOD DEED DAILY

> 'The quality of mercy is not strained . . . it is twice blessed; it blesseth him that gives and him that takes.'
> **William Shakespeare**

In a study of Harvard graduates, researchers found that those who made a conscious effort to help other people on a regular basis had greater feelings of happiness, calmer minds and suffered less depression than those who did not. The poet Samuel Taylor Coleridge once wrote: 'We receive but what we give.' It follows that the more positivity you can put out into the world, the more will flow back your way. Today, try to do at least one good deed. For instance:

Take out a subscription to a play or join a friend up for an evening class you know they're interested in.

Buy fresh flowers on the way to work, and give them to the person on the front desk.

Get in touch with someone you haven't seen for years — like an old school friend — and take them out for a meal.

On your next walk, pop a coin into a parking meter that's about to expire.

Once a week don't buy a coffee or a sandwich, and give the $2 to someone less fortunate.

## 334. BE AN INCURABLE ROMANTIC

'Things do not change — we do.'
**Henri David Thoreau**

And before you leap to the conclusion that this automatically means you have to have a partner — you don't. Being an incurable romantic means re-igniting the flame of passion in your life, it means turning the ordinary into the special, it means having a touch of class. Here are some creative, unusual and wonderful ideas and gestures to celebrate your life, with or without a significant other.

Propose a toast to life at every meal.

Hire a pianist to play during dinner at home.

Copy a romantic, inspirational poem or the lyrics to a great song onto beautiful parchment paper. Frame it.

When's the last time you attended the ballet? The opera? A jazz concert?

Hire a limousine for a memorable evening out with friends.

Use a special fountain pen to write important notes and letters.

Always keep a bottle of excellent champagne in the fridge. Celebrate tonight, or save it for a special occasion.

Eat dinner by candlelight.

Hang fairy lights outside your house or flat so you can see them from your window or balcony.

Trade homes with a friend for the weekend. It won't cost you a cent, and the change of environment is refreshing.

Make your own greeting cards. You don't have to be artistic, just sincere.

Snuggle up in front of a roaring fire.

Take a course in ikebana, the Japanese art of flower arrangement.

## 335. STOP WORRYING

On my fridge I have the following quote from Ralph Waldo Emerson: 'Some of your hurts you have cured, and the sharpest you've even survived. But what torments of grief you've endured from evils which never arrived!' I must have looked at it a hundred times to remind myself that there are few things more draining and mind-deadening than focusing on problems that haven't even happened, and may not ever happen!

Still, it's a tough call to learn to stop worrying. Everyone worries — it's a part of everyday life. But what really bothers us? Researchers say that women worry most about their future, maintaining a spark in their relationship, pursuing their career, child concerns, and financial security, usually in that order — which pretty much means they worry about everything! Here are some ways to deal with worry:

**Look at the reasonable evidence for your beliefs**. If a friend ignores you, for example, it could be because they're busy and not because they don't like you anymore.

**Stop 'what-iffing' in your mind**. Try thinking aloud — it will make any illogical flaws in your thinking more obvious.

**Distract yourself from negative, depressing thoughts**. See a film or socialise with someone who's fun to be with.

**Ask yourself what's the worst that could happen**. Whatever's happened may be unpleasant, embarrassing, inconvenient, upsetting — but will it actually kill you?

**Schedule an hour of unbridled worry time a week — but no more**. Some problems demand immediate attention — a smoke alarm siren, or a police car's whirling lights. But many low-grade stressors can be dealt with at a later time, when it's more convenient. File them away in a little mental compartment, or make a note, then deal with them when the time is right. Don't let them control you.

**See a counsellor**. It could be useful if you really don't think you can handle your worries by yourself.

# 336. LET IT OUT

If you've ever felt angry with your partner or children and then felt guilty about your anger, you'll probably know that it made you feel even worse. Look at your emotions as you would a newspaper or signal: they are an attempt to alert you to the need for change and they provide you with the energy for the actions that are needed to bring about that change.

**Know what you want**. This is trickier than it looks on paper. If you're feeling down, you need to work out the cause. To rediscover your own needs, think about your present situation. Look at all the things you feel unhappy about. Imagine how life could be ideally. At this stage, don't get bogged down in working out exactly *how* you are going to achieve the change.

**Express yourself**. If you are unhappy about something, you need to say so. Your colleagues, partner, children, friends and parents are not mind-readers. Unless you say something, nothing is going to happen. You don't have to be loud, impolite or aggressive when uttering your wishes. And the sooner you give voice to an emotion, the less likely you are to become 'emotional' about it, by shouting or crying.

**Challenge your fears with hard evidence**. A fear of emotions is really a fear of the consequences of expressing them. If, for instance, your partner suggests separate holidays and this makes you unhappy, what are you afraid will happen if you say no? A row, a rejection, or a refusal to take your opinion on board? These are all possibilities, but better to risk the reaction than to repress the feeling. Keeping feelings to yourself won't help you to get rid of them. One possibility is that you will one day lose control and let your anger explode.

**Have a good cry**. Shedding tears can give you a new lease of life. Physically, the lubrication in the eye supplies oxygen to the cornea and carries away carbon dioxide and debris. Emotionally, tears relieve stress. They contain hormones which, if kept bottled up, could prolong depression.

# 337. ACCEPT IMPERFECTION

'Whatever is flexible and loving will tend to grow. Whatever is rigid and blocked will wither and die.'
**Lao-tzu**

Perfectionists are most at risk of losing the plot when the going gets tough.

Someone with a more flexible, easygoing approach to life might say to themselves when they're under pressure: 'I'll just go out there and do my best with the time and resources available to me.' A perfectionist, on the other hand, says: 'I must do an absolutely fantastic job and the results must be flawless', often adding 'and if I don't I'm completely stupid/hopeless/a failure.'

Everyone makes mistakes. Learn to take responsibility for yours and be able to move on. Don't blame others or criticise yourself and make yourself feel as though there could have been any other possible outcome. It's over, and it's happened. And remember that there are very few people in the world that can give 100 per cent of their talent and skill to every single project that comes their way — and even if they were to manage that sort of commitment and thoroughness, they couldn't do it 24 hours a day.

## 338. DISCOVER YOUR PASSION

'Whatever you can do — or dream you can do — begin it.'
**Johann W. von Goethe**

The culture we live in sets very high expectations for us: for one thing, we are supposed to be 'on track' all the time and to know precisely what we're doing. It can be very intimidating to think that other people, the ones we admire, have found that elusive 'thing' that makes their lives meaningful — most usually, a partner or a career, or even a calling, like motherhood. If you are not focused — if, in fact, you're vague and dreamy, or just plain confused and burnt out, don't worry. Everyone has off-days, off-months, even longer off-periods where they just don't know what they want to do. Here are a few things to think about that will help you winkle out those inner dreams and aspirations that have been tamped down for so long.

Leave aside the fact that you don't have a particular aspiration right now: assuming you did, who are the people whose permission you need before you can get started? What are the things in your life that are stopping you? Ask yourself: what do I daydream about when I'm waiting in supermarket queues? What do I think about when I'm alone? What activities make me feel really connected to others, and 'in tune' with myself?

And, the most powerful question of all: what things did you love to make or do when you were little? This one will nearly always give you the answer. Psychologists tracking the development of children through adolescence and adulthood have found that children often act out their life purpose in favourite games, and the stories and toys they identify with most strongly also provide plenty of clues as to what they're going to be like as adults, and tasks they're going to be good at later in life. So, what was your passion as a child? Building doll's houses? Making rock gardens? Reading? Camping? Electronics? Solving jigsaws? Did you make up a newspaper with friends? Sell and swap toys?

Remember all the different things that interested you and gave you pleasure. Listen to your inner voice, the one that tells you your innermost longings, as you sift among your memories. Are there clues to your dreams in your childhood memories? Don't listen to those ever-ready demons in your head, the ones that are always ready to jump in with budgets and other boring practicalities that say why something can't be done. Look past what you think — trust what you feel.

# 339. EARTH YOURSELF

It isn't the garden that's important — it's the gardening. It's a wonderful all-round body tonic, with one recent study finding that gardening at least once a week can help combat the bone-thinning disease osteoporosis. The study looked at bone-mass measurements in women aged 50 and older and how often they did gardening, compared with aerobics, jogging, walking, weightlifting, cycling and dancing. The results? Regular gardening — digging, mowing, weeding, raking — was the optimal choice for maintaining bone density.

Gardening is also one of the best ways to tune into the natural world and soothe your mind and spirit. Even if you live in an apartment, you may be able to establish a container-garden on a roof or balcony. Just being outside, digging with low-tech tools, and spending time with those silent friends, the plants, and watching their periods of growth, you will find that your intuitive abilities will also grow and that you will feel more peaceful and centred. A lot more grows in a garden than plants — the blissful puttering about is an ideal form of meditation and psychotherapy rolled into one.

So — let the sunlight play on your shoulders, the breeze at your hat brim. Get up close, knees on the earth, and look at the pattern and translucency of petals, examine the progress of bees — their industrious and sensuous twirls through pollen — and watch sparrows hop, cats prowl, and earthworms loop through the soil. The repetition of weeding, watering, pulling hoses around, and staking up vines causes everything else to leave the mind, so you can return to your indoor life with small inspirations, insights and a sense of renewed capability. Little wonder that garden lovers talk about how relaxed they feel after their green hours: when we garden, we cultivate ourselves.

## 340. ROLL UP YOUR SLEEVES

Does your suburb need a little spring cleaning? Join the thousands of volunteers who take part in national community beautification programs. Under the leadership of these nonprofit litter-prevention and education organisations, volunteers will collect rubbish, plant trees, remove graffiti and refurbish parks in their areas. To join, call your local government department and ask for guidelines.

# 341. FAKE IT

Smiling is a two-way mechanism. We do it when we're relaxed and happy — but doing it can also make us feel relaxed and happy, even if we're not. How? Smiling transmits nerve impulses from the facial muscles to the limbic system, a key emotional centre in the brain, tilting the neurochemical balance toward calm. So, go ahead and grin. Merely moving your mouth into the shape of a smile — even if you have to pretend and just hold a pen between your teeth in the approximate shape of a smile! — can lift your mood. Grin at strangers on the bus; be extra polite to the postie. Project the mood that you want to get back. Never underestimate how contagious moods are between people. Often others will just automatically react and be nice back to you, even if they weren't planning to. Don't you feel better already?

## 342. REWIND YOUR MIND

'Very little is needed to make a happy life. It is all within you, it is your way of thinking.'
**Marcus Aurelius**

To help you clear out mentally, you need first to remove the clutter in your mind.

Start with anger, especially the petty things in life. Imagine you have delete and rewind buttons in your brain, and when you have a negative thought, press the delete button. Then rewind and rethink the matter in a more positive light. Follow this with a positive daydream. Sit quietly with a straight spine and visualise a sequence of events you would like to happen. The thought is the blueprint of the action that — in theory — can become a reality.

## 343. Get things in perspective

> 'Being able to persist is not the most important thing — the ability to start over is.'
> F. Scott Fitzgerald

Try to be more aware of the snowball effect that negative thinking can have. Here's how to stop the misery train before 'Poor Me' has a chance to get on board:

**Accept that life isn't fair**. Just saying this statement to yourself, and knowing it to be true, can stop you feeling sorry for yourself. Pity is a self-defeating emotion that only makes you feel worse.

**Ask yourself, 'Will this really matter a year from now?'** Is the problem really as important as you make it out to be? Chances are, a year from now, it will be a long-forgotten minor incident.

**Think of what you have, rather than what you want to have**. Consider all you have to be grateful for and focus on enjoying yourself in the present. As spiritual teacher Ram Dass says: 'Be. Here. Now.'

# 344. SAY YOU CAN

'Anybody can do anything' says my mother, a 'housewife' who has become, through the years and her own efforts, an inspired cook, excellent gardener, competent nurse, skilful seamstress, reliable source of all sorts of general information, dependable accountant, ikebana expert, book-a-day reader, amateur ornithologist, and tireless bargain hunter. And she's right. According to a study of law students at America's Johns Hopkins University, optimism improves your health and your chances of success. By mid-semester, students who had reported a positive give-it-a-go outlook at the beginning of the term had immune-system cells that were a whopping 33 per cent more effective than the cells of those who approached their work with low or negative expectations.

## 345. Make your garden a sanctuary

Since the sixteenth-century poet Andrew Marvell wrote of the 'sweete and wholsome Houres spent in a green shade' to now, when scientists are steadily accumulating a body of evidence proving nature's positive effects on our bodies and minds, we have known that more grows in a garden than plants and flowers. Here's how to turn your garden into a sanctuary for your body and soul:

**Keep it private**. Plan to include walls or fences, where possible, a row of shrubs, or even low hedges. All provide a feeling of being enclosed and safe, as well as giving protection against the weather or intruders.

**Make an entrance**. Even if it's just a plain wooden gate, it marks the transition from the outer world to your personal space. Paint your gate a welcoming colour, like red or bright yellow; if you enter your garden via an arch or a driveway, plant a beautiful flowering vine overhead.

**Consider features**. No matter how small, there should be room in your garden for a bench conducive to contemplation, or tinkling wind chimes. **Add water**. A tiny birdbath, a ceramic dish where you can float a single bloom, a small pond or fountain, even a dry pebble stream can all add to feelings of tranquillity and balance. **Encourage wildlife to come**. Butterflies are an ancient emblem of the soul. To lure them, plant the nectar-rich flowers they love, such as lilac or honeysuckle. If you're a birdlover, include a feeder.

## 346. GROW HERBS

Herbs are easy to grow, inexpensive, and a much-needed daily treat for your jaded senses. Even if you've only got a teensy windowsill, you can still grow and harvest lush handfuls of your own richly aromatic fresh herbs. All you need is seeds, potting mix and a terracotta pot or planter box. Growing your own herbs and stirring them into hearty soups, whisking them into omelette mixtures, or tucking them into a thick, simmering casserole will make you feel connected with the soil and the season, no matter how many floors up your kitchen is.

Fresh herbs offer an astonishing variety of vibrant and glorious flavours, and experimenting with them in recipes will make your food sing. And their gifts go beyond the mere culinary: there is delight in simply handling fresh herbs in the kitchen, crushing and rubbing them between your fingers. Who can resist sniffing a purple basil leaf or crushing a piece of crinkly green mint? Then there are the creative joys of pairing herbs successfully with other ingredients, the wonderful opportunities to invent and improvise, and to create your own treasured recipes to hand down to the next generation. Just a few ideas: you know about adding mint to fruit . . . but have you tried it with ginger? Chocolate? And minted fresh beetroot is one of life's most exquisitely simple summer pleasures. Same goes for basil: you know what it tastes like with tomatoes or in spaghetti sauce — but try it with potatoes for a sublime treat, or snip a little over soft cheese. Yum!

## 347. COME HOME TO YOURSELF

Like Dorothy in *The Wizard of Oz*, we all long for home. What does home mean to you? Close your eyes: what does it look like, what can you smell and see? Pay attention to details.

Chances are, your feelings about your home are not just to do with nostalgia, or where you've been in the past. Regardless of your childhood experiences, your home is rightfully a place where you belong, in safety and comfort, and one where your precious treasures are kept. But your home also speaks of where you are going, and with whom and what. Your home is your destiny. When you come into your home, be overjoyed. Shut the door behind you and appreciate every single thing about getting home, and about being where you are in your life, and where you are going. Breathe in and out, feel the satisfaction of being in your sacred domain.

# 348. BLESS YOUR HOME

Many spiritual traditions say that homes absorb the psychic vibrations of past and present inhabitants and events. These energies can haunt the space, keeping you from feeling truly 'at home'. Cultures from China to the Americas have always practised house blessing rituals to renew a house's psychic energy, clearing any energy that's stuck. You can find ideas for house blessing rituals in such diverse traditions as Catholicism (prayer circles), Native American (burning sage leaves), Wicca (asking household members to visualise healing beams of light), and Judaism (lighting candles). Or you can make up your own. Here are some ideas:

**Plant a prayer**. Write down a prayer or a blessing and bury it in a favourite plant. When you water the plant, the prayer is symbolically energised.

**Create a blessing altar**. Use your intuition in selecting the objects. A purple cloth symbolises spirituality, salt is for cleansing, candles mean inner light, and shells represent feminine energy. Crystals or white feathers are said to clear the atmosphere of negativity and open the way for love. Photographs of loved ones help generate positive energy.

**Offer plants and flowers**. Traditionally found on altars around the world. Specific meanings include: daffodil (joy), daisy (innocence), lily of the valley (new start), rose (love), apple (health), pomegranate (fertility, abundance), rice (luck, plenty) and mustard seeds (strength).

**Ring bells**. Historically, bells, gongs and chimes have been associated with restoring vibrational balance. In many traditions, the ringing of metal was thought to drive away evil spirits. Any bell or chime can be used to clear energy in your home and create sacred space.

**Burn incense or oil**. Use aromatherapy candles, incense or essential oils to purify the atmosphere in your home. Peppermint releases mental fog, lavender soothes tension and rose gives warmth and love.

**Use flower essences**. Essences such as Bach Flower Essences and Australian Bush Flower Essences are said to contain spiritual properties which help heal many different conditions. They may be sprinkled around the home to create a delicate web of energy which is very conducive to bringing joy. Choose Centaury for calm, Mimulus to overcome fear, and Rescue Remedy to harmonise the atmosphere after trauma or argument.

# 349. GET IN TOUCH

Think about this: everything you touch sends a message to your brain. Depending on what it is, this could be a message of comfort and connectedness — or one of alienation. Make your home and, where possible, your workplace a sensual haven where everything your hands, feet and body make contact will help you to feel good.

**Live in a material world.** Choose fabric not just for utilitarian purposes, but for what it says to you, how it feels when you touch it, the effect it has on the mood of your room. For a bright, brisk feel, buy cotton curtains and covers. For a warm, cocooning, cosy ambience, opt for chenille and brushed cotton. Place a soft woolly rug in front of the fire to create a welcoming spot. Toss mohair throws over sofas, make velvet cushions and scatter them on your bed for the ultimate sensual touch. Satin is also sensual, with its slippery feel, catching the light — but avoid the cliché of satin sheets. (Who can take them seriously?) Leather is great for making you feel at home — the more battered, the better!

**Don't forget your feet.** Just walking on a cool tiled floor or smooth wooden floorboards can boost your mood, though scratchy synthetic carpets can make you feel irritated without even knowing why. Best of all — go outside, kick off your shoes and feel the texture of the grass between your bare toes.
**Little touches mean a lot.** Fill a bowl with shells or smooth river stones and place it on a table you pass often: you'll appreciate the roughness of the shells or the smooth roundness of the stones every time you pick them up and let them fall through your fingers.

# 350. Avoid scary cleaning products

Every day, commercial household cleaners expose you to toxic chemicals like lye, chlorine and petrochemical solvents. Many of these have well-established short-term effects on health. Ammonia, for example, can irritate the skin and lungs; chlorine is an eye irritant. What's more of a worry is that no one is quite sure of the effects of *long-term* exposure to lots of little quantities of these chemicals, and whether and how they are stored in the body.

What can you do? First, learn to decode the labels, and look for products with the fewest warnings. 'Caution' is the mildest; 'Danger' the strongest. Avoid 'extra strength' products — all-purpose cleaners are generally milder. Stop using the worst offenders — oven cleaners, drain cleaners and toilet bowl cleaners. Most of these contain lye or some sort of acid. And be aware that the increased saleability of 'green' products has led to some rather grey areas when it comes to marketing claims, so be sceptical of vague phrases such as 'environmentally friendly' or 'natural'. If in doubt, write to the manufacturer and ask for a more thorough explanation. If they don't respond to your letter — well, there's your answer!

The good news is that making your house less toxic doesn't mean you have to tolerate dirt. There are plenty of cleaning alternatives, ranging from a wide variety of good quality ecologically designed products to many common kitchen staples which double as environmentally friendly (and cheap) cleansers. Here are a few examples:

**Bicarbonate of soda** Use as a gentle scouring powder for tiles and bench tops. Just sprinkle on and rub with a wet sponge.

**Vinegar** In a 50:50 mixture with water, this makes an excellent glass cleaner. Use full strength to disinfect cutting boards and bathroom fixtures.

**Soda water** Simply fill a spray bottle for an all-purpose cleaner. It doesn't need to be fizzy — the alkalines in the water give it its cleaning power.

**Soda crystals** Try these as an alternative to chlorine-based bleaches, biological washing powders and chemical cleaners. They really do work, removing dirt without resorting to bleach, phosphates or enzymes.

# 351. RESTOCK YOUR KITCHEN CUPBOARDS

Don't leave these items off your shopping list — otherwise it's all too easy to eat rubbish. Plus, they all taste good!

**Baked beans** High in fibre, beans also provide lots of carbohydrate and B vitamins. They have a really low glycaemic index, which means they release their energy slowly and help to keep hunger pangs at bay longer.

**Eggs** Provide high-quality protein, along with iron and vitamins A, B complex and D, and they're super-quick to prepare.

**Garlic** Contains sulphur compounds, which improve resistance to infections, reduce cholesterol and thin the blood.

**Olive oil** Rich in monounsaturates that lower cholesterol. It's also less likely to form free radicals (which can damage cells) at high temperatures.

**Sardines** A great source of the omega-3 fatty acids needed for the heart and circulation.

**Tomato purée** It contains lots of lycopene, the carotenoid that makes tomatoes red. Recent studies show it protects against cancer, especially prostate cancer.

**Yoghurt** Full of calcium, for strong bones. Yoghurt containing the bacteria *Lactobacillus acidophilus* can help the digestion and may ease fungal infections such as thrush.

## 352. GIVE YOUR BED THE ONCE-OVER

Say 'yes' to any of the following questions and you should think about getting new bedding — a good mattress and pillow are the key to preventing back problems in later life, not to mention lack of sleep, the main reason for tiredness and fatigue.

Is your mattress over ten years old?

Do you wake up with a backache or pain in the neck?

When lying in bed, can you feel the springs or ridges beneath the surface?

Do you hear creaks or crunches when moving around?

Do you and your partner roll towards each other unintentionally?

Is the base uneven or sagging?

Has your pillow lost its thickness? Is it misshapen?

Do your bedclothes need replacing? Do they keep you comfortably warm?

## 353. BEAT THE HYPE

'Earth provides enough for everyone's need — not for everyone's greed.'
**Mahatma Ghandi**

An international email newsletter, 'Whose Birthday Is It Anyway?', gives ideas on how to avoid the 'gimme' habits that seem to be inextricably linked to Christmas. If ever there was a time of year to start putting into practice the ideas I've covered in this book, about 'spring-cleaning' your life, paring down at home, at work, and in your community, streamlining your lifestyle, and making positive changes to bring more health and happiness into your life — it's Christmas. Here are a few ideas that are specific to making the 'silly season' a simpler, more truly joyous time:

**Have a swap-a-present party**. Invite friends to bring over things they no longer want. The fun begins as everyone grabs whatever they do want, and leftovers go to charity.

**Resist buying things you'll only use once or twice**. Hire dishes and glasses. Wash and re-use plastic cups and plates instead of throwing them away.

**Buy longer rolls of film**. You can save nearly 40 per cent by purchasing rolls of 36 exposures instead of 12.

**Cater sensibly**. If you're having a party, get everyone to bring a plate of food. Make your own Christmas and birthday cards. Cut up and recycle kids' paintings. Make sure your cards are the same size as the 'Post Office preferred' ones in the shops so that they will only cost you 40 cents to mail.

**Don't buy chips or soft drinks for kids**. Homemade popcorn is cheaper, and litre-for-litre, cordial costs about one-tenth of a glass of soft drink!

**Make your own presents**. Save all re-useable lidded jars, and have a big cooking day where you fill them with home-made jam or chutney.

**Be creative when wrapping presents**. Use fabrics or newspaper and decorate brown paper bags.

**Get savvy about present-buying**. Have the family agree that you'll only buy presents for the under-15s. And think simple when it comes to kids' toys. It's the classics like beach balls, teddy bears, Lego and games like Scrabble, Twister and Uno that remain the favourites every year. If you do buy for adults, stick to your money-saving principles and give 'time vouchers' instead: one hour's babysitting, an afternoon's weed-pulling – you get the idea. Or put all the family's names into a hat, and each person draws out one. They then buy a gift for that person.

## 354. DEAL WITH DIFFICULT DAYS

'Harmony is never granted. It has to be conquered indefinitely.'
**Simone de Beauvoir**

I know all about Difficult Days. I just had one. Staggered through the door with ten enormous bags of shopping, the mail, bread and whisky. One boy was trying to dig a tunnel in the backyard and the other was in the bathroom with the tap running — a very bad sign. The cat had thrown up in the laundry basket and there was a message on the answering machine from the bank to say I was overdrawn (sometimes they just can't wait to send a letter to give me bad news). If you've had a horrible day, try these quick, calming remedies . . .

**Brew up some passionflower tea**. It will relax you, lift your spirits and help you sleep.

**Breathe correctly**. Stand up straight and breathe from your abdomen rather than the top of your lungs. Place one hand on your abdomen and take several deep, slow breaths through your nose.

**Try DIY shiatsu**. (1) Tap the top of your head with your fingers, keeping your wrists loose. (2) Smooth your fingers across your forehead, making circles at your temples with your fingertips. Squeeze along your eyebrows. (3) Using your thumbs, press firmly on points all around your eye sockets. (4) Rub your cheeks and the end of your nose. (5) Press your thumbs under each cheekbone and work out as far as your ears. (6) Pull your ears: up, down, forwards and backwards, then rub them all over with your fingers. (7) Pinch along your lower jaw; press your thumbs on any nodules or glands to help drain away toxins.

## 355. CHERISH THE ORDINARY

'What is living? Not to eat and drink and breathe, but to feel the life deep down in you, passionately and joyfully.'
**Elizabeth Barrett Browning**

It's odd that birthdays and Christmas can be the most depressing times of the year for many. There are many reasons, but one is that we build them up as being far too special, and have unrealistic expectations of how others will behave and how we will or should feel.

Try this exercise: instead of celebrating the special, celebrate the ordinary instead. Did you realise that the word ordinary comes from 'order'? So, celebrating the ordinary should not mean you are being boring or mundane; instead, it means you are approaching your life in an orderly, measured way. Rather than agonising over life's mysteries and problems, share the gift of being ordinary and simple, and of being grateful for the small things that are the source of true joy and satisfaction in your life. For example, if it's someone's birthday, celebrate by pulling weeds in their garden. At Christmas, celebrate by straightening your linen press. Living an orderly life helps keep expectations low and contentment high.

## 356. TRUST IN THE UNIVERSE

'You got to walk that lonesome valley
You got to walk it by yourself
Ain't nobody here can walk it for you
You got to walk it by yourself.'
**Old Negro spiritual song**

The word 'addiction' probably makes you think first of drugs and alcohol. They're horrific addictions, but they're nowhere near as widespread as another one: the addiction to control. With its partners in crime — worry, overmanagement and guilt — control addiction stealthily takes over every aspect of your life, making it as joyless and grim as any junkie's.

The only way to beat control addiction is cold turkey. Resist, resist, resist the temptation. Don't listen to the insidious little voice in your mind that says you're the one that has to be in charge; that without you, nothing will get done; that you have to check and re-check everyone else's jobs as well as your own. Instead, sit back, turn off, and let your inner self find a different path. Your deep knowledge of what is right for you, your instincts, feelings and intentions — the ones that are usually buried beneath daily to-do lists — are the most powerful tools you have. If you sense you are following a path of constant vigilance, revise your intentions: say the old Celtic prayer: 'All will be well, and all will be well, and all will be well' out loud — and let go.

Whether it's one particular work issue you're bogged down on, or it's to do with a bigger attitude change that you want to bring about, opportunities and openings cannot come your way unless you leave some room for them. The more you try to force an outcome — the tighter you stitch everything up — the harder it is for things to turn out as they should. Invariably the outcome that is right for you will be the one that drifts towards you from where you would least expect it, not the one that you organise. From today, plan to turn over one per cent of your life to the universe. Give up something, anything — a daily ritual, a habit, some sort of regular behaviour — and see what comes to fill its place.

## 357. REPROGRAM YOUR DREAMS

'The world of reality has its limits. The world of imagination
is boundless.'
**Jean-Jacques Rousseau**

Dreams are a powerful and effective way to connect with your unconscious mind.
By learning to introduce more positive messages to your dreams, you can boost
your confidence, change your daytime behaviour and reactions, and improve your
relationships.

The first step is to let your mind 'get used' to the dream you want to have. If,
for example, you want to dream about having a better relationship with a work
associate you've been having problems with, think about them, as neutrally as
possible, during the day. Visualise them clearly — but take them out of the
context of arguments or negative situations that may have happened previously.
Instead, see them in a clear bubble, waiting for you, and watching you. Now, start
to visualise what will happen with them in your dream, and in what context. Be
thorough — imagine details, scents, light and colours. Perhaps you'll just be
talking pleasantly with them, or perhaps you've got a more complicated scenario
in mind, involving seeing yourself behaving in a more confident, assertive manner.
Last thing at night, as you lie in your bed, visualise them clearly, then tell yourself
you'll definitely dream about them. Keeping a dream diary (writing down your
dream as soon as you wake up) will help you to remember things and tap into
your unconscious thoughts.

# 358. SURROUND YOURSELF WITH OPTIMISTS

'Those who wish to sing will always find a song.'
**Swedish proverb**

I have a tatty old Charlie Brown newspaper clipping that I think says it all about being the cock-eyed optimist that I am. In it, Charlie Brown is saying: 'I don't know where I'm going, but I'm on my way.'

Most of us probably worry about something at some time or another — our finances, family gossip, the odd health problem. But for some people, anxiety is unremitting and constant, it's a way of life. Everything and anything is a possible cause of calamity. This doesn't necessarily mean that they complain the whole time, nor does it mean that they are negative or defeatists, who just give up before they've even had a go at something. They are, however, pessimists, and what they will have in common is the characteristic of being very vulnerable to the moods of others, real or imagined. They are particularly susceptible to free-floating emotions like anger, scorn, guilt, anxiety, and sadness that are occurring in the lives of family, friends — or even in the lives of strangers on television — and take them up as their own.

No one is 100 per cent immune to this sort of susceptibility — it's part of being human to identify with other people and how they feel. However, it's easy to take it too far and get dragged down by anxiety and anger that actually has nothing to do with your own situation. A critical weapon in the battle against negativity is to surround yourself with people who have a positive, optimistic attitude to life, people who, like Charlie Brown, are 'on their way'. Your mind and spirit will subconsciously model themselves on happiness and contentment, rather than negativity, without trying to figure out the whys and wherefores if they're not immediately apparent. Then, when anxiety does attack, it will be easier to look at the real reasons you're feeling anxious, rather than getting swayed by other people's difficulties. As a bonus, being optimistic is said to help you live a healthier life. Researchers from the University of Kentucky have found that, when the pressure was on, optimists' immune systems got stronger, protecting them from infections. Pessimists, however, were more prone to sickness when under stress.

# 359. HAVE A STRESS-FREE CHRISTMAS

> 'Blood is thicker than water — and it boils quicker.'
> **Anon.**

The truth is, Christmas has never been much fun for those working behind the scenes. All in all, it can be a nerve-wracking experience, even for die-hard softies like me, who get sentimental at the sight of a fruit cake (and who are invariably still up at 2 a.m. on Christmas morning, putting the finishing touches on presents! Here's how to avoid the pitfalls.

**Lower your expectations**. Decide that you'll be happy if you have a calm day with agreeable food and the odd moment of enjoyment. You'll then avoid feeling resentment if your Christmas is not living up to a fantasy.

**Don't try to change your parents or your siblings**. They will always see you as the child you once were. Don't get up in arms. Just grin and bear it. In-laws can be more difficult. If you do get on, count your blessings, If you don't, try to find some neutral ground on which you all agree. Do safe things like play board games, or go for a walk after lunch or dinner.

**If you're on your own and feeling left out, volunteer at your local hospital or shelter**. Many charities run events for local homeless people or the elderly and always need volunteers.

# 360.  DIGEST FOOD PROPERLY

Here are five must-haves for your shopping list:

**Live yoghurt** 'Friendly bacteria' which help digestion are already present in your gut, but they can also be found in some foods. Live yoghurt, which contains *Lactobacillus acidophilus*, is a great example.

**Pineapple and pawpaw** The enzymes bromelain, found in pineapple, and papain, an ingredient of pawpaw, both aid the body's digestive processes because they break down protein. Blend both fruits with skim milk to make a healthy smoothie, or use them in a fruit salad.

**Peppermint tea** Has a relaxing effect on the digestive system and can help reduce embarrassing problems such as flatulence and diarrhoea.

**Beans** Haricot, butter and red kidney beans are all excellent sources of fibre, which is important for avoiding constipation and haemorrhoids.

**Fennel** Eaten as a vegetable — either steamed or roasted — or drunk as a herbal tea, fennel has a soothing effect on the gut, so can help ease digestive problems.

## 361. LET GO OF YOUR MISTAKES

'Failure is only the opportunity to begin again — more intelligently.'
**Henry Ford**

Brooding over errors you've made in the past, telling yourself 'That wouldn't have happened if I'd done this instead of that' or 'It was all my fault, I didn't try hard enough' not only stops you getting on with that one particular aspect of your life, but it can make you feel bad about all sorts of other issues, leaving you with a sort of free-floating anxiety about anything and everything.

If you're otherwise competent, it doesn't make any sense to obsessively mull over mistakes. Next time you hear yourself say something starting with 'I wish I hadn't . . .' or 'I really stuffed up when . . .' try, instead, to get things into perspective. Accept that you're not perfect, and that you don't have to be. Rather than fret about things that haven't gone to plan, take a look at your 'batting averages' — at your successes along with your failures — and such negative thoughts might simply disappear.

## 362.  PUT A SPIN ON IT

> 'Life is 10 per cent what you make it, and 90 per cent how you take it.'
> **Irving Berlin**

Taking time out is especially important when things aren't going well — say, during a heated argument with your partner or when a friend cancels dinner plans after you've got everything ready. The edge comes off the situation and things become less irritating or disappointing if you step back and force yourself to like some part of what's happened: your partner's passion and determination while standing up to you, or the unexpected bonus of a couple of hours to spend as you choose — and some terrific leftovers!

# 363. Get help

If unresolved issues are holding you back, see if there is a group of like-minded people who can help you cope, such as a support group for the bereaved. Your library will hold a list of these organisations.

## 364. MAKE LOTS OF LITTLE CHANGES

'We know how to sacrifice ten years for a diploma, and we are willing to work very hard to get a job, a house, a car, and so on. But we have difficulty remembering that we are alive in the present moment, the only moment. We need only to be awake.'
**Thich Nhat Hanh**

Consider a pebble plopping into a still pond. Imagine all those ripples circling out, over and over again, eventually reaching the shore. It's a metaphor I like: that, so very often, it's the tiny, almost unnoticeable shifts in consciousness or behaviour that really make a difference in our lives. Here are some gems:

Buy yourself one beautiful piece of artwork that inspires you.

Buy an outrageous pair of underwear — satin boxers, a gold G-string — it will make you smile when you remember you're wearing it.

Give yourself a two-minute scalp massage every time you shampoo.

Dance in the lift while you're alone.

Wear comfy slippers.

Create a photo mural. Put your favourite snaps of family and friends in a large clip frame — looking at it will give you an instant boost.

Take naps. Lots of them. Fill a small pillow with dried lavender to inspire you.

Always take a brisk, brief cold shower after your hot one. It's an instant tonic.

Escape. Take a day off work and go to see a film on your own.

Chew your food and eat slowly. If food is chewed to perfection, it is easier to digest, so you can extract more goodness from it.

Add a few drops of eucalyptus oil to your wash water to reduce allergens and make you go 'Ahhh' when you put on your fresh-smelling clothes.

# 365. FIND YOUR FEEL-GOOD STRATEGY

**Sit in silence for a few minutes each day**. Researchers use noise to induce stress in people. Overwhelming noise of any kind creates profound aversion and confusion. It is devastating to the brain's capacity to maintain itself.

**Remember your peak experiences**. If you've felt great in the past, you can feel great again. Psychologist Abraham Maslow studied people who were very energetic, creative and happy and found they shared a capacity to make the most of good experiences. By recalling your happy moments as vividly as possible, you can conjure up the accompanying feelings.

**Change frequencies**. For most of our waking day, our brains operate on beta waves: this is our thinking mind. The relaxation wavelength is the alpha, and you can tap into it with a simple breathing exercise. Become aware of your breathing, making it deeper and slower. Count the outgoing breath up to ten. Thinking should naturally slow down, and you should feel refreshed by the time you are ready to switch back into beta mode. Yoga and meditation take this one step further.

**Find your happy side**. Simple visualisation techniques can put you in touch with your happy self. Close your eyes or focus on a fixed point. Count backwards from 300, imagining you are descending steps. Visualise a person coming up the steps to meet you. It is yourself and you are happy, energetic and vivacious.

# Recipes & Remedies

# Conversions

| Metric | Imperial | Metric | Imperial | |
|---|---|---|---|---|
| 15g | ½ oz | 15ml | ½ fl oz | 1 tablespoon |
| 30g | 1 oz | 30ml | 1 fl oz | |
| 120g | 4oz (¼ lb) | 60ml | 2 fl oz | ¼ cup |
| 250g | 8 oz (½ lb) | 125ml | 4 fl oz | ½ cup |
| 500g | 16oz (1 lb) | 150ml | 5 fl oz | ⅔ cup |
| | | 175ml | 6 fl oz | ¾ cup |
| | | 250ml | 8 fl oz | 1 cup (½ pint) |

These conversions are workable approximates for the recipes in this book.